UPROOTED

UPROOTED

Race, Public Housing, and the Archaeology of Four Lost New Orleans Neighborhoods

D. Ryan Gray

THE UNIVERSITY OF ALABAMA PRESS
Tuscaloosa

The University of Alabama Press
Tuscaloosa, Alabama 35487-0380
uapress.ua.edu

A Dan Josselyn Memorial Publication

Inquiries about reproducing material from this work should be
addressed to the University of Alabama Press.

Typeface: Scala and Scala Sans

Cover image: *Magic Archway*, on the site of the former Lafitte housing
project in New Orleans, was designed and created by Laurel True and
True Mosaics Studio with the help of Lafitte community members and
is a site of contemplation and gathering; see http://truemosaics.com
/magic-archway; courtesy of Laurel True
Cover design: David Nees

Cataloging-in-Publication data is available from the Library of Congress.
ISBN: 978-0-8173-2047-8
E-ISBN: 978-0-8173-9277-2

Contents

Illustrations

TABLES

Preface

The lives of many New Orleanians are glimpsed in these pages. There is Julia Metoyer, a Creole of Color midwife, whose family passed back and forth across the color line as it negotiated the politics of race, class, and gender in postemancipation New Orleans. There are the Bruenns, a German Jewish family in the Irish Channel, upwardly mobile but still struggling with class and social divisions in a city that increasingly divided things into stark terms of Black and white. There are the African American residents of the Red Devil tenement in the now-obliterated Belmont neighborhood, a shifting array of renters on the urban fringes who sometimes disappear in documentary sources, even as they staked out claims on rights and citizenship in the Jim Crow–era city. There are other working-class African American households too, sometimes finding common cause with white immigrant neighbors, and sometimes finding conflict. And there are the women of Storyville, the city's red-light district, where the city was eventually faced with its own inability to police sexuality and a color line that was never as precise as the proponents of white supremacy liked to pretend.

For the most part, the neighborhoods in which each of these stories took place no longer exist. They were uprooted, their houses and outbuildings demolished during an ambitious slum clearance project that began just before World War II, to be replaced by some of the nation's first federal public housing projects. In recent decades, these housing projects—new neighborhoods themselves—became targets for clearance and redevelopment, a process that uprooted residents and linked conceptually stories of people whose everyday existences were regulated by racist institutions and class hierarchies, but who found new ways of bringing energy and life to the places that they called home. The process had already begun before Hurricane Katrina made landfall, but its pace was dramatically hastened by the events set in motion on that day in August 2005. Many would say that the era of large-scale public housing in New Orleans has now ended, marked by the demolition of the Iberville Public Housing Project in 2013. I am thankful that grassroots activists, ethnographers, oral historians, and former residents themselves are telling the stories of those who made these housing projects the distinctive neighborhoods that they became: sites of political activism, of cultural production and innovation, of families, and of friendships. The housing projects of New Orleans were beset by problems, too, and to remember them fully means acknowledging those issues. They had been neglected for decades, largely abandoned by the state since the Civil Rights era, and buildings had deteriorated and fallen into disrepair. They were stigmatized, isolating residents and exacerbating social problems such as poverty, crime, and violence. After experiencing the results of years of disinvestment, former residents were naturally distrustful of the rush to privatize and redevelop, though many were also in no rush to return to the status quo.

The redevelopment of Iberville, an iconic feature of the city's landscape for almost seventy-five years, was a signal moment in this regard. It was located just a couple of blocks from the city's French Quarter, nestled between Canal Street, one of the city's primary arteries, and the complex of St. Louis Cemeteries No. 1 and No. 2, some of New Orleans's oldest aboveground cities of the dead. Its well-constructed two- and three-story brick buildings frequently were visible in the background of tourists' photos of the much-visited St. Louis No. 1, where they somehow seemed right at home as a tableau for the crumbling brick tombs and the stacked wall vaults at the cemetery's edges. Iberville's scale and massing were so harmonious with its surroundings that it had come to be loved by the city's notoriously fastidious preservationists, who feared that its demolition would pave the way for more of the large-scale developments popping up around the city's downtown, part of a post-Katrina building boom that was transforming the area just outside the Quarter. Blocks away, a massive new medical complex was under construction, and just beyond it, the Lafitte Housing Project, the similarly aged counterpart to the Iberville complex, was in the process of becoming Faubourg Lafitte, another mixed-income redevelopment. A new streetcar line (operational as of 2016) was planned for nearby North Rampart Street, the traditional lakeside boundary of the French Quarter, and ground breaking for the construction of the Lafitte Greenway, a 2.6-mile bike path and pedestrian park connecting downtown to the Mid-City neighborhood, would take place in March 2014.

Of course, Iberville had been much more than just a scenic backdrop for the city's visitors. Since the integration of New Orleans public housing in the latter part of the 1960s, the formerly segregated, white-only Iberville Project had become an important core of housing for the city's African American working class. For people employed in restaurants, hotels, bars, and music venues in the city's tourist areas, the easy walking distance of both Iberville and Lafitte made residence at the complexes highly desirable. Located almost adjacent to Armstrong Park and the Tremé, which was experiencing something of a tourist renaissance of its own thanks in part to the HBO series of the same name, Iberville and Lafitte formed a nexus for African American culture in the city. Every year, the Zulu Social Aid and Pleasure Club culminated its Mardi Gras parade by going past the Lafitte Project on Orleans Avenue. The intersection of Basin Street and Claiborne Avenue, just past Iberville and alongside Lafitte, became a rallying point for Black New Orleans, where families, parading groups, brass bands, and Mardi Gras Indians met and celebrated in the shadow of the freeway overpass that had bifurcated and almost destroyed the Tremé in the 1960s.

The decision to demolish Iberville, the best preserved of the projects from the first generation of public housing in New Orleans, was controversial. It was a controversy that had been simmering since at least the 1990s, part of a move to eliminate large public housing complexes in favor of scattered site units and mixed-income redevelopments. Back in 2007, with the city still experiencing acute housing shortages in the wake of the devastation of Hurricane Katrina, the Department of Housing and Urban Development (HUD) and the Housing Authority of New Orleans (HANO) had initiated plans to redevelop all other remaining housing projects in the city. The "big four" developments—C. J. Peete (originally Magnolia), Lafitte, B. W. Cooper (originally Calliope), and St. Bernard, all dating from roughly the same era as Iberville, and all comprising the same sturdy, low-density brick housing stock—were targeted. HANO and HUD claimed that all of them had been so badly damaged during the storm that to do anything else but wholesale demolition was too expensive and time consuming to be feasible. At that point, most had been closed for almost two years, with moisture, rot, and mold eating away at the interiors. The exact plans for the future of each of those housing projects varied in their details, though they all involved the construction of a mixture of market-rate and subsidized or low-income housing. Some incorporated much broader community revitalization initiatives as well, with off-site plans including community centers, schools, housing for the elderly, and parks. Perhaps a few historic buildings would be left to be rehabbed or mothballed, a nod to the architectural significance (and presumed National Register eligibility) of the complexes, but most would be razed. It seemed clear that the city was moving in a new direction, one that would have profound implications for the future of housing within it.

Despite ostensible commitments for one-to-one replacements of low-income units, these redevelopments became flashpoints in the charged emotional atmosphere of post-Katrina New Orleans, where thousands were still displaced from their homes. Many of the new plans dispersed affordable housing as scattered site units, with little clarity on timelines for these being ready for habitation. As public housing remained closed and inaccessible to former residents after the 2005 storm, activists staged protests and filed lawsuits, advocating for the right of return of tenants, an idea that even managed to get some legislative traction in H.R. 1227, the Gulf Coast Housing Recovery Act of 2007. This bill, introduced by Maxine Waters of California, was passed by the House before dying in the Senate. Protestors tried to occupy buildings and block heavy equipment during the demolitions, which began in earnest in 2008 and 2009. While some of those efforts brought much-needed attention to the problems of rebuilding and recovery in the city, they had little impact on the plans for public housing in the long term. As demolition and new construction pushed forward, protest groups were plagued by diffused goals and infighting, a situation not helped by the fact that at least some involved were new to the city, with little knowledge of its longer history of public housing and racial inequality.

Still, the decision to actually raze Iberville came as something of a shock, even if the general trajectory of public housing in the United States in the years since the 1980s had made it seem an inevitability. The Iberville location had been coveted by developers for years even before Katrina, and activists had rallied around its protection as a sort of last stand since it was proposed for demolition after Katrina in 2005. A group called C3/Hands Off Iberville claimed that any demolition was tantamount to racial and ethnic cleansing of the city's downtown. Iberville had scarcely been affected by Katrina's floodwaters, and former residents had returned in substantial numbers. Thus, there was also a resident population that would have to be relocated before any redevelopment. It seemed then that, for once, the interests of activists, current residents, and establishment preservationists might actually align to create a coalition that would make Iberville, in essence, untouchable.

As someone who both worked in cultural resource management and considered myself to be concerned with social justice, I certainly felt this way. I had toured one of the Lafitte units soon after demolition had been approved. The apartment had been sealed since the storm, with protective plating placed over the doors and windows to prevent "trespassing," a manifestation of HANO's concerns that former residents would return, unsanctioned, to reoccupy their old apartments. As a result, the former resident's possessions were left essentially as they had been since August 29, 2005. Glasses and plates remained, half filled and moldering, on a coffee table. Open DVD cases sat alongside the television. Clothing scattered about the floor suggested the hurried gathering of possessions as floodwaters rose in the surrounding area. There was mold and moisture damage in the buildings, to be sure, and perhaps some waters had penetrated into the ground floor. But standing water had not affected this area to any significant degree, and most of the damage seemed to me to be from moisture entering the unit from roofs and windows and then being sealed inside. Neglect of the buildings since Katrina had exacerbated whatever problems had thus been created. Having helped numerous friends clean flood-ravaged homes, I had seen much worse. Iberville had been even less affected and had already been reopened at the time, at the insistence of residents and activists. It was difficult to fathom that the same logic for redevelopment could be applied there.

Furthermore, as someone whose specialty was archaeology and historic preservation, I knew that the redevelopment of Iberville would present a daunting additional set of challenges. As with all the city's other housing project redevelopments, any plans would fall under the purview of Section 106 of the National Historic Preservation Act (NHPA), which calls for federal agencies to take into account the effects of their undertakings on historic properties. In the case of Iberville, this taking account would be a particularly complex process. Like many of the housing projects where redevelopments were already getting started, not only was Iberville historic itself, it was located on property with a long trajectory of urban use prior to its construction. But Iberville was also uniquely sensitive in this regard. It was located directly adjacent to some of the city's oldest extant cemeteries, the boundaries of which shifted on nineteenth-century maps, suggesting the possibility that burials could stretch under certain portions of its existing footprint. On top of that, the project had been placed almost exactly to coincide with the former location of Storyville, the city's infamous experiment in regulating prostitution. Storyville looms large in the city's imagination of its own exceptionalism, and the name is emblazoned on business signs across the city. It is notorious for its connections to the origins of New Orleans's tourist trade, its marketing of sex across the color line, and its reputation as the birthplace of New Orleans jazz. With its sheer size, the archaeological remains of Storyville would be a historic resource that would take considerable time, labor, and expense to address.

My own entry into the archaeology of the city came as a result of the Greater New Orleans Archaeology Program's "Archaeology in Tremé" project, directed by Christopher Matthews. This project, in the churchyard of St. Augustine Catholic Church, at the heart of what is sometimes called America's first Black neighborhood, emphasized public outreach as a central component of its methods. At the time, I had just relocated to New Orleans. My background had been in the archaeology of the ancient Maya, but I soon discovered that there were few jobs for a budding Maya epigrapher with only an undergraduate degree. I had moved to the city with the vague intent of making it back to Central America, but the Tremé dig opened my eyes to the possibilities of a socially and politically engaged archaeology. Soon afterward, I landed at the local cultural resource management firm Earth Search, Inc. (ESI), at what turned out to be a propitious time for doing archaeology in the city. I volunteered to work on the archaeological monitoring at St. Thomas, as it was just a few blocks from my apartment, and I gradually became more and more invested in the archaeology of the city. I was still doing research on St. Thomas—and on a number of other urban projects—when Hurricane Katrina made landfall in 2005. Many of the oldest areas of the city, located as they were on the high ground of the natural levee of the Mississippi River, did not severely flood. However, the low-lying areas at the foot of the natural levees, the traditional locus of African American settlement in the city dating to the years of residential segregation, were overwhelmed with water. When HUD and HANO made the decision to move forward with mixed-income re-developments to replace most of the projects, my research expanded in scope and came to bear on contemporary sociopolitics. The archaeological data re-coveries and background research mandated by federal law vastly increased the breadth of the data to which I had access, making it possible for me to begin to pose broader questions about the role of slum clearance and urban renewal in producing the contemporary racial landscape of New Orleans.

I was involved in varying capacities in the archaeological work and back-ground research that went into the projects discussed in this book. The sin-gular factor that made all of these data recoveries possible was the necessity for federal agencies (in this case, HUD and HANO) to comply with Section 106 of the NHPA. Beyond that, the exact situations of fieldwork varied consid-erably, as did the circumstances of my involvement. I supervised all phases of the archaeological data recovery at St. Thomas and the laboratory analyses of the material recovered there while I was employed at ESI, which performed the fieldwork under contract to Historic Restoration, Inc., of New Orleans. Even though the technical reports for those excavations have been slow to ma-terialize, I have presented and published on this work in both formal and in-formal settings often over the years, and as a result some of my analysis here draws on that previous work. Also for ESI, under a HANO contract, I devel-oped research designs for data recoveries and assisted in some field investi-gations at the Magnolia/C. J. Peete and Lafitte Housing Projects. I have then drawn on the laboratory inventories compiled by ESI as I developed more in-tensive independent analyses, reexamined collections, and used its general background research as a foundation for my work.

Iberville is something of a more complex case. While I contributed ideas and issues for a research design meant to govern the larger project there (in a field effort that was being led by ESI), I conducted independent fieldwork at a single historic block within Iberville, City Square 130. Over three seasons with a field school conducted through the University of New Orleans (UNO), we focused on a single courtyard in the modern complex, intensively investigating features associated with a group of lots near the center of the block. This work was intended to inform the archaeological project being conducted concurrently by ESI, which was done for the purpose of compliance with the NHPA and thus sometimes had to proceed rapidly to stay ahead of the redevelopment. ESI's field effort also had to cover a great deal of ground, and sometimes management decisions had to be based on the contingencies of the redevelopment project. There was, quite simply, too much of archaeological significance at the site to be able to address it all. Our work at Iberville, only some of which will be discussed here, was meant to supplement the federally mandated project with qualitatively different categories of data.

Ultimately, the City of New Orleans, HANO, and HUD proceeded with demolition at Iberville, and the resistance to the redevelopment there was replaced with negotiations over the minutiae of the plan. My direct involvement with Iberville—and with all the housing project redevelopments discussed in this book—is as an archaeologist. The subject of this book is the archaeology of New Orleans, and more specifically the archaeology of four urban neighborhoods eventually chosen as the locations of the city's first housing projects, neighborhoods where the cast of characters mentioned earlier made their homes. Their stories are, for me, intertwined with those of the people whose lives have been affected by these newest redevelopments. The logic of slum clearance in the past can help us understand the process of urban displacements in the present, particularly the ways in which redevelopments are wielded instrumentally, as tools meant to produce certain types of subjects and certain types of normality that serve the interests of a dominant group. Archaeology is my own tool, and it is one that I believe can help us understand the world that these redevelopments were trying to remake. By showing how different types of inequalities are normalized in the past and in the present, whether these inequalities are conceived along axes of race, ethnicity, class, religion, or gender, archaeology can hopefully also serve as a tool that can break down these hierarchies, or at least the imaginations of them that make them so persistent.

A Note on Terminology

I have chosen to capitalize *Black* as a term that is generally applied to denote ethnicity, to emphasize its importance in this discussion. I leave *white* lowercased except in cases where the word is capitalized in historical sources. In New Orleans, racial terminology is particularly complex, with categories that overlap in some periods, that disappear and reappear, and that sometimes shift in meaning. I try to stay close to the original sources except when it might cause confusion; as a result, the terms *African American, Black, Mulatto, Negro, Creole of Color,* and *person of color* all show up in this work in reference to particular categories of identity, which are sometimes interchangeable and sometimes not.

Acknowledgments

Archaeological work tends to be social by its nature, and many of the projects discussed in this work involved numerous individuals: field archaeologists, analysts, historians, students, and volunteers. However, I must express thanks at the outset of these acknowledgments to two people: Jill-Karen Yakubik, president of Earth Search, Inc. (ESI), of New Orleans, and Shannon Dawdy of the Department of Anthropology at the University of Chicago. Jill-Karen's guidance and support got me started in historical archaeology and gave my interest in New Orleans archaeology a chance to develop and grow. She was willing to give me a chance when I had practically no experience in cultural resources management (CRM) archaeology, and she taught me everything she could about historical pottery. She also allowed me to continue working with collections generated by ESI's projects in New Orleans after I had moved on to the University of Chicago. There, Shannon guided and supervised my work with a steady hand, as a friend, a mentor, and a scholar. While I alone am responsible for any shortcomings of this book, it could not have happened without their influence and support, and I am enormously grateful for how they have helped me throughout the years.

Many others at ESI also played a part in this research, some working on these projects for only days, others for months and even years. Benjamin Maygarden, former historian at ESI, conducted a great deal of initial research that was foundational to this effort. Ben provided a critical foil as I developed my own understanding of the relationship between archaeology and historical research; he and Mary Beth Maygarden demonstrated what a thorough research effort looked like with their work on St. Thomas. Michael Godzinski, project manager at ESI, ran projects at Peete and Lafitte and shared his insights with me. I cannot begin to hope to name everyone who worked on all these projects as field and lab techs, something that continued after I left. Thanks to Rhonda Smith (who served as co-project manager with me on the first part of the St. Thomas data recovery), Anthony White, Kathryn Lintott, Kimberly Eppler, David Harlan, Stuart Nolan, Jessica McNiel, Angele Montana, Tatum Evans, Todd Mayberry, Christine Hernandez, Erin Sneddon, Christa Clement, Wendy Bosma, Aidan McCarty, Anne Titelbaum, Amanda Garvin, Sarah Riley, Tania Mahato, Kevin McMahon, Ryan Murray, Ryan Hale, Crorey Lawton, and Jason and Eylene Parrish. There are many others too, and I apologize to anyone whom I may have missed, or who worked on the later iterations of these field projects after I left.

Francois Richard and Alan Kolata, my other mentors at the University of Chicago, were significant influences on the development of this work, as were Adela Amaral Lugo, Christopher Grant, Brian Wilson, Sarah Kautz, Elizabeth Fagan, Beth Brummel, Bill Feeney, Anna Guengrich, Karim Mata, Maureen Marshall, and Kate Franklin. Of course, I benefited from discussion with many of my other classmates at Chicago as well. A special thanks to Beth and Pip Potter, without whom I never would have made it through those winters in Chicago. I will always be grateful.

Thanks also to Christopher Matthews, who provided my first opportunity to volunteer on a project in New Orleans, and who has been a friend and frequent commentator over the years. My colleagues and students at UNO have also played a key role in the development of this work, especially its later chapters. Thanks in particular to Rachel Breunlin of UNO and the Neighborhood Story Project, who has been a collaborator on many events and projects since I arrived here, and to David Beriss, our departmental chair, who has supported my work. Thanks to Andrea White, of the now defunct Greater New Orleans Archaeology Program, who codirected the first season of excavations with me at Iberville, and to all the UNO field school students who worked there and in the lab, including Blair Bordelon, Austen Dooley, Janet Greenfield, Kyle Knighten, Alex Leigh, Christopher Lewis, Blaine Lirette, Michael Montgomery, Alahna Moore, Jonelle Schmidt, Elizabeth Seleen, Jermaine Taylor, Krystal Weber, Elizabeth Williams, Catherine Lorelli, Stephen Hagan, Hien Hoang, Sam Malone, Cortney Marsh, Victoria Nätell, Christy Becnel, Ryan Borel, and Elizabeth Rogers. Thanks also to a number of graduate students who have volunteered and collaborated on the Iberville project, including Grace Krause, Mia Carey, and Christopher Grant (again!). And thanks to the Housing Authority of New Orleans (HANO) and the City of New Orleans, who allowed access to the Iberville site for the field school. Permission always seemed to come down to the wire, but we somehow made it happen!

The many local institutions that provide support and opportunities for outreach in archaeology, and that provide facilities for research on the city's history, also deserve thanks in an endeavor like this. The City Archives at the New Orleans Public Library were essential in the research for this project, particularly before so many of the resources had been digitized by on-line databases like America's Historical Newspapers and Ancestry.com. Of course, these too eventually played a role in this work, as did the Louisiana Collection at the University of New Orleans, the Hogan Jazz Archive and the Southeastern Architectural Archives at Tulane University, the Historic New Orleans Collection (HNOC), the Louisiana State Museum, and the New Orleans Notarial Archives. Thanks also to Chip McGimsey, state archaeologist of Louisiana, and to the Louisiana Division of Archaeology. Chip and the staff of the division have supported these efforts, and they have worked hard to create an environment that fosters archaeology of all kinds, both in the private sector and in scholarly research.

A final thanks to friends and family. My family back in Alabama supported me back when it seemed a pretty remote dream that someone could actually make a living doing archaeology, and I will always appreciate that, as I appreciate that it was no small feat for my mom, dad, and grandparents to get me to New York City to start my undergrad career at Columbia. I now have my own family here in New Orleans, ones who continue to provide love, guidance, and friendship. Thanks to my long-time friend Karl, who has been there through many ups and downs over two decades in New Orleans. Thanks most of all to my wife, Elizabeth, and my daughter, Brita. They both changed my life for the better in more ways than I can possibly quantify, and it is their love that has inspired me to keep going, in everything that we do, now, together. Beth has read through numerous drafts of these chapters; she has tortured over book titles along with me, been patient when I was frustrated, and given the encouragement that I needed to get through this. Brita was born the day that the final version of my doctoral thesis was submitted, marking the close of one chapter in my life and the opening of a new one. Her first years filled us with happiness, but they were years also tempered with sadness, from the loss of another close friend, unexpectedly and far too early. This book is thus dedicated to my daughter, Brita Rose Gray, born in 2012, who gave us hope and joy, and to my friend Ryan Riddle, who left us in 2014.

Abbreviations

ESI	Earth Search, Inc.
HANO	Housing Authority of New Orleans
HNOC	Historic New Orleans Collection
HUD	Department of Housing and Urban Development
MNI	minimum number of individuals
NHPA	National Historic Preservation Act
PWA	Public Works Administration
UNO	University of New Orleans
WPA	Works Progress Administration

UPROOTED

I

Renewing New Orleans,
Past and Present

After Hurricane Katrina struck the Gulf Coast in August 2005 and set off a series of engineering failures that inundated the majority of New Orleans, planning for how (or even whether) to rebuild the city became an almost immediate concern. It would help determine who could come back and when this might happen, issues that were clouded with uncertainty for many of the city's residents. Well before the decision had been made to demolish and redevelop public housing, numerous reconstruction plans and blueprints for the city had been fiercely contested in public media and in closed meetings, often with contradictory or confusing results. The Bring New Orleans Back Commission, convened by Mayor C. Ray Nagin a month after Katrina's landfall, had called for a "bigger" city, "a sustainable, environmentally safe, socially equitable community with a vibrant economy,"[1] but it did so only after one of its consultants, the Washington-based nonprofit Urban Land Institute, had caused dissension by recommending that the city be restored to a smaller footprint. The "New Orleans Neighborhood Rebuilding Plan," prepared at the instigation of the city council, advocated instead for a neighborhood-based recovery focusing on the immediate needs of those most able to return to the city quickly, typically upper- and middle-class residents. Such plans operated through trickle-down logic, with the implicit assumption that lower-class residents would follow, in order to resume their traditional places in the service sector. In the wake of acute shortages of affordable housing following the storm, many observers saw these plans as ploys to whiten the city by discouraging the return of poor African American residents, who were disproportionately affected by displacement after the storm. To many former tenants, the demolition of public housing that began in 2007 (figure 1.1) just seemed to be the latest of the indignities to be aimed at the city's most marginalized populations, and protests inevitably followed.[2]

While part of a nationwide trend toward the elimination of large public

Figure 1.1. Demolition of the Iberville Housing Project. (Barry South, courtesy of Earth Search, Inc.)

housing complexes, the redevelopments were only the latest expression of the idea (common in American urban planning since at least the end of the nineteenth century) that social relations and the possibilities for social action in the city could be transformed through changes in the built environment. Since the 1980s, public housing in the United States had been discursively situated as a failed experiment, an attempt at social engineering that had gone disastrously wrong. Planners and administrators looked to replace monolithic housing complexes with mixed-income redevelopments as the remedy for this failure, often with a commercial component included to sweeten the deal for private developers. Beginning in 1992, many such redevelopments were undertaken under the auspices of the HOPE VI grant program of the Department of Housing and Urban Development (HUD). HOPE VI sought to remake deteriorated and isolated urban public housing according to the principles of New Urbanism, which emphasized the creation of functionally integrated communities organized around private ownership of smaller-scale housing units. This transformation entailed the replacement of dense high-rise units with single-family homes, duplexes, and/or townhouses, which would have improved linkages with vital city services and commercial zones. HOPE VI was criticized almost from its inception, mainly because of its poor track record with regard to the return of former public housing residents to the new mixed-income developments built under its auspices. It came to be seen as a tool of gentrification, with the poor minority populations displaced by demolitions shifted to scattered-site units or left to fend for themselves with Section 8 vouchers.[3]

The Desire Housing Project was the first in New Orleans to fall under HOPE VI, and it certainly seemed like a good candidate for redevelopment. Opened in the 1950s, Desire and the nearby Florida Projects represented the low point in New Orleans's experiment with public housing. They had been a dramatic departure from the earlier generation of projects. Desire became the city's largest housing project, a sprawling complex of some thirteen thousand residents at its most populous. The development, hastily and shoddily constructed, was located over a former dump in a low-lying industrial corridor at the periphery of the city. Even before it opened, Desire was feared to be unsafe for human habitation, and conditions only declined further after flooding from Hurricane Betsy in 1965. Desire was isolated and all but abandoned by city services, and, as activists and community-based groups helped fill that void with social service programs, it became fertile ground for organizing in the 1960s. This organizing culminated in 1970 in a series of violent confrontations between the New Orleans Committee to Combat Fascism (an offshoot of the Black Panther Party that was active in Desire) and the New Orleans Police Department. Sporadic attempts to improve Desire throughout the 1970s failed from a lack of money, a lack of resolve, or both. By the 1990s, when demolition of Desire began, few were sad to see the crumbling buildings go, though many residents and activists wondered what was next.[4]

The St. Thomas Housing Project, targeted for HOPE VI redevelopment in 1996, was another matter. The first part of St. Thomas was opened in 1939, just before Iberville, making it one of the first housing developments in the country built with funding from the New Deal–era Housing Act of 1937. It was located on the desirable high ground of the city's riverfront, adjacent to the Lower Garden District, a National Register Historic District and much-touted destination for visitors to the city. The redevelopment that began in 1999 encapsulated many of the controversies associated with the HOPE VI program. To city boosters, St. Thomas appeared to be a failure, a crime-ridden and decaying island in what should have been a thriving riverfront area with a booming tourist-driven economy. But St. Thomas was also a center of Black political activism and organization with a strong neighborhood identity, and residents immediately expressed concern about the lack of sufficient low-income replacement units in the redevelopment. Many of those residents were eventually resettled in the St. Bernard Housing Project, located in a portion of the city far removed from St. Thomas and not nearly as easily accessible by pedestrian or public transportation. As the redevelopment proceeded, it also raised the ire of local historic preservationists, particularly after Historic Restoration, Inc., the local real estate developer coordinating the project, incorporated a big-box Walmart Supercenter as the primary occupant of the commercial component of the site.[5] The new neighborhood was rechristened as River Gardens, and, after Katrina, it would be lauded by then-mayor C. Ray Nagin as a vision of how badly damaged areas of the city could be revitalized. Others remained skeptical of this brand of New Urbanism, both for its cavalier approach to the historic fabric of the city, and for its seeming myopia regarding preexisting racial and class divides.[6]

The redevelopment of the housing projects announced in 2007 represented a drastic scaling up of the mixed-income template that had already proven controversial at St. Thomas. Demolition of Peete/Magnolia, Cooper/Calliope, Lafitte, and St. Bernard marked a massive intervention into the built environment of the city, one affecting a number of very different neighborhoods (figure 1.2). Peete/Magnolia, located in a low-lying backswamp zone adjacent to the Central City neighborhood, had been constructed as the segregated Black counterpart of the white-only St. Thomas Project in 1939–40. Similarly, Lafitte, located at the edge of the Mid-City neighborhood along Orleans Avenue, a major thoroughfare, had been paired with the white-only Iberville Housing Project and constructed around the same time. B. W. Cooper, between Central City and a series of rail yards, and St. Bernard, in the Gentilly/Seventh Ward area, were also products of the first years of public housing construction in New Orleans, focused specifically on supplying the housing needs of the growing African American population of the city. Most were subsequently expanded further, and even as additional larger-scale projects like Desire were built, this earliest generation was distinguished by the quality of its construction. Unfortunately, after desegregation in the 1960s, these projects were all increasingly neglected by city services and by federal funding, allowing them to physically deteriorate and become notoriously unsafe. While conditions in each of the projects prior to Katrina certainly merited significant action (and, in fact, plans for a partial redevelopment of C. J. Peete had begun even before 2005, with its later expansion section already demolished), the wholesale destruction of what was seen as solid, well-constructed housing stock seemed drastic, if not willfully neglectful of former residents' needs.

All these early housing projects were originally conceived and constructed as part of a large-scale campaign to eradicate supposed slum housing conditions in the city. The compromise that had allowed the federal Housing Act of 1937 to pass Congress let local authorities determine the locations for federally funded housing. New Orleans had been positioning itself in this regard for some time already. A 1934 survey had estimated that over half the city's

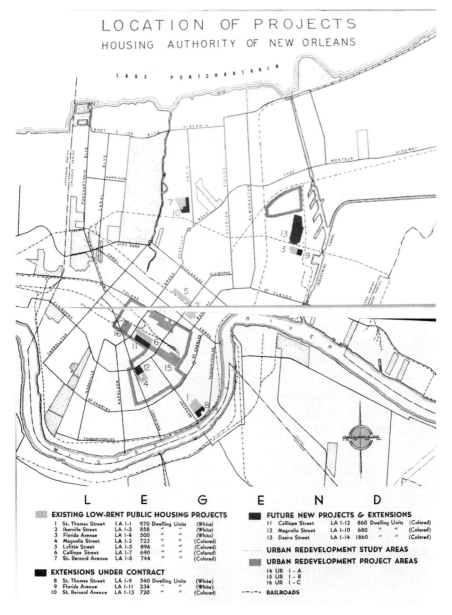

LOCATION OF PROJECTS
HOUSING AUTHORITY OF NEW ORLEANS

LEGEND

EXISTING LOW-RENT PUBLIC HOUSING PROJECTS

1	St. Thomas Street	LA 1-1	970	Dwelling Units	(White)
2	Iberville Street	LA 1-3	858	" "	(White)
3	Florida Avenue	LA 1-4	500	" "	(White)
4	Magnolia Street	LA 1-2	723	" "	(Colored)
5	Lafitte Street	LA 1-5	896	" "	(Colored)
6	Calliope Street	LA 1-7	690	" "	(Colored)
7	St. Bernard Avenue	LA 1-8	744	" "	(Colored)

EXTENSIONS UNDER CONTRACT

8	St. Thomas Street	LA 1-9	540	Dwelling Units	(White)
9	Florida Avenue	LA 1-11	234	" "	(White)
10	St. Bernard Avenue	LA 1-13	720	" "	(Colored)

FUTURE NEW PROJECTS & EXTENSIONS

11	Calliope Street	LA 1-12	860	Dwelling Units	(Colored)
12	Magnolia Street	LA 1-10	680	" "	(Colored)
13	Desire Street	LA 1-14	1860	" "	(Colored)

‑ ‑ ‑ **URBAN REDEVELOPMENT STUDY AREAS**

URBAN REDEVELOPMENT PROJECT AREAS

14 UR 1 - A
15 UR 1 - B
16 UR 1 - C

‑‑‑‑ **RAILROADS**

Figure 1.2. Map of major public housing projects of New Orleans. (From the 1951 *Report of the Housing Authority of New Orleans*)

population of 550,000 lived in "overcrowded hovels of decay," and one of the surveyors purportedly discovered "9 people, 2 dogs, 1 cat, 6 chickens, and a duck" sharing a one-room apartment as illustrative of the state of affairs in the purported slums.[7] The Housing Authority of New Orleans (HANO) ostensibly based its decisions about the sites for the new projects on a further series of surveys of conditions around the city that carefully quantified the physical condition of the city's housing stock, even as the city gathered information about the social and racial profile of neighborhoods. The public housing units constructed to replace the designated areas would provide modern amenities like electricity, indoor plumbing, heat, and gas ranges, while also opening green space, ameliorating overcrowding, and improving sanitary conditions. Unlike the high-rise projects built in the North, the housing complexes in New Orleans were intended to be low density, with solid brick construction and appealing aesthetic qualities, designed by well-known local architects. The openings of the St. Thomas and Magnolia Projects in 1939–40 attracted considerable attention, with crowds estimated at twenty-five thousand visiting Magnolia on opening day, and even more subsequently lining up to see St. Thomas.[8] By HANO's own accounts, at least, the evictions necessary for clearance of the project areas had been an unqualified success, proceeding rapidly and with minimal resistance from the population of renters that made up most of the occupants of the neighborhoods. A passing note was made of the fact that, at St. Thomas, relocations had been delayed by some families' insistence on staying for first communions at their local parish churches.[9]

While the placement of the 2007 demolitions within the context of the post-Katrina reconfiguration of New Orleans had made them seem exceptional, they were conceived along the same logics according to which the housing projects were first deemed necessary in the 1930s. Through much of the nineteenth century, urban reformers had focused on the moral uplift of the poor as a remedy for social disorder in the city. Reform efforts had, as a result, emphasized programs based on providing outreach to individuals through charitable institutions, especially ones targeting children. During this time, the slum as a geographic locale within the city was simply coterminous with those spaces in which the "depraved" rather than the deserving poor resided, and thus it could be located anywhere in the urban zone.[10] However, with the growth of the Progressive movement in the years before World War I, there was an increasing shift toward the idea that the physical environment of the city itself could be productive of moral and social order, and that well-planned cities could thus be curative, remedying the social ills of the impoverished.[11] By the 1930s, residents and city officials confronted crowded and decaying urban centers, shortages of affordable housing stock, and rising racial tensions over access to decent homes. The era of Jim Crow segregation was reaching its peak, further circumscribing the possibilities for housing for Black Americans. It is within this historical context that the birth (and death) of public housing in New Orleans must be reconsidered.

Archaeology in the Housing Projects

Nobody had given much thought to doing archaeology in the housing projects in New Orleans until relatively recently. After all, why should they? Urban historical archaeology as a subdiscipline of archaeology was slow to develop in New Orleans just as elsewhere in the United States.[12] There were some excavations in the 1970s at historic homes in the French Quarter, notably at Madame John's Legacy and the Hermann-Grima House, but the most intensive investigations had been reserved for the prehistoric sites near the lakefront in the city's eastern section, many of them threatened by post–World War II suburbs. These sites, shell middens dating back some two thousand years or more, had been essential in defining the Early Woodland period's Tchefuncte culture, a term referring to the lifeways of hunter-gatherers who exploited the brackish water shellfish of inland marshes and made large quantities of low-fired pottery with a surprising range of decorations. Such sites were obviously significant in themselves, but a broader interpretation of Section 106 of the NHPA developing through the 1970s meant that the archaeology of historic sites also became a greater consideration in planning federal undertakings. The focus still tended to be the colonial and antebellum eras, and many early reports of such investigations emphasize chronology and architecture, paying only passing attention to assemblages and materials from the more recent past.[13]

There were signs that this was changing by the 1980s. Large federally mandated projects conducted by private cultural resource management companies drastically increased the body of archaeological data available across the country, and such projects began to consciously address broader interpretive questions of neighborhood development and identity. One of the largest such projects of the 1980s in New Orleans took place in conjunction with the expansion of the Greater New Orleans (GNO) Bridge No. 2, adjacent to the Lower Garden District. Eventually, portions of at least fourteen city blocks were examined in some detail by Coastal Environments, Inc., of Baton Rouge, with numerous artifact-rich pit features excavated (figure 1.3). Such features, like abandoned wells, cesspits, and outhouse (or privy) shafts, are often filled rapidly when no longer in use, and the artifacts found within them may then be linked to specific households identifiable through documentary evidence like census records or city directories. This documentary evidence allows variations in material remains to be potentially connected to specific types of social

Figure 1.3. Excavations during the Greater New Orleans Bridge Expansion project, ca. 1985. (Courtesy of Coastal Environments, Inc.)

or cultural difference. The GNO Bridge assemblages seemed especially well suited to addressing variability in socioeconomic class and ethnicity, as the area historically contained a high proportion of first- and second-generation immigrants from Ireland, Germany, and Italy, engaged in a diverse array of occupations. Unfortunately, it proved to be difficult to control for any one factor in interpreting the assemblages; it was often impossible to determine whether similarities or differences in material culture were due most to race, to class, to ethnicity, or to some other factor entirely.[14]

The GNO Bridge excavations were indicative of the new standard for doing urban archaeology in New Orleans. Other well-reported digs around the city, like those conducted by cultural resource management firm R. C. Goodwin and Associates at the New Orleans General Hospital Site and Algiers Point and by Earth Search, Inc. (ESI), at sites in the French Quarter, expanded the available data still further.[15] Such projects helped establish the need for professional archaeologists who specialized in the archaeology of New Orleans, and by the 1990s, the scope of archaeology in the city had expanded considerably. In addition to compliance-based projects around the city, excavations were sponsored by organizations like the Historic New Orleans Collection (HNOC) on sites that they owned or planned to develop. The Greater New

Figure 1.4. Public archaeology in the Greater New Orleans Archaeology Program's "Archaeology in Tremé" project. (Courtesy of Christopher Matthews and the Greater New Orleans Archaeology Program/University of New Orleans Department of Anthropology)

Orleans Archaeology Program was based out of UNO beginning in 1995, and under the direction of first Shannon Dawdy and then Christopher Matthews, it developed an active field presence around the city. Dawdy's work at the Maginnis Cotton Mill and at Madame John's Legacy, and Matthews's "Archaeology in Tremé" project, were dynamic, theoretically engaged urban projects, often actively incorporating public involvement and community engagement as a component of their methodology (figure 1.4). Dawdy's and Matthews's work in the city addressed issues like creolization and hybridity, capitalism and inequality, racialization, identity, and memory, and it continues to do so.[16]

Despite the increased attention to urban archaeology from both regulators and scholars, most were slow to recognize the potential of the city's housing projects for archaeological research. HANO in this era was notoriously dysfunctional, so much so that HUD, in 1996, declared the agency in breach of its service contract and negotiated an agreement with the mayor's office to administer its properties directly. With so many existing historic homes and neighborhoods still standing, many in constant threat of demolition, the housing projects seemed a low priority for historic preservationists and archaeologists. This situation began to change in 1999, when a HANO contractor dug a trench alongside an administrative building at Iberville during routine renovations. Such things had apparently been done before without much oversight from the Louisiana State Historic Preservation Office (home of the state's Division of Archaeology). However, this time, Robert Florence, a local historian who specialized in New Orleans cemeteries, saw the backdirt piles and recognized bits of bone within them. Fearing that the backhoes had hit human burials associated with St. Louis Cemetery No. 1—something that had recently happened nearby on Conti Street during utility work by the Sewerage and Water Board—Florence contacted the Division of Archaeology, which in turn contacted ESI about visiting the site. No graves had been disturbed, but rich archaeological deposits spanning the era from the beginning of the nineteenth century to the Storyville years had been partially destroyed. ESI began what was a salvage project more than an excavation, trying to make sense of what was exposed, a process hampered by gushing water from a main busted by the heavy equipment on site. The project garnered a fair amount of publicity, which was only increased by the demolition of two of the last standing Storyville cribs, on private property a couple of blocks away.[17]

The density of the archaeological deposits at Iberville was something of an eye opener to those concerned with the city's historical resources. When the HOPE VI redevelopment of the St. Thomas Housing Project was announced, impact on potential archaeological resources was an immediate concern, as St. Thomas, like Iberville, was situated on the high ground of the natural levee, in an area that had a long history of development. During the colonial era, it was part of some of the many plantation concessions that dotted the riverfront upriver and downriver of the city proper. Those plantations were later subdivided into a series of faubourgs, small suburban neighborhoods, that were eventually swallowed into the growing city. Since any of those eras of development could be represented by archaeological remains throughout the project area, ESI began monitoring the demolition of housing project buildings and conducting testing on the twenty city blocks in the area encompassed by St. Thomas. Eventually five city blocks would be selected for more complete excavation, ranging from the location of the St. Joseph Orphan Asylum, a long-lasting Catholic institution founded in 1853 to serve the multitude of orphans left by the city's frequent yellow fever epidemics, to that of a waterfront boardinghouse and tavern from the antebellum era.

From an archaeological standpoint, the project was fascinating. When the neighborhood had been razed in 1939, the subsurface features like wells, privies, and trash pits that provide some of the best data for urban historical archaeology had been preserved wherever new buildings were not constructed, particularly in courtyards and parking lots. In many areas of the city, such subsurface features are regularly targeted by an active network of bottle hunters and relic diggers. Unless protected under pavements or by individual property owners, they are often looted without documentation. The housing project areas, however, had been mostly ignored, with the archaeological resources located there assumed to have already been destroyed. As a result, over the course of some four years, proceeding intermittently ahead of the planned development, archaeologists were able to document and excavate a rich material record dating from the beginning of the nineteenth century up to the present. Tens of thousands of artifacts were recovered, including ceramics, glassware, architectural debris, food remains, and numerous personal items such as buttons, smoking pipes, rosaries, shoes, marbles, dolls, and medicinal supplies.

Much of the public interest in the archaeological component of the project centered on the reputation of Adele Street and the area surrounding it as the location of the city's original Irish Channel, a working-class Irish immigrant neighborhood near dock facilities and a saloon called Noud's Ocean Home.[18] In more recent years, the neighborhood just upriver from the St. Thomas Housing Project has adopted the Irish Channel designation, and since 1947 an Irish Channel St. Patrick's Day parade has run along Magazine Street nearby. Perhaps the most famous neighborhood institutions are the paired Catholic churches, St. Alphonsus and St. Mary's Assumption, founded in the mid-nineteenth century to serve Irish and German-speaking residents, respectively. One of the first locations where information about the archaeological dig was publicly presented was the Irish Channel Roots symposium at St. Alphonsus, which also hosted a display of some of the artifacts recovered. Predictably, the notion of a monolithic Irish heritage at some point in the history of the neighborhood has glossed over problematic racial attitudes, while helping fuel gentrification in the area, particularly after the demolition of St. Thomas and the more recent dislocations of poorer residents following Hurricane Katrina in 2005.[19]

Despite the enthusiasm in some segments of the public about the Irish heritage of the area, ESI's preliminary research suggested that a focus on Irish ethnicity would neglect a huge segment of the historical population of the neighborhood. Detailed census records for many of the blocks within it demonstrated that, while there had been significant numbers of individuals of Irish heritage residing there, the area was characterized by substantial diversity, both ethnic and racial.[20] It came as no surprise then that—whether in the crowded boardinghouses of the riverfront of what was then the separate uptown city of Lafayette (within what is now New Orleans) or in the biracial meetings of riverfront workers in the Dock and Cotton Council of the early 1900s—working-class residents had occasionally made common cause across ethnic and racial lines. Also unsurprising was that tensions between racial groups were exploited by the city's elite and occasionally erupted into violence, especially with the increasing codification of Jim Crow separation in New Orleans in the first decades of the twentieth century. In light of the controversies that coalesced around the modern St. Thomas/River Garden redevelopment, the straightforward narrative of the construction of the housing project itself began to seem questionable. Why was the neighborhood that became St. Thomas characterized as a slum in 1939? How did it compare with other neighborhoods in the city? Alan Mayne has observed that the material conditions in the imagined slums of late nineteenth- and early twentieth-century cities were often not appreciably different than those in surrounding neighborhoods.[21] If improving these conditions was not the primary goal of slum clearance at St. Thomas, what transformations in the social fabric of the city were meant to be effected by its redevelopment? Were there specific social forms that such interventions were intended to produce, and how did this objective impact the possibilities for subject action for the residents of the areas targeted for change?

Producing the "Normal"

I assume as a starting point for my analysis of slum clearance that all subject positions are naturalized within specific systems of knowledge and power, and that, in being materialized as forms of identity, they become both the means by which inequality is reproduced in society, and, conversely, potential positions from which to mobilize resistance by disrupting or transforming its assumed categories. Race, of course, is a particularly cogent example of such a subject formation in the United States. While constructed to facilitate capitalist economic exploitation and social domination in the form of race-based slavery and segregation, Blackness also became a site of resistance and counterorganization. Throughout this work, there will be examples in which those in power—people claiming whiteness as a position of privilege that allowed them to subjugate others, both socially and economically—attempted to instantiate a two-tiered racial hierarchy, through everything from large-scale state interventions to de facto and de jure discrimination. The populations affected by these processes were not passive observers, nor were they simply in a position of merely responding to the exertion of power. After all, while specific subject categories may be delimited very strictly within a society, in themselves they do not account for the entirety of social action, and this work is full of examples of those whose everyday lives pushed against these hierarchies. However, rather more subtly, racial ideologies positioned a particular vision of whiteness as a norm against which all other modes of social action were defined as illegitimate, pathological, or representative of social disorder.

In this work, I approach the spaces characterized by dominant groups as zones of disorder—urban slums, ghettos, environmentally and socially mar-ginalized spaces—through an archaeological method, in both a literal and a Foucauldian sense.[22] I focus on the other forms of sociality at work in these spaces—alternative, oppositional, heterogeneous, "illegitimate"—by tracing the everyday lives of some of the people who made their homes in the neigh-borhoods prior to clearance. These lives were often deeply impacted by pov-erty and by material need, and the twin strategies of clearance and the con-struction of public housing were ostensibly meant to remedy some of the ills thought to characterize slums, like overcrowding and unhealthy living conditions. However, they were also meant to be productive, constitutive of a middle-class vision of normality centered on a family engaged in produc-tive wage labor. This vision was also one fundamentally rooted in racial hi-erarchy, an ideology in which a monolithic white category was inherently dominant, and in which Black labor was assigned to the service sector. Ulti-mately, public housing would serve as a tool to this end, whether intended or not. It would segregate urban neighborhoods that had been filled with un-ruly subjects, ones that did not conform to the rules of racial and class divi-sions and to those of a middle-class domesticity rooted in a separate and un-equal whiteness.

The language of slum clearance linked this type of disorder to people and the social spaces they inhabited rather than to the material conditions of those spaces. Of course, spaces are never simply empty, open to boundless possi-bilities; they are always themselves social products that set limits and con-ditions for human action, ones inflected by the ghosts of dominant norms. These norms, whether visibly or invisibly, inscribe parameters on the social environment, parameters that are inevitably structured by power relation-ships, inequalities, and hierarchies. While I emphasize the possibilities for experiment and cultural production that were emergent in certain moments and in certain spaces in the city, such possibilities too represent the results of very specific genealogies of power, and any one of them might also rep-resent a closure, a sedimentation, a blockage. I do not intend to represent life in those neighborhoods that were characterized as slums as utopic, full of possibilities. Rather, I seek to interrogate what possibilities were radically circumscribed by slum clearance. The material record of daily life in each of the neighborhoods examined here will form an anchor that will help to resist the dehumanizing tendency of social theory, in which, as João Biehl, Byron Good, and Arthur Kleinman put it, "people who are subject to the most pro-found human experiences . . . have too often been transformed into remote abstractions, discursive forms, or subject positions" by a theoretical focus on subjectivity.[23]

After emancipation and the end of race-based slavery in the United States, there were many methods used to reproduce racial hierarchy: Jim Crow seg-regation, antimiscegenation laws, racist immigration regulations, redlining and racial covenants, lynching, and the terrorist violence of white supremacy. Urban redevelopment and renewal—slum clearance efforts, highway projects, private demolitions, commercial and industrial developments, beautification projects, or other interventions into the built environment—have also been implicated in this process, even though such spatial transformations are pre-sented in the name of progress and improvement, whether material, social, or moral. An examination of these attempts at transforming the urban envi-ronment reveals a complex relationship between space, social production, and material culture. The so-called high modernist tradition of city planning, in which spatial order is seen as a means to regulate social identities and create legible subjects, targeted both densely populated residential clusters near city centers and informal periurban developments at their edges.[24] In the Ameri-can context, such modernist tendencies became fragmented, instituted in fits and starts, with local interests influencing outcomes as much as any mono-lithic state vision. The consequences of such changes in urban space have been analyzed in some detail in a number of cases around the United States, particularly with regard to their role in racial ghettoization and the creation of contemporary urban hyperghettos.[25] Whether as a result of intention or ne-glect, in cities with large African American populations, such interventions materialized systematic residential segregation along racial axes at the level of the everyday and thereby created structural conditions by which those di-visions were reproduced.

To urban planners seeking to understand the disasters connected to Hurri-cane Katrina, the influence of the environment appeared to offer some ready-made answers to the question of what went wrong. In this deterministic reading of urban development, poor and Black residents of the city had been relegated by decades of discriminatory housing policies to the most margin-alized and disadvantaged parts of the city. Such areas, isolated from city ser-vices, coinciding with industrial zones or environmental hazards, and char-acterized by decay and neglect, were seen as acutely delimiting the subject possibilities for those residing there, in a process of physical and social ghetto-ization. Public housing, at least at its inception, had seemed to offer an alter-native to this narrative. With its ordered rows of nearly identical units and large open courtyards, the housing projects would discipline urban space. In contrast to slums or ghettos, with their seeming opacity, such ordered areas could be observed and controlled, and they were thus more conducive to the production of particular kinds of subjects, who could be diagnosed, normal-ized, and reintegrated into the city at large along very particular lines of order. Here, too, the possibilities for social action on the part of residents would be circumscribed, in this case through the acquiescence to an urban order actualized by the visibility of public housing.[26]

Ironically, in the period after World War II, as public housing developments also increasingly became restricted to environmentally marginal spaces at the city's fringes, the vision for what they could do would change. They were still meant to produce something, to be sure: combining together social isolation, segregation, stigmatization, insecurity, and surveillance, the resulting spaces created a state of what the sociologist Loïc Wacquant has termed *advanced marginality* for their resident populations.[27] By looking at the historical (and social) production of these spaces, we can interrogate a reading of African American urban history that sees the present as an inevitable outcome of racist housing policies. In New Orleans, after Hurricane Katrina, residential patterns in the city were discussed as if they were a product of a series of rational consumer choices by residents. The process by which Black residents had come to occupy the lowest-lying, most vulnerable lands in the city—a result of explicitly racial housing covenants, redlining, and decades of de facto and de jure segregation—was ignored, excluded from the very contentious discussions about the direction for the city's future growth. This myopia, in turn, gave the vast inequalities that were exposed in the traumatic post-Katrina scenes of disaster an aura of economic inescapability: it only seemed natural, after all, that the poor would live in what were presumably the cheapest, most vulnerable parts of the city.

There is always a challenge in examining the lives of people in the past through the objects that they consumed, particularly in the era of industrial-level mass production. Everyday consumer goods both reflect and are themselves meant to be constitutive of the norms and values of the dominant society in which they are produced. It is here that historical archaeology, and its theoretical emphasis on materiality, can offer an additional perspective on the past. In cities like New Orleans, authorities (whether urban reformers, city administrators, or police) denied the legitimacy of the everyday survival strategies of the urban poor. The study of everyday life in the areas identified as slums, expressed through the material practices of consumption and through the spatial practices revealed in the material record of the built environment, can be coupled with a critical reading of documentary evidence to advance understandings of urban sociality outside of the binaries of order and disorder. An archaeological focus on materiality helps us examine the active role of marginalized and racialized populations in reshaping and reterritorializing urban spaces, and thus in shaping the city itself.

This, too, is a project that is meant to engage with contemporary politics and claims on power, ones with practical effects on the lives of those affected by urban redevelopment and displacement. The archaeological record gives us a means to examine both the daily lives and the subjectivities of the residents of these neighborhoods, as a necessary step in understanding what kind of normality the housing projects were meant to produce. While the archaeological remains from any of these areas could be incorporated into a narrative based on class aspirations and struggles to adhere to bourgeois ideals, the evidence also suggests that other forms of sociality offered meaningful alternatives for subject action for residents. Just as the construction of the housing projects effaced the physical space of the St. Thomas, Magnolia, Iberville, and Lafitte neighborhoods, so too did it obscure the complexity of social life at their hearts.

Structure of This Book

This book examines four New Orleans neighborhoods (four of the six locations chosen for redevelopment in the first era of slum clearance, just before World War II): St Thomas, Magnolia/Peete, Lafitte, and Iberville. At first, these neighborhoods appear to be a disparate group. St. Thomas and Magnolia, and Lafitte and Iberville shortly thereafter, were planned as racially segregated pairings, but the neighborhoods that they replaced varied in racial, ethnic, and class composition. The degree of resident home ownership varied as well, and in some cases, the neighborhoods even looked very different physically, with different logics of spatial organization structuring them. This book examines why these neighborhoods were classified as having a common singular feature, that of being a "slum," despite this diversity. I use archaeological and historical data to address how these spaces were discursively linked and, moreover, how the tensions, contradictions, and dissonances in the data allow this singular narrative to be contested.

Chapter 2 provides background information, both theoretical and historical, that informs the subsequent chapters. I address some of the theories of subjectivity, the social, and the relationship between space, material practices, and social production that inform this work as a whole, and I engage with archaeological and historical approaches to race and racialized subjectivities. The chapter also examines the issue of race in the city of New Orleans from the colonial period until approximately World War II, particularly as it pertains to African American urban development and the working class in the city after Reconstruction, and as it became connected to ideas about urban planning and renewal that gained prevalence in the years before the growth of federally funded public housing in the United States. Many issues raised in this chapter are revisited within the body of the work, as each of the four individual cases here illuminates a different axis along which disorder was conceived in the view of the proponents of slum clearance. Ultimately, all these axes intersect with race, which remains a constant concern throughout the work.

Chapters 3 and 4 deal with the first two federal housing projects to be constructed in New Orleans. St. Thomas and Magnolia/C. J. Peete were constructed in a structurally similar but racially segregated pair, one, St. Thomas, in desirable, well-drained land on the city's natural levee, and the other, Belmont/Magnolia, in a poorly drained backswamp zone. These chapters examine historical accounts, censuses, insurance maps, and other historical documents to investigate the official account of life in the neighborhoods replaced by these housing projects in the years prior to clearance. Archaeological data from excavations at each of the housing projects provides a means of drawing out tensions in the historical evidence to explore the daily practices—living arrangements, economic strategies, modes of social action, and so on—that made these spaces slums for the proponents of urban renewal. While St. Thomas had become a racially mixed neighborhood by the time it was cleared, the Belmont neighborhood was conceived as mostly Black space for much of the twentieth century. However, it was also a space that was becoming increasingly opaque to governance, as part of an environment that potentially fostered disorder, resistance, and the development of aesthetics and attitudes that contested notions of racial hierarchies within the Jim Crow city. To maintain that order, a certain level of visibility had to be maintained. Public housing, at both St. Thomas and Belmont/Magnolia, represented a reassertion of a normality that had racial separation at its apex.

Chapters 5 and 6 address a second pair of racially segregated housing projects, the Black-only Lafitte and the white-only Iberville Projects. The logics behind the selection of these locations are perhaps even more complex than those at St. Thomas and Magnolia, though they too revolve around unique constellations of perceived racial disorder. Lafitte was within an area with a long connection to the city's Creole of Color community, something reflected in racial identifications in the census (with large numbers of individuals identifying racially as Mulatto from 1900 to 1920), in French surnames for families, and in frequent occupation in skilled trades for residents. By the time of clearance, the neighborhoods' demographic profile was heterogeneous along lines of color and of class, inverting traditional hierarchies of race along the way. Such inversions offered up unique possibilities for the city's Black residents to claim social status and economic power. Chapter 5 examines some of these opportunities through an assemblage from a single feature at Lafitte, a collection of artifacts apparently associated with the household of a midwife and conjure worker from the early 1900s. Such workers crossed the lines between Black and white social worlds in a manner that was troublesome to city and state authorities who sought to regulate their work. Eventually, a neighborhood like Lafitte would create too many contradictions to Victorian ideologies (of race, of class, and of gender) to be tolerated.

Iberville, discussed in chapter 6, is something of a special case in that its boundaries corresponded almost precisely with those of the Storyville district. Storyville was long gone by the time that the housing project was planned and constructed, but its legacy was perceived as tainting the urban environment. In this chapter, I discuss a small segment of a larger archaeological effort within Iberville to examine Storyville, the creation of which in some ways prefigures the sort of large-scale social engineering represented by later slum clearance. I also examine its decline and afterlives to consider why the area was selected as a site for a white-only public housing complex. The decision erased an embarrassing moment from the city's consciousness; after all, many of the city's prominent citizens profited from the district, both directly and indirectly, and its supposed boundaries were always more permeable than they were portrayed. However, what made the Iberville area a slum, and thus subject to clearance, was something more complex. It involved race, gender, and sexuality, particularly the question of sex across a color line that was sometimes still a fluid boundary. The Story ordinance, which created the district, had been meant to address this by making sex work more visible and thereby simpler to police. Storyville eventually failed in this regard, but that failure had echoes and impacts long after the district was gone. Iberville made the district white in a way that an ambiguously worded city ordinance never could.

The chapters shift in scale, from the individual to the family, and from the household to the block and neighborhood. Chapter 7 concludes with a discussion of the common connections and themes that emerge in consideration of these four sites. In short, slum clearance at the inception of the city's public housing became a tool that naturalized the two-tiered racial hierarchy of Jim Crow and effaced the social spaces in which this hierarchy was contradicted. In the years after this first generation of public housing was constructed, its goals and forms changed. The conclusion to this work therefore also considers urban development in modern New Orleans more broadly, including the ways in which these sites and those of the city's other former public housing projects have been transformed and contested in the period before and after Hurricane Katrina. As racial segregation became inscribed on the residential landscape, and as progressive goals were abandoned in public housing policy, these inequalities were reified in the city's housing patterns, something that has sometimes been ignored in planning for the city's post-Katrina development. A consideration of this legacy forms a postscript to my narrative and, perhaps, a nod to the city's future.

2

Subjectivity, Race, and the Birth of Public Housing in New Orleans

In the February 11, 1939, edition of the *Louisiana Weekly*, New Orleans's last major newspaper aimed at an exclusively African American audience, there was a small report of Negro families being forced to abandon the white neighborhood around 1200–1202 Short Street, part of the modern Carrollton/Riverbend area, after a bombing attempt at their home. While local white newspapers at the time seemed to mostly ignore the event, the *Wichita Star* published a fuller account of the three families being terrorized. The "terrific explosion" of the bomb on the front upper porch of the multiunit apartment building was the culmination of a sustained campaign of intimidation that had already progressed through petty police reports (when white neighbors complained about a moving van obstructing the sidewalk) and threatening letters and phone calls. The white landlord of the families had attempted to help by "securing police vigilance . . . when intimidating violence was threatened," but apparently to no avail.[1] This part of the Carrollton neighborhood would remain white space, at least for a little while longer.

Such acts of terror and violence around the issue of housing have been documented in many American cities during the early and mid-twentieth century, but New Orleans has been seen as having a somewhat exceptional history in this regard, with a tradition of integrated housing persisting well into the era of Jim Crow segregation, and with a purportedly greater tolerance of the contradictions inherent in the attempt to racially categorize a heterogeneous population at the level of the everyday.[2] And at least in some sense, New Orleans *was* a special case. The city's African American community was internally complex even before emancipation, with stratification based on class and color, and many neighborhoods continued to display a multiracial residential pattern even after the influx of a rural Black population from former plantations in the post-Reconstruction period. Nevertheless, as Jim Crow separation became reified into urban social, political, and economic power structures, the disorder that was perceived in these patterns could not be tolerated if a two-tiered racial hierarchy was to be sustained. Given the heterogeneity of the experience of race and racialization in the city, violence like the attempted bombings at Short Street would not be sufficient to segregate New Orleans. To re-race the city would require much larger-scale interventions into the built environment. Slum clearance was wielded as one of those tools, meant to create racialized subjects in a white supremacist social order.

In the first half of this chapter, I briefly explore some of the ways that archaeologists have approached the study of race, racialization, and the ideologies that support segregation and racial hierarchies. In subsequent chapters I turn to work from historians, anthropologists, and archaeologists who examine race and Blackness more explicitly, and who attempt to connect them to consumption as a meaningful practice. The second half of this chapter provides a brief history of race and urban development in Black New Orleans, along with a discussion of how this history broadly figured into the city's first big slum clearance movement of the 1930s. This chapter provides both the historical and the theoretical backdrop for a more detailed discussion of the St. Thomas, Magnolia, Lafitte, and Iberville neighborhoods in the chapters that follow. In each of those individual chapters, I introduce additional works that help us understand the experience of marginalized populations in urban America, especially those affected by the racial hierarchy of Jim Crow.

Subjectivity, Space, and Material Culture

How are the actions of individuals constrained by the structural forces that shape their everyday lives? How do *things*, whether it be buildings and the spaces that they form, items that mark and identify the body such as clothing and objects of adornment, or objects that people use to eat, to drink, to treat illness, to work, to relax, even to play, help form and position us as subjects? And what happens when those subjects become unruly or disorderly? How do they reassert their agency to push the range of possibilities in any larger system of "structured structures predisposed to function as structuring structures," to borrow Pierre Bourdieu's somewhat opaque formulation?[3] I approach the rise of public housing in this book not as a historian charting its course, but as one who seeks to understand how race and racial hierarchy became so deeply embedded in American cities as to seem inevitable, and how objects and spaces are implicated in the production of a conception of normality that is rooted in inequality and power.

Throughout this book, I draw on a Marxian tradition in anthropological and social theory that treats the concept of the individual as a stable and unified subject as itself historically situated, the product of a specifically modern (and Western) philosophical tradition of Cartesian dualism that is inherently connected to the economic relations of capitalism.[4] By the twentieth century, many researchers inspired by Marx were examining the ways that people were positioned as subjects in more depth, in part to consider just how powerful ideology might be in determining one's self-perception as an individual and as part of a collective. It is an intellectual tradition that encompasses theorists like Louis Althusser, who emphasized the repressive power of Ideological State Apparatuses, the institutions that interpellate people as subjects and inculcate individuals with an ideology—"a system of ideas and representations"—that only gives meaning to the specific subject positions that reproduce the state's authority, and Michel Foucault, who instead emphasized how power is suffused through the social body, and how the constitution of subjects, through systems of identification, discipline, and classification, is something that occurs at the level of the everyday.[5] Others, drawing on the distinction made between ideology and hegemony by the Italian Marxist Antonio Gramsci, have emphasized the divisions between agentive and nonagentive power, and the potential of daily practice to affect deeply embedded structures and hierarchies, even as those structures set parameters for the choices that can be made within a social system. In the analysis of Pierre Bourdieu, for instance, subjects are formed relationally, and while their lives are shaped by the dominant structures around them, they maintain the ability to affect those structures and assert new positions within them.[6]

One's position as a subject with the ability to act in a social system is also necessarily connected to space, a fact that has received increasing attention stemming from the work of Henri Lefebvre but that has been expressed most vehemently in the work of geographers like Edward Soja and David Harvey. Lefebvre examines space itself as a social product, with social space composed simultaneously of the spaces of the lived, the conceived, and the perceived, where the subjectivities that sustain specific modes of production are constituted and reproduced. However, even as subjects are positioned in abstract spaces of domination, their positions as actors in lived space enable them to generate opposition to the dominant order.[7] Similarly, though proceeding from a somewhat different conceptualization of space, Michel de Certeau has also focused on the unique spatial stories created by individual subjects in their movements to draw attention to the tactics that make subjects more than just passive consumers defined in terms of their surroundings. Certeau's focus is on what Fran Tonkiss has called "urban spaces overdetermined by maps, plans, rules, codes, and schemes," equivalent to what Lefebvre has dubbed *conceived spaces*.[8]

Anthropologists have previously recognized that "the experience of space is always socially constructed," but it is also constitutive, with space and place inextricably linked to how subjects and their identities are defined.[9] If such is the case, urban restructurings like the slum clearance projects discussed in this work provide evidence of how dominant ideologies, expressed in the work of planners, architects, politicians, and reformers, are meant to mold and produce subjects. However, contemporary anthropological and social theory has actively reclaimed the margins of urban order—"spaces of insurgent citizenship" or "spaces of vulnerability"—as loci of cultural production as well.[10] This capacity can be obscured in historical accounts, which privilege the dominant viewpoint and its evidentiary traces, thereby rendering it as timeless, unquestioned and unquestionable, even hegemonic. The analysis in this work draws on historical research as a starting point, but it also incorporates the results of archaeological work as a means to explore the possibilities for social action in those places characterized as slums during the period between the turn of the century and World War II. The data derived from material residues are here considered not just as things that illustrate the historical narrative or that define the dominant norm of a social and cultural moment. Rather, they serve to create tensions; they illuminate gaps, vacancies, and lacunae; they incite conflict and expose ruptures and disjunctures.

Many archaeological studies have attempted to address social life in urban neighborhoods and supposed slums in the modern era, but these studies have varied in how they connect material culture—artifacts, architecture, landscapes—to the populations being studied. In nineteenth-century industrial capitalism, there was a proliferation of technologies designed to categorize populations and make them more governable by fixing identities along certain stable axes of difference, with the legal recognition and codification of naming practices and the increasing specificity of censuses seen as symptomatic (if not constitutive) of this trend. Thus a robust chain of documents may exist that ostensibly describes in great detail the individuals who made up a household or neighborhood, defining them by age, gender, race, ethnicity, nationality, language, religion, occupation, familial relationship, or some other criterion. Whether we take a hard approach to identity, one that sees particular attributes as primordial, fixed, and regulated, or a soft one that emphasizes their constructedness and situational fluidity, such information can provide a useful starting point for analyses. After all, the identities ascribed and recognized by the agents of the state, whether census takers, police officials, or tax collectors, mean *something*: they provide overt insights into subjectivities and the limits that are intended for subject action.[11]

At a large scale, the ideology of a socially or politically dominant group seems to permeate and shape urban spaces. Stephen Mrozowski has argued, for instance, that urban landscapes were "direct expressions of the spatial requirements of both economic regimes [here referring to mercantile and industrial capitalism] and the inequalities they engendered," particularly as these requirements were expressed in the separation of home and work space.[12] Mark Leone has gone so far as to assert that William Paca's garden in colonial Annapolis, Maryland, was fundamentally about power, meant "to naturalize the conflict between slaveholding, diminishing power, and Paca's strong desire to be better able to control the political influences on his own wealth,"[13] while Martin Hall has noted how monumentality and "public manifestations of power" in the colonial Chesapeake and South Africa "worked to frame and form the relationships between people." These "facades of order" concealed the violence of slavery and colonial control, even as they were meant to produce ordered subjects. This process was always imperfect, and many recent studies of landscape have shifted their analysis to the multiple and overlapping landscapes constituted by the everyday actions of individuals or groups.[14]

Individual artifacts, too, may express the dominant ideology, although whether as active attempts to emulate it, as passive expressions of values and worldviews, or as simple embodiments of economic class has been a source of debate as well. In an interpretation of assemblages from late nineteenth-century Sacramento, Adrian Praetzellis and Mary Praetzellis see the material trappings of Victorianism (in the form of fashionable ceramic wares, cups with slogans celebrating work and temperance, and dolls and miniature tea sets) as attempts to "influence the future social order" through the "symbolic and didactic power of artifacts to reinforce 'appropriate' attitudes."[15] This has been a particular theme in archaeological studies of areas identified historically as urban slums, with the apparent banality of the material record taken to indicate that consumption served primarily as a vehicle for class aspirations and respectability for poor and working-class residents of the city.[16] In other words, what is so striking about the excavated material from tenements and slums is just how much it looks like assemblages from middle-class households.

Objects may be intended to express and promote middle-class values and dominant ideologies, and the apparent homogenization of assemblages in the Victorian era may likewise be attributed to the forces of industrial mass production, through which manufactured objects became cheaper and more widely available than ever before. Nevertheless, the meanings imparted to objects by consumers (as well as the actual uses to which the objects were put) do not necessarily correspond with those intended by a dominant group and in fact may diverge from those intents dramatically. Daniel Miller has emphasized that consumption is a meaningful practice, and that to consumers "the authenticity of artifacts as culture derives . . . from their active participation in a process of social self-creation in which they are directly constitutive of our understanding of ourselves and others."[17] While Miller is speaking about capitalist mass production, it has also been argued that any objects, just by virtue of being exchanged, may be transformed into commodities with socially relevant qualities and "regimes of value," loci for both sending and receiving social messages. Considered in this way, material objects mediate notions of identity and subjectivity, and a nuanced reading of the contexts in which objects occur may show the dialectical relationship between material culture as a passive expression of one's subject position and as an active assertion of subjectivities that are not coincident with it.[18]

Archaeological studies of race and consumption in the United States provide some useful examples of the dual role of material culture in society. In the postemancipation United States, racial identity, built on a history of race-based slavery, became a fundamental component of a dominant ideology that justified continued unequal relations between social groups and classes. Particularly in the Jim Crow South, racial difference would come to be portrayed as absolute, with the gulf between Black and white represented as inviolable. Practice-based theories in archaeology have previously dealt with the social identities produced by racialization and the subsequent efforts on the parts of elites to naturalize them.[19] Archaeological studies of African American consumption have further served both to contest the supposed homogeneity of Black life (at least as portrayed by ideologies of racial segregation) and to demonstrate the importance of consumer goods in claims to subject positions that used Blackness as a point of resistance. For instance, Mark S. Warner has used a detailed analysis of ceramic and glass assemblages from African and Anglo-American sites in Annapolis, Maryland, to show that African American consumers were not simply emulating the dominant material culture but in fact using it to "delineate social and/or economic distinctions within African American Annapolis."[20] Paul R. Mullins, also using archaeological materials from Annapolis as a foundation, has presented a much more elaborate treatment of African American consumer culture, incorporating both the effects of racism and the heterogeneity of African American interests to look at the daily struggles that characterized the use of consumer space. By examining commodity consumption and the multiple meanings held by objects for consumers, Mullins explores both how material goods "shaped consumers' understandings of significant social issues, including racial ideology, nationalism, and affluence," and how those goods could be used to challenge those ideologies.[21]

Looking at the social construction of race within historical contexts and in specific fields such as that of consumer culture may help challenge the very ideologies that promulgate racism in the present. As a result, many archaeologists in recent decades who have researched the African American experience in the United States have attempted to actively engage with contemporary politics, with an implicit or explicit goal of positively affecting the everyday lives of Black Americans. While some of those working in this mode have turned to critical self-reflexivity as a method for examining how their own social positions and biases may unintentionally affect interpretations, more often archaeologists have emphasized inclusiveness and public engagement as tools to make research relevant to the populations who might be affected by it. Perhaps partially as a response to these concerns, the one-time relatively circumscribed field of African American archaeology is now much more broadly constituted, to encompass the African diaspora in all its locations, and the Black Atlantic as a social and political field in which a shared experience of race and racialization united African-descended populations in the past and present. Despite the positive impacts of much of this work, and the best intentions on the part of its practitioners, the ability of a publicly engaged and politically involved archaeology of Black America to engage with a subject as daunting as race is still open to debate. As Terrence Epperson has noted, archaeologists should be vigilant of a "vulgar-anti-essentialism" that allows them to only superficially engage with the concerns of the communities who have an interest in their work.[22] Race may be a social construction, but it is one with material consequences, and it is a subjectivity that is experienced in very real ways every day.

Race and Urban Development in New Orleans

The problems of racial classification in New Orleans were apparent quite early in the city's history, and they have received considerable attention in historical studies of the city.[23] Although the area around what is now New Orleans has a long history of indigenous use and occupation, the city was established in 1718, and most of the enslaved Africans brought to the city during the subsequent French colonial era came during the first years of French rule, with all but 190 of the 5,951 documented arrivals of slaves happening prior to 1732. Many of this first generation of enslaved Africans appear to have originated from the Senegambian region of West Africa, perhaps enhancing their ability to maintain interconnections and cultural continuities. Imports of slaves all but ceased between 1732 and 1769, but the institution of slavery, initially unfamiliar to many in the Louisiana colony, was codified and made increasingly strict in these years. A revised version of the French Code Noir, the official crown policy toward slavery, was promulgated in Louisiana in 1724, establishing directives for punishments (to be administered by royal judges rather than private citizens), prohibiting interracial marriages, requiring masters to feed and care for the enslaved and provide them religious instruction, and ostensibly preventing the separation of families during sales. These regulations were rather selectively enforced during the French era, particularly in the fluid society of New Orleans.[24]

The African-descended population of the colony occasionally found common cause with local indigenous populations, alongside of whom they were sometimes enslaved, and with whom they participated in the Natchez rebellion of 1729, in which over two hundred French settlers were killed.[25] Archaeological data from the St. Peter Street Cemetery in New Orleans attest to the closeness between Native Americans and the founding generation of enslaved Africans. There, an archaeological project in 2011 recovered the remains of at least fifteen individuals, most of whom were likely of at least partial African descent. At least four of these individuals also had shoveling of the incisors, a genetic trait associated with Asian and Native American populations, suggesting that these remains were of people of mixed parentage, born during the era of the hiatus in the slave trade.[26] New births probably help account for the fact that, even though the enslaved were typically intended for agricultural labor outside of the city, they still made up over a quarter of New Orleans's roughly 4,500-person population in 1769. Records of free people of color (or *gens du couleur libre*) in Louisiana first appear in 1722, and, although the official count of 165 is often cited for numbers of free Blacks in the city by the end of the French regime, this figure is doubtless an underestimation, as categories of race were enumerated differently (when at all) by the French administration.[27]

During the period of Spanish colonial control of New Orleans, while *gente de color* were distinguished from *blancos*, people of color were also internally differentiated into categories like *mulato, pardo, moreno, grifo,* and *indio*, with the designations (derived from the Spanish casta system) indicating degrees of European, African, and Native American descent. At the same time, the African population of the city was replenished by a renewal of the slave trade, with a shift in geographic focus to the Kongo/Angola region in Central Africa. The greater cognizance to the details of presumed ancestry, along with more liberal Spanish policies toward manumission, helped establish the foundations of a group identity for free Black Creoles by the beginning of the American period.[28] As the racial character of the city was reordered along Spanish lines, the physical character of the city was also transformed, thanks in no small part to devastating fires in 1788 and 1794 that destroyed large swathes of the city's most densely developed center. The city was almost entirely reconstructed according to new building codes in the years afterward, even as Spain was negotiating a return of lands west of the Mississippi River to France. This retrocession had little effect on the city's administration, other than allowing France to sell these same holdings to the United States in the Louisiana Purchase of 1803. It is no small irony that a city that celebrates its

French heritage so strongly has little architecture that dates to the period of French colonization; much of the French Quarter dates from the late Spanish and American antebellum eras.

By the time of the first American census in 1810, a substantial number of both the enslaved (5,961) and free people of color (4,950) were resident in the city, with their numbers together outnumbering the white population of 6,316.[29] The distinctiveness of the city's African American population was further enhanced between 1791 and 1815 by the migration of as many as twenty thousand French-speaking refugees from the revolution in Saint-Domingue, many coming via Cuba.[30] Despite the official end of the importation of slaves to the United States in 1808, New Orleans became a major market for the trade in humans throughout the plantation South, and slavery in southern Louisiana finally found its economic wherewithal in the form of plantation sugar at the beginning of the American period.[31] Throughout the antebellum period, many small farm cessions along the Mississippi River were consolidated into large plantation holdings, which, in turn, required a large number of captive laborers to be economically profitable. It was a boom and bust economy, with its periods of boom constructed on brutal violence and fear.

In New Orleans, as in many cities in the South, urban slaves had lived in proximity to owners, often residing in detached but nearby structures that doubled as kitchens, and free people of color lived in neighborhoods arranged along lines defined more by economic class than by race. This living arrangement resulted in what has been termed the *backyard pattern* of residential integration, in which both free and enslaved Black people regularly interacted with white populations.[32] This situation facilitated surveillance and control, but in a society underpinned by race-based slavery, it also remained a source of considerable anxiety for slave holders in the years leading up the Civil War, probably for good reason. A major slave uprising had been planned in Pointe Coupée, upriver of New Orleans, in 1795, and influences of the Jacobinism of the French Revolution and its Haitian counterpart echoed into the American period. In 1811, another insurrection was attempted, with some five hundred slaves led by a Mulatto man named Charles Deslondes from Saint-Domingue eventually marching toward New Orleans before being stopped by armed militias. Resistance, both overt and covert, from the enslaved and from free people of color, continued throughout the antebellum era. As a result, increasing restrictions were placed on the movements of free people of color, the rights of the enslaved, and the legal requirements for manumission, in a continuing effort to maintain dominance over a defiant population.[33]

The Civil War and the subsequent abolition of slavery marked the beginning of massive shifts in population in the South, and between 1860, just before emancipation, and 1900, the African American population of New

Orleans more than tripled, from around twenty-five thousand (including both urban slaves and free people of color) to over seventy-five thousand. Large-scale street violence marked both the beginning and the end of Reconstruction, from the race riot of 1866 to the so-called Battle of Liberty Place of 1874, which effectively restored white supremacist control of state and local governments. Even though the promises of Reconstruction were unfulfilled, the end of slavery signaled profound transformations in notions of identity and citizenship for the African American population of Louisiana and elsewhere.[34] In New Orleans, freed men and women entered a society unlike many in the South, in which a vocal, property-holding, politically active group of *gens du couleur*, many claiming European descent, formed a ready-made Black upper class. Despite the heterogeneity of African American urban life in this period, and internal stratification on the basis of class and color, many of the Black Creole elite saw it as their duty to make common cause with other Black citizens to challenge white supremacy in newspapers, in legal cases, and in social and economic arenas.[35]

Despite this tradition of activism, by the end of the nineteenth century, increasing legal and social barriers were being instituted across the nation to ensure that Black people as a whole would be relegated to a permanent racial underclass, even if they were still internally differentiated by social or economic status. A few signal events marked the codification of Jim Crow segregation in New Orleans. Interracial marriage was outlawed in Louisiana in 1894, with this prohibition extended to concubinage in 1908. In 1896, in the infamous *Plessy v. Ferguson* legal decision, the US Supreme Court made a ruling that sanctioned the separate-but-equal clause that defined Jim Crow racial separation. To instigate the legal action that resulted in this test case, Homer Plessy, a light-skinned Creole of Color who could easily pass as white, had to inform a conductor that he was violating the state law that mandated segregation of passenger railcars. The city's Black political elite felt confident that this case would expose the inherent absurdity of race-based segregation laws. Instead, the decision paved the way for the Louisiana legislature to effectively repeal the protections of the Thirteenth and Fourteenth Amendments and disenfranchise Black voters in the Louisiana Constitution of 1898, distinguishing the right of citizenship from the "privilege" of voting. An example of the impact of this decision can be seen in the rapid decline of registered Black voters. Between 1888 and 1898, the registration of "colored" voters in Louisiana dropped by around 90 percent, from a high of 128,150 to only 12,902, and by 1930 only 2,128 registered voters in Louisiana were identified as Black.[36]

Between 1900 and 1940, the Black population of New Orleans doubled again, to near 150,000.[37] In the antebellum period, many neighborhoods in the city had been substantially mixed in racial composition, but by the twentieth century, African American migrants to the city increasingly were confined to what geographers have termed *backswamp ghettos* or *back-of-town clusters*, poorly drained and flood-prone zones just off of the higher natural levee of the Mississippi River along the historical periphery of the city.[38] These lowlying areas were also often circumscribed within superblocks with perimeters formed by major radial boulevards and commercial thoroughfares. Typically, more affluent white populations concentrated along the outer portions of these superblocks, and poor and/or Black residents, often employed in the service sector, clustered in the interior.[39] Nevertheless, pockets of racial heterogeneity, some on valuable riverfront property, persisted well into the twentieth century, even as Jim Crow segregation became increasingly entrenched in state and federal courts and in society at large.

While backswamp areas along the edge of the river levees had been the sites of extensive development on the part of African Americans and poor white immigrants in the post-Reconstruction period, the decision in the 1890s to undertake large-scale drainage projects converted many of these areas into valuable real estate.[40] As a result, populations that identified racially as Black or Negro, displaced by rising rents and exclusive housing covenants, were pushed into even more marginal landscapes, which in turn received lower priority for connections to city services and minimal investment for maintenance of public works. Furthermore, the extension of the city streetcar system to encompass larger geographic areas of the city facilitated segregation, in that it eliminated the necessity for African American domestic workers to live in proximity to their employers. By 1940, around the time that the first major federally funded housing projects were constructed in New Orleans, much of the city's Black population resided in a belt through some of the lowest elevations in the city, between the toe of the natural levee and the slightly higher ground of the Gentilly Ridge and Bayou St. John.[41]

Slum Clearance and Public Housing in New Orleans

In the colonial and antebellum eras, developments on the peripheries of towns and cities had often been characterized as loci of social disorder because they provided a refuge for the so-called strolling poor, along with vagrants, maroons, and other marginalized groups. But as the administrative arm of governance improved methods for regulating populations in the latter half of the nineteenth century, it was the densely populated inner-city neighborhoods, often the home of ethnically mixed and/or immigrant populations, that epitomized the chaos of city life.[42] Large-scale modernization projects became one remedy for this situation, with the so-called Haussmannization of Paris representative of the top-down nineteenth-century approach to slum clearance.

With authority coming directly from Napoleon III, Baron Georges-Eugène Haussmann's project, running from the 1850s until 1870, opened large boulevards into crowded neighborhoods of winding streets, accompanying this effort with renovations to sewage and sanitation, provisions for parks and public spaces, and improvements to churches and public buildings. This project was intended to benefit public health, even as it made it easier to police the city and forestall political unrest.[43]

The dense urban slums that developed in England during the nineteenth century became a particular source of fascination for Victorian-era reformers. Rapid industrialization and a concurrent growth in population in London (which, by the end of the nineteenth century, had reached a population of over six million), had created crowded, squalid, often-desperate conditions in the inner city, and a literature dedicated to exploring slums developed in England and soon spread to the United States. This literature blended sensationalist accounts and titillation with supposedly objective reporting on life in impoverished neighborhoods. Coupled with what Dell Upton has termed a *republican imagination*, which sought to order, classify, and rank the disorder of city life, reformist literature impelled the burgeoning slum clearance movement domestically. Jacob Riis's *How the Other Half Lives* (1890) was only the most prominent of the American genre of slum reportage that involved supposed exposés of the dark and alien worlds of the city's center. The slums, and the lower classes who resided there, were feared as a source of contagion, potentially contaminating middle-class values and spreading vice.[44]

Material conditions in urban tenement areas, particularly problems in health, sanitation, and access to adequate living space, were typically due to stark inequalities in the provision of basic city services for the urban poor, but these conditions also made them an appealing target for clearance for ambitious new city planning projects, like those proposed for Washington, DC, Cleveland, San Francisco, and Philadelphia, and perhaps most famously in Daniel Burnham's 1909 plan for Chicago. Such plans treated densely occupied downtown areas as blank slates, ready for replacement with monumental civic buildings and grand radial thoroughfares, and they rarely if ever dealt with the problem of urban housing in a substantive way.[45] Attempts at reform were initially linked to private philanthropy and, often, the women's movement, with Jane Addams's Hull House in Chicago being one of the more famous examples from the late nineteenth century. Hull House, founded in 1889, was a settlement house intended to provide services to new immigrants to the city and to help them integrate into American society. Other private developers experimented with providing low-cost but high-quality tenement housing for working-class families in the first decades of the twentieth century, but with at best mixed results.[46]

After 1909, a new generation of City Beautiful and City Functional planners applied their designs chiefly to the construction of middle- and upperclass suburbs outside of the densely developed city center. As the growth of such suburbs gained momentum in the 1920s, it only served to circumscribe the possibilities for housing the city's poor, especially the growing African American population of cities in the North and South. The new suburbs were zones of control, where the tool of the restrictive covenant was used to limit the possibilities for how property could be developed. While the obligations that such covenants inserted as contractual terms for purchasing property could be used to regulate commonplace aspects of the physical environment (the heights of buildings, colors of paint, and so on), many such obligations were also intended to guarantee a socially and racially homogeneous neighborhood in perpetuity. While the US Supreme Court ruled that racial zoning was unconstitutional in the 1917 *Buchanan v. Warley* decision, this ruling did not apply to private racial covenants, which had already been sanctioned by Louisiana courts the same year. Such patterns persisted long after World War II, even though the Supreme Court added that private racial covenants were unenforceable in 1948. The National Association of Real Estate Boards officially discouraged integration in its Code of Ethics until 1950, and it considered the right to exclude minorities as fundamental in its Property Owners' Bill of Rights as late as 1963. The tools for discrimination in housing were expanded further in these decades to include redlining, the practice in which banks would refuse to issue housing loans to specific areas because of their racial composition, undermining the economic possibilities for Black citizens in a way that was particularly insidious, as it was so invisible.[47]

By the end of the nineteenth century, two chief strategies had emerged for creating order out of the perceived chaos of slum life. One focused on the individual as a subject to be disciplined, corrected, and made moral, often through repressive means, while the other focused on reshaping the urban environment as a means to this end, under the assumption that physical order could produce moral order. These strategies would ultimately come together in slum clearance projects like those that gave birth to public housing in New Orleans. The housing situation—and, moreover, the situation of the urban poor in general—was dire in New Orleans by the 1900s. Funding for public relief in New Orleans, particularly for Black residents, was practically nonexistent, with the city ranking last among thirty-one major American cities in spending for social welfare. During World War I, the federal government had announced the intention to build special war housing in the city, and the state legislature passed an act to form a housing commission in response. However, most early agitation for housing reform came from private philanthropic groups like the New Orleans Community Chest, a coalition of the city's charities that was formed in 1924. Advertising itself as "Builders of Future Citizens . . . Impartial, Non-Sectarian—For the Welfare of All Races and Creeds," it focused on social uplift through programs of "Team Work" like the Boy Scouts rather than the "Gang Work" of the alleys that "develops the type of men who tear at the very vitals of society." The organization claimed wide support from city authorities and considerable success in fund-raising in the years leading up to the stock market crash of 1929, even as the city's shortage of housing for Black residents grew more and more acute.[48]

Despite early attempts to ignore the severity of the crisis, the realities of the Great Depression set in rapidly after 1930, when vast numbers of the broke and unemployed set on the move in a futile search for work. Hoovervilles, temporary encampments of the transient homeless unflatteringly named for President Herbert Hoover, formed around many American cities. Groups like the Community Chest, representing the old private model of philanthropy, could not even hope to keep up with the demands for support, their campaigns to raise money falling far short of their stated goals, and even farther short of the needs of the poor. Upon assuming office in 1933, new president Franklin Delano Roosevelt immediately initiated the New Deal, including a number of far-reaching programs intended to stabilize the country's financial crisis, provide practical relief, and put the unemployed back to work, often through massive public works projects. In New Orleans, Public Works Administration (PWA) funds were used to build the new Charity Hospital building and to complete the Huey P. Long Bridge over the Mississippi River. The Works Progress Administration (WPA) was also particularly active in the city, with WPA workers employed to renovate historic buildings like the Cabildo, improve bridges, restore public markets, and expand and beautify parks.[49]

The New Deal marked a dramatic change in federal policy on urban housing. In 1933, Secretary of the Interior Harold Ickes announced the formation of the Public Works Emergency Housing Corporation to "engage in low-cost housing and slum clearance projects which otherwise would not be undertaken."[50] This was followed soon after by the National Housing Act of 1934, which created agencies like the Federal Housing Administration, the Federal National Mortgage Association, and the Federal Savings and Loan Insurance Corporation.[51] While reformers began planning for redevelopments in many urban areas, the exact form that housing reform should take (and the level of federal involvement in it) was deeply contested in subsequent years, and courts effectively blocked attempts by the government to acquire large tracts by condemnation. Even at this early period, reformers and planners recognized that the racial composition of public housing would be a contentious issue. As a result, Ickes developed what was known as the Neighborhood Composition Rule, by which any new housing project should not change the

racial composition of the area in which it was located. It was simply understood that public housing itself would be segregated.[52]

Plans for the construction of public housing in many urban areas in the
United States were already underway by the early 1930s, but construction
typically languished until the end of the decade. In a few cases, like that of
Neighborhood Gardens in Saint Louis, smaller-scale housing units were built
as potential models for the more extensive ones that would come later.[53] In
New Orleans, Belmont, the neighborhood eventually replaced by the Magnolia Project (discussed in chapter 4), was targeted as a potential locus of slum
clearance by the first part of the 1930s, but these initial plans were repeatedly
undermined by friction between local, state, and federal authorities over who
had the power to select sites and condemn land for redevelopment. This debate was also taking place at a national level, and a compromise was eventually reached in the form of the US Housing Act of 1937. This act, also known
as the Wagner-Steagall Act, was passed to provide federal assistance to "the
States and political subdivisions thereof" for the construction of residences
for low-income families.[54] Many problems in the equitable implementation
of public housing stemmed from language in this act (and, later, in the 1949
Taft-Ellender-Wagner Act), which placed ultimate control of planning, placement, and construction of housing complexes in the hands of local authorities like HANO.[55] Even though many administrators of the PWA Housing
Division and of its successor, the Public Housing Administration, were proponents of integrationist policies, the wording of the act removed them from
direct supervision of decisions that might affect housing's racial composition.
Furthermore, until the 1960s, to obtain support from segregationist legisla-
tors, whose votes were essential for the housing acts to pass, no provision for
integration of public housing could be inserted in the federal law. Groups op-
posing public housing, among them the National Association of Real Estate
Boards, National Association of Home Builders, and US Savings and Loan
Leagues, often allying themselves with segregationist forces, organized their
opposition at the local level, forcing housing advocates to compromise larger
goals of social reform.[56]

The New Orleans City Council, recognizing the urgent need for affordable housing in the city, was proactive in its approach to slum clearance, and
it created HANO to prepare applications for federal funds even before the
Wagner-Steagall Act was passed. In 1938–39, with authority stemming from
the 1937 act, HANO, working in conjunction with the WPA, conducted surveys of housing conditions throughout portions of the city, quantifying residences along criteria like "cold water only," "no lighting facilities," "major repairs needed," or simply "unfit for use."[57] Descriptions of this survey in the
local paper couched its goals in euphemisms: the survey would "provide the

Figure 2.1. Buildings (described as "ramshackle" in the 1950 HANO report) at Toledano and Magnolia Streets in the Magnolia extension area.

basis for a better city" and "determine the future trend of new building," for instance.[58] In the metropolitan area as a whole, of 145,039 dwelling units surveyed, 62,758 were found to be substandard, either in condition, in occupancy, or in both (figure 2.1, table 2.1).[59] In addition, blocks throughout the city were mapped according to their racial composition. According to the "Definitions of Terms Used" for the surveys, "if any member of the household, other than a servant, is negro or of a race other than white, the entire household is considered as belonging to that race."[60] Thus, the surveys applied the social equivalent of the biological one-drop rule, serving to obscure the level of close cross-racial interaction in the city at the level of the everyday. Soon, the city would be remade in an attempt to inscribe this dichotomy into the landscape.

The specific trajectory of the development of public housing in New Orleans has previously been explored in some detail.[61] New Orleans was considered a leader in this field, in no small part because of the energetic stewardship of Colonel Kemper Williams, the chairman of HANO in these formative years, and vice-chairman William Guste, both of whom were nationally recognized for their dedication to bringing federal investment in housing to the city. Williams himself described New Orleans as the "guinea pig" of US cities in the application of the Housing Act, as the first to fully implement it.[62] The first six sites selected were paired conceptually, if not geographically. The white-only St. Thomas Housing Project would be located at the riverfront adjacent to the present-day Lower Garden District, while the Black-only Magnolia

Street Housing Project was located in a low-lying backswamp zone. The location of the white-only Iberville Housing Project almost precisely corresponded to the footprint of the former Storyville red light district, and its counterpart, the Black-only Lafitte Project, would occupy a location between Orleans Avenue and the former course of the Old Basin Canal. Two other Black-only projects, the Calliope (later renamed B. W. Cooper) and St. Bernard, were meant specifically to address the shortage of urban housing for the city's African American residents. They would be located farther afield: the Calliope was built largely over a dump adjacent to a railroad, and the St. Bernard was located at the isolated lakeward edge of the Seventh Ward. Property acquisition for these projects took place rapidly, with relatively few disagreements over the valuations of homes in the areas selected, and the tool of condemnation proceedings only used as a last resort.[63]

Relocation of families living within the areas to be cleared took place rapidly. The Magnolia area, for instance, was apparently vacated in just over a month. According to official accounts by HANO, the "evacuations" at St. Thomas and Magnolia proceeded with minimal controversy, with area newspapers cooperating by refusing to circulate and publicize rumors that might cause a panic. Coverage in the *Louisiana Weekly*, directed at an African American audience, was almost exclusively concerned with issues related to the administration of the Magnolia Project. By the time of site clearance, the racial segregation of the new projects was a foregone conclusion. The paper cooperated with HANO by printing editorials encouraging affected families to vacate promptly, so that the slum could be replaced exclusively with those having a "background of decency" and "good morals." Some evidence of occasional disquiet appears in the paper: concerns were expressed about "abusive interviewers" in charge of selecting new residents, and Black community leaders were worried about the new, exclusively residential zoning in the area immediately surrounding Magnolia, which might force away business owners. Nevertheless, as far as the newspaper was concerned, the chief issue regarding the new project between 1939 and 1940 that required editorial activism was the racial composition of those in management positions. After occasional protests and amid near-weekly coverage of the issue through summer 1940, HANO finally caved on the "Negro manager question," with the proviso that any Black manager would still be subordinate to a manager for St. Thomas and Magnolia together, a position formally reserved for "a member of the white race."[64]

Although it was known at the outset that the new housing would be segregated, the potential composition of new residents was the subject of a considerable number of rumors. At the end of 1939, when St. Thomas was all

Table 2.1. Data Collected in 1938–39 by the Housing Authority of New Orleans on the Neighborhoods to Be Replaced by Housing Projects

Housing Project Area	No. of Units Surveyed	Cold water only	No lighting facilities (no gas or electricity)	No heating arrangements	Major repairs needed
LA 1-1 (St. Thomas)	513	451	183	116	129
LA 1-2 (Magnolia)	869	854	471	168	309
LA 1-3 (Iberville)	723	714	485	168	364
LA 1-5 (Lafitte)	567	552	172	171	141
LA 1-7 (Calliope)	25	25	8	2	3
LA 1-8 (St. Bernard)	67	64	35	33	32

Source: Compiled from the 1939 *Report of the Housing Authority of New Orleans.*

but finished, the *Times-Picayune* reported that applicants were still uncertain whether children would be allowed, and some potential residents thought that they would only be allowed to leave the project once a week if admitted. There certainly were many rules, and many of them seemed almost specifically aimed to exclude the sort of families that had resided in the areas previously. Residents of the new units had to be "bona fide families of no less than two and no more than seven members," with no boarders, no pets, and no unrelated people in the household. The applicants had to be living in a derelict building at present, and they could have no police record or "reputation for rowdyism."[65] Such requirements seemed to betray the stated intent of public housing: if only the elements of the poor who fit with such ideal versions of a family were allowed into public housing, then what should happen to those excluded? The story of what happened to public housing in the years after World War II, in both New Orleans and elsewhere around the country, is a subject to which I return later in this book. More public housing projects were built in the city in the years after the war, each larger, more isolated, and

Table 2.1. *continued*

Unfit for use	Indoor shared toilets	Outdoor shared toilets	Stove only in kitchen	Sink only in kitchen	No stove or sink	No bathing facilities
41	37	78	92	1	42	207
70	127	311	226	31	116	454
101	196	341	329	5	229	476
40	27	81	138	2	27	220
2	0	2	0	0	0	10
9	0	1	40	1	1	62

more shoddily constructed than the last. At the same time, the lofty goals of social uplift initially attached to slum clearance were abandoned, with urban renewal policies increasingly concerned with warehousing and confining the poor. After the 1960s, when public housing was finally integrated in New Orleans, public housing had become almost exclusively Black space, and its demolition and redevelopment would be seen by some as an even more pernicious attempt to remake a more segregated city.

3

St. Thomas

Effacing Heterogeneity in the Irish Channel

The Irish Channel in New Orleans has a long-fabled reputation and a certain mythic quality. Today, the name is applied to an area of small shotgun houses and larger townhouses, many with ornate late Victorian detailing, located along the riverfront from Jackson Avenue to Louisiana Avenue. This area was codified as the Irish Channel after being listed as a National Register Historic District in 1976, with the designation later applied to a somewhat larger area by the city's Historic District Landmark Commission in 2002. It is a scene of booming real estate, with its claim to Irishness cemented by an active neighborhood association, Irish-themed corner bars, and a raucous St. Patrick's Day parade and block party. From rather modest beginnings in 1947, the parade has become a massive event in a busy calendar of such happenings, enhanced by the surreal scene of cabbages, onions, carrots, and potatoes (the ingredients of Irish stew, of course), along with stuffed animals, beads, panties, Irish Spring soap, and, inexplicably, packages of ramen noodles—all of it raining from floats. This parade was founded in part to reunite families and friends from the neighborhood who had long since moved out of the city to St. Bernard and Jefferson Parishes, a process of combined white flight and displacement in which the construction of the St. Thomas Housing Project in 1939 is said to have played a substantial part. The president of the Irish Channel St. Patrick's Day Club reminisced in 2012 about the old channel neighborhood as "a melting pot of Italians, Germans, and French," along with the Irish, united by a shared Catholic heritage.[1]

There is little evidence today that the modern historic districts of the Irish Channel were known historically by that name, and the location of the original channel—if there was one—is open to debate. Most would locate the historic Irish Channel in the area around the two blocks of Adele Street, a tradition that was given voice in accounts recorded during the WPA era by researchers of the Louisiana Writers' Project.[2] Adele Street is now all but obliterated.

Its former location sits under the once-controversial Super Walmart complex that forms the commercial anchor of the River Gardens redevelopment, which replaced the St. Thomas Housing Project by 2002. The 1950s expansion of St. Thomas had already left Adele Street a near-deserted cul-de-sac, though a small historic Baptist church with an African American congregation and a few workshops and residences had persisted into the 1990s. The loss of the physical space of Adele Street perhaps makes it easier to propagate the long-standing legend of the Irish Channel as an oddly homogeneous melting pot: diverse in ethnic background, but held together by a working-class, Catholic, and white identity. This legend holds that the projects helped to destroy this insular, closely knit neighborhood, and that it is now coming back despite pockets of persistent Black poverty within it. Parades are, after all, a way of reclaiming public space and reterritorializing it; whatever the intentions of organizers, the Irish Channel St. Patrick's Day parade valorizes a very particular—and very white—version of the past of the neighborhood.[3]

Despite the negative view of the housing projects today, when HANO embarked on its program of slum clearance in New Orleans in 1939, it was initially met with plenty of excitement, even apparently among those to be displaced by the new construction. The government-funded projects provided state-of-the-art amenities like refrigerators and indoor plumbing, many of which were rare in the city's poorest communities, and crowds lined up around the block to tour model apartments opened at St. Thomas and Magnolia. Particular pride was taken in the fact that the new structures themselves would occupy only 25 percent of the built footprint of the areas selected for redevelopment, so that the salubrious effects of light and open space could be felt by all new residents.[4] New Orleans was cited nationally as a model for US cities in the practical application of the 1937 Wagner-Steagall Act, which provided federal assistance for the construction of low-income housing. Under the guidance of chairman Colonel Kemper Williams, a philanthropist and businessman, HANO was seen as a prime example of the energetic application of the law to housing the urban poor. As preparations were made for tenant selection, Colonel Williams was rewarded with the Times-Picayune Loving Cup for his service to the city, even as the housing program was steadily expanded.[5] Only occasional notes were sounded about the loss of the former neighborhood. A feature in the Times-Picayune, for instance, told the story of the three Breslin brothers, who were delaying moving out of their home for as long as possible. The Breslins were the bachelor sons of an Irish immigrant, and the family had resided at 624 St. Andrew Street for sixty years. The story emphasized that even they knew that change in the neighborhood was inevitable.[6]

Some of the initial excitement rapidly gave way to disappointment, as many of the neediest families in the city found themselves categorically excluded from housing in the new projects, particularly in the neighborhoods in which they formerly had resided. The new projects were segregated along racial lines, with St. Thomas reserved for white residents only. This meant that roughly half of the St. Thomas neighborhood's former residents would be ineligible to return. New potential residents also faced an intensive screening and interview process that rejected many applicants as ineligible or undesirable. While the *Times-Picayune* proudly trumpeted that "dogs, criminals, and rowdies" were to be excluded, the criteria by which undesirability was measured were subjective at best. Potential occupants were eliminated from consideration based on interviewers' impressions about their "poor housekeeping" or "personality difficulties"; one otherwise neat family was rejected at the Black-only Magnolia Housing Project (discussed in more detail in chapter 4) because the husband was "insolent" and possessed "too many suits."[7]

While the improvement of decayed housing conditions was certainly a concern for those on the board of HANO, many of them would likely have agreed with David Walker, the executive director of Philadelphia's Redevelopment Authority, who expressed his faith in the ability of urban renewal to reform residents. Speaking of a new housing facility at a 1950 public hearing, Walker said, "Here . . . will be the joining together of facilities and abilities to bring normalcy into areas which today do not have normalcy."[8] This idea, that the spatial disorder of urban slums was inherently connected to social disorder and pathology, is something that has a long history in the interventions meant to deal with urban poverty in America. From a Foucauldian perspective, it underlies the disciplinary logic of prisons, schools, poorhouses, and hospitals, all of which are physical locales meant to separate, order, rank, diagnose, and correct. Joseph Heathcott has noted as much in Saint Louis, where public housing was inspired by a sort of panopticism to explicitly act "in the nature of a clinic" at its birth, providing "the basis for the cultivation of good family life" through the provision of separate, private units with modern amenities, governed by policies regulating appropriate uses of space.[9]

St. Thomas, along with the rest of the first generation of New Orleans public housing, certainly fits with this model. Each project replaced the perceived disorder of urban slums with low-density apartment blocks, divided into neat, modern residential units occupied by single families, equipped with private kitchens and sanitary facilities, ordered around wide, open courtyards. These units were meant to be productive of a very particular kind of normalcy, one characterized by families with a wage-earning man at the head and a mother keeping the home, with private spaces for family life, and with the focus of social life moved inside, away from the chaos and heterogeneity of the street. The new units at these earliest examples of public housing were architecturally appealing and well built, quite distinct both from the dense high-rise units that would soon be associated with public housing in other urban centers, and from the sometimes-ramshackle wood-frame buildings that characterized the neighborhoods that they replaced. Public housing, at its inception, was meant to be a curative, a stopover that would allow the deserving poor to rehabilitate themselves and move on to more permanent accommodations, even if the screening process for potential residents suggests some suspicion that architecture alone could not exact lasting change on individuals. By the 1960s this reformist ethos in public housing would be abandoned for one that was essentially custodial; if the projects were intended as clinics, then these clinics increasingly became simply about quarantine and confinement.

But why was the St. Thomas neighborhood selected as a slum, a space so blighted that conditions there could only be remedied by their total effacement? This is the question to which I return in this and the next three chapters. The neighborhoods selected for clearance and redevelopment had very different histories, and, on the ground, they looked very different, whether in racial and ethnic demographics, in class composition, in housing conditions, or in the built environment itself. While the obvious answer to this question would be that it was the material elements of these neighborhoods, such as decaying housing stock and substandard sanitary conditions, that made them slums, this supposition breaks down very quickly. Alan Mayne has demonstrated through historical research how the portrayal of slumlands as "existing upon the margins of tolerable living conditions and acceptable behavior" is often divorced from the material conditions within them, with the slum as something that is discursively created to contrast the progress-oriented and capitalist modern city with the subterranean, dark, and morally degenerate premodern one. This "imaginary schism" justified large-scale interventions intended to eradicate these perceived sites of disorder, even as it perpetuated the idea of the slums as sources of social and physical contagion. Such interventions allowed heterogeneous slum populations to be separated and remade as both productive workers and stable consumers, gridded into planned neighborhoods that facilitated state control and surveillance.[10]

This chapter discusses the St. Thomas/Irish Channel neighborhood in the decades prior to its razing in 1939 to identify characteristics that allowed it to be conceived as a slum and thus as a subject for redevelopment. While the public transcript of administrative sources gives a straightforward account of this process, a critical reading of those same sources, along with an analysis of the material record, can reveal ruptures and contradictions, a productive discord that can help to understand the interlinked logics by which St. Thomas and the other neighborhoods discussed in this book were identified for slum clearance.[11] Disorder in each neighborhood was marked where race intersected with other aspects of identity in such a manner as to threaten the ideological structures of whiteness, and therefore of twentieth-century America itself, structures that were intended to maintain racial hierarchy and undermine working-class cooperation. Ethnicity, at least in a constructivist view, is always about defining boundaries, either for political and economic ends or for claims of relative position in a social hierarchy. In the St. Thomas neighborhood, the logic of this hierarchy was breaking down. When that mythic character of the Irish Channel as an ethnic enclave of working-class white New Orleans was exposed, it became a source of disorder that could no longer be tolerated.[12]

From Irish Channel to Urban Slum

The St. Thomas Street Housing Project (designated LA 1-1 by HANO), as it was originally planned, occupied the entirety of ten city blocks and portions of three others, in a part of the Lower Garden District bounded by Constance, Felicity, St. Thomas, and St. Andrew Streets. During the 1950s, it was expanded to encompass seven more blocks, extending almost to Tchoupitoulas Street. This portion of the city, located on the desirable high ground of the river's natural levee, has a history dating back to the colonial era, when it was part of a series of plantation tracts and farmsteads. Development throughout the eighteenth century was concentrated directly at the riverfront, but as the city rapidly grew in this direction during the early part of the American period, these tracts were subdivided into residential lots gridded for urban use. The area that became St. Thomas was located at modern St. Andrew Street, along the dividing line of two such tracts, the Faubourg Nuns (named after the Ursuline nuns who had established a plantation in the vicinity by 1780) and the Panis Plantation tract. These tracts were surveyed for subdivision in the first decades of the nineteenth century. During the early antebellum years, they remained suburbs of the city proper. They were established as part of Jefferson Parish in 1825, and the Faubourg Nuns was incorporated into the new city of Lafayette by 1833 (not to be confused with the modern city of that name, located to the west of New Orleans). The river frontage of Lafayette thrived in the 1830s and 1840s, particularly after a series of wharves was constructed, and industries associated with the stock landing at Jackson Avenue, like slaughterhouses, tanneries, and tallow renderers, became particularly prominent.[13]

Immigrants flooded into New Orleans in these antebellum years, and the suburb of Lafayette expanded from an official population of only 1,200 in 1840 to over 14,000 in 1850. These new residents were employed in a variety of trades, with many naturally gravitating to shipping, both at the docks and at newly established rail lines. Much of Lafayette retained a somewhat rural character throughout these years, with more affluent residents concentrated along the mule-drawn railcar line on Nayades Street (now St. Charles Avenue) and along the commercial thoroughfare of Jackson Avenue.[14] The blocks closest to the river were something of an exception, becoming densely developed with a mixture of crowded small cottages, tenements, and boardinghouses. Many of these blocks catered specifically to the transient populations who worked the river trade, and something of a rough-hewn entertainment district sprang up along Tchoupitoulas between St. Mary and Josephine Streets, with numerous coffeehouses, billiard halls, oyster saloons, cigar stores, and liquor sellers in proximity. Particularly prominent in this period was the Bull's Head, a tavern located at the foot of St. Mary where Mississippi River boatmen, after delivering goods to the wharves, would dismantle their flatboats and sell the wood for lumber and scrap.[15]

Archaeological vestiges of this early riverfront development were found in an area now occupied by the parking lot of a Walmart in the block historically bounded by Tchoupitoulas, St. Mary, Religious, and St. Andrew Streets. A warehouse for the Pelican Cotton Press had been built on the block in the 1850s, but when it was constructed, a layer of industrial fill had sealed the remains of an apparent tavern and boardinghouse from the city of Lafayette beneath it. Archaeologists found a brick surface that apparently represented an outdoor public area at the business, which would have been covered over in part by a second-floor gallery on wooden posts, in a style still commonly seen around the city (figure 3.1). Records of businesses are often a bit unclear about precise geographic locations in the city's antebellum era, but this may have been the location of a coffeehouse operated by James Mut, a Spaniard who shows up in an 1846 City Directory for Lafayette and in the 1850 census. In the latter, he is enumerated in a household with his family, along with a Portuguese bartender at the coffeehouse, a bottle washer from Spain, and an English clerk. Some unusual patterns were noted for the assemblage of archaeological remains at the site, including an abundance of small plates, cups, and bowls, many of them from long-outdated ceramic wares and decorative styles, and a paucity of those personal items traditionally associated with women and children (toys, beads, jewelry, etc.). At least two pipe bowls decorated with Masonic emblems and Irish harps were collected, along with a pocket watch and a pewter mercury syringe for treating venereal diseases. Most unusually, a number of the broken ceramic vessels recovered had apparently been reworked into small saucer-like dishes, perhaps well suited to casual dining in a raucous tavern setting. Overall, the material suggested a social environment characterized by informality, one dominated by a multiethnic, transient population who took advantage of the opportunities offered by life on the fringes of the city.[16]

Figure 3.1. Excavations at antebellum riverfront coffeehouse in City Square 33, St. Thomas Housing Project retail extension area, summer 2002. (Courtesy of Earth Search, Inc.)

Lafayette was reincorporated into the expanding city of New Orleans in 1852. By the 1850s, this portion of the city had become associated especially with Irish immigrants, and it is presumably in this period that Adele Street gained its reputation as the city's original Irish Channel. However, the surrounding riverfront area quickly assumed a multiethnic character. Census records from the city of Lafayette attest to a polyglot population in boardinghouses along the riverfront, and a substantial German population was resident in the area quite early. The diversity of religious institutions founded in these years helps to track the shifting neighborhood demographics. At least three different Catholic parishes, divided along ethnic and linguistic lines, were needed to serve the local population by 1860: St. Mary's Assumption for Germans, St. Alphonsus for the Irish, and Notre Dame de Bon Secours for French speakers. In addition, a Jewish synagogue was opened on Jackson Avenue soon after 1852, and an assortment of Protestant denominations dotted the area.[17] In 1853, the St. Joseph German Catholic Orphan Asylum was opened along Annunciation Street, as a response to the devastating yellow fever epidemic of the same year. This imposing brick-walled structure remained a fixture in the neighborhood through various incarnations until the redevelopment of the 1930s; it, too, would be investigated archaeologically as part of the efforts discussed in this chapter.

New Orleans was included in engineer George Waring's 1879 surveys of sanitary conditions in major American cities, and the statistics there provide systematic data organized by city district (table 3.1). The future St. Thomas area was included in the Fourth District of New Orleans, encompassing the river frontage above Felicity Street and extending across St. Charles into the low-lying areas that now make up the Central City neighborhood. Of 7,387 premises surveyed in the district, the vast majority relied on aboveground rainwater cisterns as water sources. The district contained 37,761 rooms in dwellings, which served a population of 33,231 (divided between 27,175 people listed as white and 6,056 as Colored), for a typical ratio of 1.14 rooms per person or 4.6 people for each dwelling. Conditions in the First District (including the modern French Quarter) and the Second District (including the modern Central Business and Warehouse Districts) were comparable, if not more crowded, with a ratio of 5.7 people per dwelling in the former and 5.6 people per dwelling in the latter. Sanitary conditions were somewhat less satisfactory in the Fourth District: of 9,654 privies surveyed, almost two-thirds were classified as foul or defective. While this ratio is not significantly different from that of the First District, the oldest portion of the city, this part of town was much less densely developed at the time and could have been expected to have fared better in comparison. Nevertheless, the majority of inspected premises in the Fourth District were classified as being in good condition overall; only eight, for instance, were categorized as having a roof in bad condition.[18]

A more precise picture of the development of the St. Thomas area comes into focus in the decades after the Waring survey was completed, as US Census records were enumerated by street address beginning in 1880. The romanticized notion of the Irish Channel also begins to take shape in this period, even though (or perhaps *because*) any distinct Irish ethnic character of the neighborhood was rapidly disappearing. The neighborhood remained largely residential throughout the period, interspersed with a variety of small businesses, such as corner stores, groceries, drugstores, bars, cooperages, and carpentry shops. Much of the residential development of the St. Thomas area in these years consisted of the construction of houses built on the single- or double-shotgun pattern, with long, narrow floor plans consisting of rooms in a front-to-back row with no connecting hallways. In many cases, smaller units at the rear of properties, including some that had served as detached kitchens or residences of the enslaved in the antebellum period, were also converted into rental units. Although many larger homes were subdivided into smaller units in the course of the twentieth century, few were intentionally built as tenements on the pattern of those in many northern cities.[19] Nevertheless, the perception of the area along the riverfront as a slum was certainly

Table 3.1. Data Compiled by George Waring on Housing Conditions by District in New Orleans, 1879

	First District	Second District
Housing stock		
Number of premises inspected	11,188	8,013
Number used as dwellings	9,195	7,164
Premises described as "bad" condition	625	n/l
Total number of rooms in dwellings	48,997	33,243
Population		
Persons occupying dwellings	52,344	40,431
Number designated "White"	39,764	29,050
Number designated "Colored"	12,580	11,381
Persons per dwelling	5.7	5.6
Persons per room	1.1	1.2
Sanitary conditions		
Privies in good condition	3,180	5,481
Privies in foul condition	6,880	3,250
Privies classified as defective	995	239
Number of nuisances requiring abatement	9,377	3,520
Percentage of privies classified as foul or defective	71.2	38.9

Note: The rows detailing persons per dwelling, persons per room, and percentage of privies classified as foul or defective have been added by Gray. The Fifth District is omitted in the original. The abbreviation *n/l* stands for *not listed.*

beginning to form in these years. In 1904, when John Ker Towles from Tulane University made a study of slum housing in New Orleans, he included the neighborhood as part of a much larger area with the worst housing conditions in the city. Although the Sewerage and Water Board began to extend sewerage and water mains into the area between 1906 and 1908, individual connections were made sporadically on a house-by-house basis.[20] Based on archaeological evidence, some houses in the vicinity were likely not connected to city services until the 1920s or later.

Excavations along Adele Street, the reputed heart of the Irish Channel, undertaken in the latter phase of the St. Thomas redevelopment, give a sense of the paradigmatic Americanization of families of Irish background in the

Table 3.1. *continued*

Third District	Fourth District	Sixth District	Seventh District
6,269	7,387	3,586	1,327
6,215	7,196	3,300	1,161
178	n/l	n/l	n/l
28,172	37,761	11,561	4,346.0
33,787	33,231	15,341	4,979
25,220	27,175	11,236	2,476
8,567	6,056	4,105	2,503
5.4	4.6	4.6	4.3
1.2	0.9	1.3	1.1
4,308	3,127	2,422	1,144
1,812	4,260	1,164	184
1,188	2,267	11	0
1,085	244	2,493	920
41.0	67.6	32.7	13.8

Source: Compiled from George E. Waring Jr., *Report on the Social Statistics of Cities,* 1886–87, 2 vols. (New York: Arno Press, 1970).

area. A number of privies were investigated in City Square 32, associated both with addresses along Adele and with ones fronting on the other side of the block, along St. Andrew Street. These privies ranged from deep wood-lined shafts from the mid-nineteenth century to large, fully lined brick enclosures, some of which were filled with a staggering amount of ceramic and glassware. One of these privies, a double privy with interior chambers separated by a central dividing wall, served the two sides of a double-shotgun home at 466–470 St. Andrew Street. At the time that the privy was filled, the home had been the residence of the Heffner family for almost thirty years. William Heffner, a native-born son of German immigrants to the neighborhood, and his wife, Catherine Butler Heffner, daughter of Irish parents, moved into the house around 1890. William worked in various unskilled and semiskilled jobs until his death in 1898 at the age of forty-eight; the Heffners' seven children slowly moved out of the house over the next few years, except for daughter Kate, who married a boilermaker of French parentage, James Follain, and moved into the other side of the double, next to her mother. Many other family members stayed in the neighborhood as well. The assemblages from either side of the privy were distinct in composition, with differences particularly related to how both ethnicity and class were expressed to communicate social connections.[21]

Though existing buildings aged, the type of housing in the St. Thomas area did not radically change in the subsequent decades. What did begin to shift was the ethnic and racial makeup of the neighborhood. The African American population of the city increased rapidly in the years before and after World War I, particularly from the migration of former plantation workers, who, dissatisfied with plummeting wages and exploitative conditions, hoped for expanded opportunities in the urban environment.[22] These former rural workers typically occupied some of the lowest-earning jobs in the city, and they often found opportunities for housing limited to swampy, low-lying zones on the fringes of the city. Despite its deteriorating housing stock, the St. Thomas area may have seemed desirable to these new migrants, as it was located along the comparably dry, valuable land of the natural levee of the river. A detailed analysis of the demographics of three households in a single block in the St. Thomas area, City Square 70, helps to illustrate the trends affecting the area as a whole. This analysis provides a more nuanced glimpse of the social heterogeneity that characterized life in the neighborhood in the years preceding clearance.

Excavations at St. Thomas Square 70

City Square 70, the block bounded by Annunciation, Felicity, Chippewa, and St. Mary Streets, appeared to be a good candidate for intensive study for a number of reasons.[23] In the antebellum period, Annunciation Street had been a fashionable address, with large homes built for more affluent residents, like Andrew Hero, a city notary and commissioner of deeds who lived at 320–324/1824–1826 Annunciation in 1870 and 1880.[24] At least some of these homes remained in the hands of the same families for long periods, while others were eventually split into multiunit dwellings. By the twentieth century, a few of the long, narrow, two-story apartment buildings that served as the local version of tenements were built on the block, as illustrated in the 1909 edition of the Sanborn maps of New Orleans (figure 3.2). At the time that archaeologists arrived on site in 1999, architectural features associated

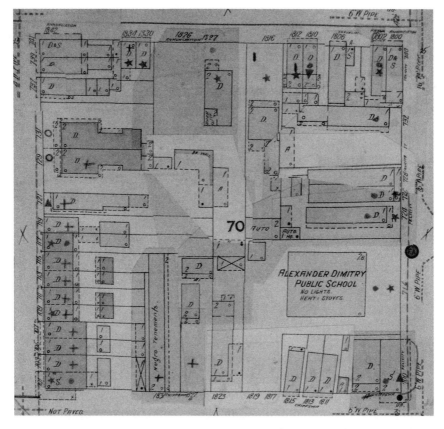

Figure 3.2. Sanborn map of City Square 70, 1909 (Vol. 4, Sheet 354). Discolored areas represent revisions done between editions by pasting in slips of paper. (Courtesy of Southeastern Architectural Archive, Tulane University)

with some of these buildings were visible in courtyard areas of the modern housing project complex, and, eventually, archaeological remains associated with a number of discrete addresses along Annunciation and St. Mary Streets were investigated.

The perception of the St. Thomas area as a slum was built around the idea that the base housing stock within the neighborhood was aging rapidly and being converted into overcrowded tenements and apartments. Conditions in these units were identified as substandard: lacking in modern amenities, prone to outbreaks of disease, and becoming ever more densely populated, particularly as back sheds were converted into living spaces. Such conditions were perceived as perpetuating unemployment, criminality, and the breakdown of nuclear families. This degeneration was thought to be manifested

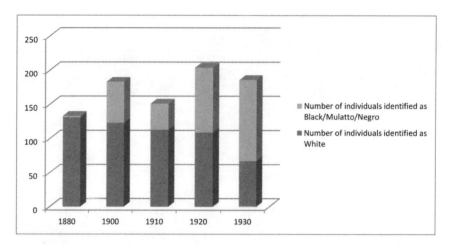

Figure 3.3. Racial composition of Square 70, 1880–1930. (D. Ryan Gray)

in more subtle ways in the urban environment: the sharing of public spaces for what should be private functions; the employment of women outside of homes and men within them, leading to a blurring of the line between public and private, home and workplace; the housing of extended or irregular families within supposed single-family units; and the inclusion of boarders and roomers within households.[25] If these criteria were the sorts of axes through which order/disorder was defined, how then did blocks like Square 70 look to the administrative apparatus of government?

Detailed census data for Square 70 for the years 1880, 1900, 1910, 1920, and 1930 were compiled and mapped on to individual addresses and units within them.[26] The overall population for the block underwent some general fluctuations over this period, tending toward increasing density, from 133 (including adults and children) in 1880, to a maximum of 204 in 1920, and then down to 186 in 1930. Some other trends are generally predictable. For instance, in 1880, many residents were first- and second-generation immigrants of German and Irish origin, supplemented by Italian immigrants after 1900. As these groups aged, the population became dominated by individuals born in Louisiana or elsewhere in the United States. As in many other parts of the St. Thomas area, the racial composition of the Square 70 block shifted over the course of the fifty years charted by the census, from only two Black residents in 1880, both domestic servants residing at the homes of white families, to over half of all residents in 1930 (figure 3.3). Notable was the prevalence of households with female family members listed as head for

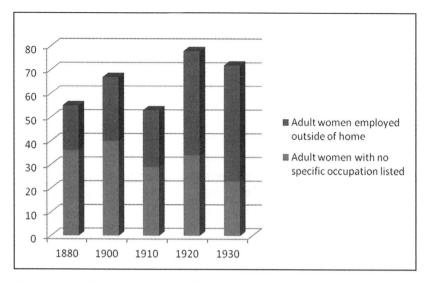

Figure 3.4. Employment data for adult women in Square 70, 1880–1930. (D. Ryan Gray)

all census years, as well as the increase in this category in the 1930 census. In all years, a substantial number of adult female family members were also employed in the workforce outside the home (figure 3.4).

In the remainder of this section, I focus on a few specific lots or groups of lots, all of which historically fronted St. Mary Street and which were investigated during the archaeological excavations at St. Thomas. Each of these lots contained remains of at least one privy shaft, outhouse pits that had been filled with household refuse. Remains from the first were found accidentally, during monitoring of the demolition of a housing project–related utility building. As the building's foundation was being extracted by a backhoe, the lower courses of a wood-lined privy were exposed, with the upper portion spilling out below the blade of the backhoe as it scraped across the ground surface. The organic and artifact-rich night soil deposit that filled the privy is likely to have accumulated in the shaft during the first years of the 1890s, based on a *terminus post quem* provided by a bisque doll head fragment with a patent date of 1894 on its reverse. In this period, a frame-constructed single dwelling occupied the lot, and, according to city directories, a carpenter by the name of Leon Cummings and his widowed sister resided there. In 1900, Laurence Cummings (presumably the same individual) still lived at the address with his wife, three daughters, and two sons. Cummings's parents were from Ireland, while those of his wife were from Ireland and Germany, and by 1900 he worked as a night watchman. The family was still residing at the address in 1910, and Cummings had returned to work as a carpenter, while his two oldest daughters were employed as stenographers.[27]

The privy at 721 St. Mary was rather lacking in ceramic vessels, with a total minimum number of twenty-nine recovered (figure 3.5). Only fifteen of those vessels reflected individual place settings (plates, saucers, cups, and bowls); platters, pitchers, a teapot, a mixing bowl, and chamber pots were also recovered, including an early Rockingham-type pitcher emblazoned with the bust of George Washington. A mean ceramic date for the assemblage of 1881 was calculated, well within the typical lag times for ceramic use and deposition.[28] The sample of glass containers collected was considerably more robust, with a minimum of sixty-six recovered. Many of these containers were at least partially intact, and at least one container, a jar of Madame M. Yale's Excelsior Complexion Cream, still contained some of its original contents. The largest portion of the bottles recovered (36 percent of the total) was medicinal in function, with both local pharmacies (like Primo's Pharmacy at the corner of Canal and Bourbon) and nationally marketed brands (like I. W. Bull's Cough Syrup from Baltimore) represented. Overall, based on embossed bottles, there was a slight preference for national brands (n=9) over locally produced or bottled ones (n=5), both of which would have been easily available in local markets.

A number of items related to other household activities were recovered from the privy fill. Among these were a variety of smoking pipes (including a complete one manufactured by the Gambier Company of Paris), clothing-related items like shoes and buckles, copper lamp burner parts, bisque doll parts, marbles, toothbrushes, eyeglasses, and an 1884 Liberty Head five-cent coin. The Catholic faith of the resident at the address was indicated by the presence of a rosary with a crucifix and a religious medallion. This medallion, marked on the obverse with a figure of the Virgin Mary and on the reverse with the saying "O MARIE CONCUE SANS PECHE PRIEZ POUR NOUS QUI AVONS RECOURS A VOUS," is an example of the so-called Miraculous Medallion of Saint Catherine Labouré. Labouré, a Daughter of Charity in France in the first half of the 1800s, had a vision of the design of this medal in 1830. It became popular, especially among French Catholic communities, and though her connection to the medal was initially a secret, Labouré was eventually canonized in 1947.[29] The most unusual find from the privy fill came when a wide-mouthed bottle was being cleaned in the lab. Hidden in the wet, brownish-black soil filling the bottle was a collection of forty-nine buttons, almost every one of them different in form. Some of these were shanked gilt-type buttons, including police and military varieties, and others consisted of glass, ceramic, and composite bodies with wire shank attachments. A collection of twelve wooden chess pieces and a brass watch fob were also recovered in the bottle.

Figure 3.5. Ceramic vessels from privy likely associated with 721 St. Mary Street. Flow black ironstone plate with sailing ship central motif, annular whiteware mixing bowl, and Rockingham ware pitcher with molded tulip decoration. (D. Ryan Gray)

The watch fob incorporates a glass wax seal with an emblem depicting a hand over a heart, along with the words "To give" and "To forgive." Although this motto has not been linked to any specific group, the sentiments are certainly consistent with the benevolent and mutual aid societies that were common in New Orleans in this period.[30]

An abundant faunal assemblage from the 721 St. Mary privy representing a diversity of species, especially fish and birds, gives some insight into foodways in the household.[31] Fresh and saltwater drum, a number of species from the catfish family, and sheepshead were represented, in addition to chicken, duck, goose, grouse, turkey, and squab, and even multiple species of turtle. Common domestic mammals likely made up a greater amount of meat than would be indicated by the number of individuals represented, but unidentified large and medium-sized mammal bone did not dominate the assemblage nearly as much as is typical in urban historical sites. Some of the collections of bone in the privy appeared to represent specific events rather than regular, sustained consumption. For instance, numerous bones from a single, unidentified juvenile ruminant were recovered, probably representing a roast of a single lamb or very young cow. The entire deposit was littered with bone from animals traditionally considered to be pets, including at least twenty-four cats and six dogs, the majority of them fetal or neonatal at the time of death. These remains would appear to represent disposal of full litters of unwanted newborns at the time of birth.

The privy at 721 St. Mary had been investigated by happenstance, and it was the only deposit associated with that particular household. A second lot on the block, located at 111–113/729–731 St. Mary Street, was investigated by design. A man named Zachary Bruenn, a Prussian Jewish clothing merchant, purchased the lot in 1861 and soon after had a large two-story double residence with wraparound galleries built on it. Initially, he rented one side of this property to an Irish drayman and his family for extra income, but as Bruenn's fortunes improved and his family expanded, he eventually came to occupy the entire building, buying adjacent homes to use as rentals. Bruenn resided at this home until his death in 1912 at the age of ninety. Only four years later, his son Bernard, who also lived at the home, would die from a stroke. Bernard, a successful lawyer, was profiled in Alcée Fortier's 1914 *Louisiana Cyclopedia*, a collection of biographical sketches of notable New Orleanians. According to it, he was known for his liberalism and sympathy to Republican causes, even while working in cooperation with the local Democratic Party. He was also a Freemason and a member "of several clubs and of the charitable organizations."[32] A succession inventory describes the elegant furnishings in the house at 729–731 St. Mary at the time of Bernard's death, including marble tabletops, mahogany armoires, a rosewood dining room set, and a piano.[33]

After 1916, Bernard Bruenn's sister retained possession of the house and rented it out. By 1920, it was occupied on one side by Charles Tolmas, the Russian Jewish proprietor of a grocery, and his family, and on the other by Matthew Hartmann, a pipeman for the fire department with his wife, child, brother, and sister-in-law. Also residing with the Hartmanns was Jacob Seifter, a seventy-six-year-old Austrian junk peddler, while a family named the Bonnevalls lived with the Tolmas family on the other side of the double. In 1930, the demographic profile of the double had changed entirely, and judging from the number of separate heads of household listed at the address (fifteen heads, some with families, along with two roomers), the structure had most likely been subdivided into a number of separate small apartments. All residents listed in the 1930 census were classified as Negro, with most of the adult men employed as laborers and the adult women as cooks, laundresses, or maids for private families. In later HANO surveys of the St. Thomas area, the former Bruenn house was selected as an example of the bygone grandeur of the area, a decaying single-family home that had been converted to tenements.[34]

Archaeologists determined that the actual footprint of the Bruenn house had been obliterated by one of the housing project buildings constructed in 1939. However, features associated with the rear yard of the property could be identified based on a comparison of archaeological remains with Sanborn maps of the block. A brick-lined pit with a smoothly plastered surface abutting a rear property wall marked the position of a privy shed that had served the Bruenn home. This privy had apparently been cleaned regularly while in active use, as was mandated by often-ignored city health ordinances, and then filled in with at least two distinct layers of material. The bottom of the shaft was filled with a fine sandy soil, apparently associated with a single cleaning episode from the approximate time of Bernard Bruenn's death, with pennies from 1911 and 1913 in the fill helping to date it, while the upper part contained additional trash and debris that accumulated around and just after that time. The assemblage associated with the Bruenn household was distinctive in that a disproportionate number of the ceramic vessels were related to hygiene, from soap dishes and a toothbrush holder to a wash pitcher and an ornate gilt and transfer-printed chamber pot decorated with a classical motif (probably the English pottery pattern called "Etruscan Vases"). The glassware from the feature was dominated by amber snuff bottles; of the forty-five glass containers recovered from the privy, at least eight complete snuff bottles were recovered. Other intact bottles may be at least somewhat indicative of the German background of the Bruenn family. In addition to bottles of the common Udolpho Wolfe's Aromatic Schnapps, a bottle of Hoyt's Cologne (famous for its Nickel Cologne and German Cologne varieties) and a bottle of the less common Doctor Petzold's German Bitters were recovered. Fancy glass tableware was also present, particularly bowls or candy dishes and tumblers. The most interesting of these items was a fine milk glass tumbler with polychrome painting and gilding, including the French word *amitie* (friendship) in cursive. Given Bernard Bruenn's connections to Freemasonry and charitable organizations in New Orleans, there may be some linkage between his social life and the vessel here.

The assemblage of ceramic vessels from this feature is curious in its lack of significant quantities of common tableware forms, but the faunal remains are even more unusual. The assemblage was dominated not by common mammal domesticates but by birds (including chicken, turkey, duck, and goose) and fish (sea trout and other unidentifiable species), and the lack of pork in particular could be related to a kosher dietary pattern on the part of at least some of the residents at the address. Even more intriguing was a single deposit occurring on top of the layer of artifact-laden sand in the base of the shaft. This deposit consisted of a piece of slate, covered in fish scales, small fish bone fragments, and fragments of eggshell. This grouping of material is consistent with the se'udat havra'ah (community meal), the traditional Jewish feast of mourning. This meal generally takes place soon after a loved one's funeral and includes food items with symbolic associations with life and fertility, particularly eggs and lentils. Fish is considered to be the only appropriate meat to serve with this meal, as most mammal domesticates are associated with celebration rather than mourning.[35] It is tempting to see the cleaning episode represented by the feature's fill and the remains of this meal on top of it as evidence of a single series of events carried out by Bernard Bruenn's sister after his death. Although this material may indicate Judaism among members of the Bruenn household, the strong Catholic identity of the neighborhood is also evident in the assemblage. A ceramic crucifix, along with a corroded saint's medal and beads that may have belonged to a rosary, would seem to indicate that someone within the Bruenn household did not practice the Jewish faith. While these artifacts could be related to one of the Irish domestic servants occasionally listed as residing at the address, they may reflect the ambiguous place of Bernard Bruenn, the politically active lawyer, in the social world of the city. The Jewish community in New Orleans undoubtedly played a strong and influential role in New Orleans, and prominent residents like Judah Touro were greatly respected as philanthropists.[36] Nevertheless, and with increasing prevalence in the late nineteenth and early twentieth centuries, Jews were often excluded from the clubs and organizations maintained by the city's elite.[37] Bernard Bruenn was a Freemason, and while policies regarding religious affiliation of members varied widely from lodge to lodge at the time, this fact may hint that he did not outwardly emphasize his Jewish background. It was perhaps convenient for him in his business and political contacts to draw attention away from this heritage, even while privately maintaining its traditions. The archaeological data minimally suggest some of the tensions and ambiguities that existed for a successful Jewish family in a society with discriminatory biases directed toward them.

A row of small brick cottages constructed during the 1850s was located just a few doors down from the home of the Bruenn family on St. Mary Street.[38] These cottages were occupied by a crowded and shifting array of renters in the period documented by the US Census. In 1880, the occupants consisted of first- and second-generation Irish and German immigrants and their extended families, all of whom were identified racially as white. Many of the men were listed in the census simply as laborers, the only exceptions being John Minnock, a policeman, and his brother, a broom maker. Of the seven households making up the row, four were headed by women. By 1900, the population of the row had become more diverse racially, with families identified as Black residing at 709, 711, 713, and 715 St. Mary. Of the ten total households identified, five had a female family member listed as the head of household. In 1910, the racial composition of the row of houses remained essentially stable, with Black families listed at 713 and 715 St. Mary, and with 709 and 711 not listed at all. The ethnic heritage of the white residents was somewhat more diverse, with individuals of Italian and Swedish parentage enumerated in addition to those of German and Irish background. In this census year, only one household was identified as having a female head, that of Clara Solomon, a forty-year-old Black woman who worked as a cook at private homes and resided with her son, a laborer at odd jobs, and her mother. The Solomon family would become the most stable occupants of the row, appearing also in the 1920 and 1930 census at the same address. By 1920, the row of cottages was occupied almost exclusively by other African American families, identified racially as both Black and Mulatto; the lone exception was the corner double at 701–703 St. Mary, where ice wagon driver Fred Young, a white native-born Louisianan, lived with his wife and eight children. The more detailed occupational listings for the residents of the row present an interesting cross-section of the professions of working-class New Orleans, including a grocery warehouseman; laborers in a molasses factory, a pickle works, and a bedspring factory; cotton mill workers; chauffeurs; and two longshoremen (one of whom, James Samuels, was racially identified as Black but was listed as of Portuguese and Palestinian descent). Most adult women were employed as domestics (maids, washwomen, and cooks), while two women worked as hullers at a pecan factory, and another took in sewing at home. Again, only one woman was listed as a head of household, thirty-two-year-old Sidonia Brown at 719 St. Mary.

As the final census taken before the period of slum clearance, the 1930 census merits some more detailed discussion. Nine households were enumerated in the row in this year. The Young family remained as the sole white family in the row at 701 St. Mary, and, while listed as renting in 1920, it now owned the corner building outright. All other families in the row were listed by race as Negro. Married couple Joseph and Maria Davis lived beside the Youngs at 705. Both husband and wife were in their forties and were employed as a laborer at a cement company and at a dispensary, respectively. James Martin, forty-five, his wife Ida, thirty-five, and their sixteen-year-old daughter lived on the other side of the double at 707. James worked as a porter, and Ida worked as a maid at a dry goods store. In the next double, at 709 and 711 St. Mary, resided the Fry and Nolan families. James Fry, forty-eight, and his wife, Rose, forty-two, lived with their five children, a sixteen-year-old nephew, and Rose's seventy-year-old mother. James was a porter at a clinic, Rose was a cotton picker at the pickery, and two sons and the nephew worked as helpers at a drug store. The family of Charles and Josephine Nolan, both in their thirties, was somewhat smaller; they lived with two sons and a seventy-year-old aunt. Charles was a longshoreman on the river, and Rose was a house girl for a private family. The oldest son, Willie, sixteen, was also employed as a helper at a grocery. As mentioned, the Solomon family, now headed by Thomas (Clara's son), resided at 713. Thomas lived with his wife, Marie; individuals who were presumably her mother (Mary Felea, sixty) and an aunt (Rosatel King, twenty-five); and two grandsons, Rosaveldt King, twenty, and Larry Kimball, ten.[39] Thomas and Marie worked as a laborer at the pickle works and as a maid for a private family, respectively. Rosaveldt and Rosatel were also both employed, he as a truck handler for cold storage and she as a dishwasher at a restaurant. At 715, Arthur Dugas, a forty-eight-year-old laborer on the river, lived with his wife, Stephenie, who was a cook for a private family, and their five daughters. The households at 717 and 719 St. Mary were somewhat smaller. At 717, cleaner and presser Henry Crittenden, fifty-five, lived with only his wife, Elizabeth, who was a dressmaker. At 719, Mary Saunders, a forty-five-year-old cook for a private family, lived with her two-year-old niece.

A single brick-lined privy associated with this brick row was identified and excavated. The upper portion of its east half had been sheared away by later construction activities on-site, but otherwise its fill appeared to be intact. The interior fill represented trash that had been deposited in the feature after the period of its primary use, probably when the row of cottages was finally connected to city sewerage. This trash accumulated rapidly, and sherds of crossmending vessels were found throughout all levels of the fill. The presence of artifacts dating to the twentieth century, including machine-made bottle glass, ceramics with decals, Bakelite and plasticoid items, and items related to electrical usage, suggests a clear *terminus post quem* in the early 1900s. However, the majority of the glass bottles in the assemblage were manufactured using the earlier multipart mold-blown techniques, suggesting that the refuse was deposited as fully automated manufacturing techniques became more widespread in the first decades of the twentieth century. Taking these factors into account, the estimated date of deposition for the assemblage is 1920–25. Based on overlays with historical maps, the privy is most likely associated with the double at 713–715 St. Mary.

Fragments of ninety-seven ceramic vessels were recovered from the privy, the vast majority (66 percent; n=64) consisting of ironstone tablewares, primarily plates, cups, and saucers. In addition, small quantities of porcelain, porcelaneous stoneware, yellowware (including Rockingham-decorated examples), utilitarian brownware, and gray stoneware were recovered. Even though the deposit dated to the twentieth century, many of the wares were manufactured substantially earlier and displayed wear resulting from long and repeated use. Although ceramic wares commonly show a considerable time lag between date of manufacture and date of deposition (often around twenty or more years), the mean ceramic date for the assemblage as a whole is 1882, a full forty years earlier than the estimated date for the filling of the privy. Back marks on ceramic vessels suggest an even more substantial lag, with dated examples from English potters like Elsmore and Forster (ca. 1853–71), Powell and Bishop (1866–78), and Jacob Furnival (1845–70) long predating deposition.[40] The white-bodied tablewares were also categorized as undecorated, decorated with molded shapes, or decorated (other), which included hand-painted, transfer-printed, edged, and annular varieties. This method of sorting was intended to provide researchers with a sense of the range of variation in household table settings. Of the seventy-three vessels represented in this group, roughly equal numbers were decorated with molding and/or embossing (n=21) and with other forms of decoration (n=20). However, within each of these categories was a large degree of variation, with few matched settings represented. The only clearly matched pieces aside from occasional molded wares, which shared generally angled gothic shapes, were a saucer and cup with simple hand-painted green and purple design.

One hundred thirty-seven glass containers were identified, representing a wide range of forms and functions, including a variety of nationally marketed patent medicines, perfumes, and hygiene products, proprietary bottles from local druggists and soda water manufacturers, liquor bottles, storage jars, ink bottles, condiment containers, and goblets and tumblers. Of identifiable embossed bottles, little preference was shown for any one brand or source, either local or national. There were two bottles each of the common Udolpho Wolfe's Aromatic Schnapps and J. Hostetter's Stomach Bitters, but all other brands were represented by only one individual. At least six different local druggists or chemists were identified through embossing on medicinal bottles, most of them in business contemporaneously. Local perfumers, many with claimed connections to France, and soda bottlers were also represented by embossed bottles, with a total of thirteen individuals representing local concerns, as opposed to nineteen individuals representing national brands. Considered by function, the glass assemblage was again diverse, with pharmaceutical/medicinal bottles forming 27 percent of the total; liquor bottles, particularly small flask bottles, forming another 14 percent; and tumblers forming 12 percent. No other single glass container type accounted for more than 10 percent of the total.

Many other artifacts were recovered from the trash deposit (figure 3.6): an irrigation syringe, toothbrushes, pipe bowls (including one in the shape of a hand presenting a bouquet of flowers and another with what may be a design associated with a fraternal order), jewelry, rosary beads, harmonica reed

Figure 3.6. Selected artifacts recovered from brick cottage privy. *Left:* fragments of porcelain and bisque figurines. *Middle, top:* molded red stoneware pipe bowl of hand presenting bouquet. *Middle, bottom:* bullets, cuprous token. *Right:* bone folding fan blade, bisque doll head fragments. (D. Ryan Gray)

plates, and a number of examples of the Victorian bric-a-brac that has been discussed at length by Paul R. Mullins and others.[41] The presence of children in the household(s) associated with the assemblage is indicated by numerous toys, particularly marbles, bisque doll parts, and fragments of toy tea services. Adult leisure activities are indicated by the presence of at least one carved bone poker chip and a bone domino. Also noteworthy were bullets in the assemblage, including .22-caliber shell casings and complete larger-caliber bullets (probably .38-caliber). While these could have been related to hunting, they could also—given the occasional outbreaks of violence in the neighborhood—represent a more pragmatic approach to self-protection in the household. A final note must be made of the many artifacts related to literacy in the assemblage, including numerous fragments of slate pencils and at least four ink bottles.

The faunal assemblage from the deposit in the privy shows a much greater reliance on typical large and medium mammal domesticates like pigs, cows, and caprids (sheep and/or goats) than that from the 721 St. Mary privy, and this analysis likely underestimates the total meat weight that these species contributed to the meals of the occupants of the cottage. Despite the bias toward common commercially available meat cuts in the assemblage, these meat sources were supplemented by fish, including catfish, jack, and sheepshead, and game animals, particularly duck and wild hare. The minimum numbers of commensal species is dramatically lower for that of the cottage privy, with no cats represented and only four fetal/neonatal dogs, likely a single litter. This absence is perhaps a sign of sanitary reforms in the neighborhood that would have made stray domestic cats and dogs less of a constant problem, or at least one addressed through other means than disposing of newborns in a privy pit.

Because of the rapid turnover of renters in most of these residences, it cannot be stated with complete certainty with which household the assemblage from the privy is associated. The privy may have served both sides of the double at 713–715 St. Mary, which suggests that minimally it may have some relationship to the Solomon family, but multiple units could feasibly have shared the use of this privy, a common practice for outdoor toilet facilities. In 1920, among the relevant heads of household are Thomas Solomon, then a laborer at the pickle works; Victor Wheeler, a spring maker at the bed factory; George Tiles, a longshoreman on the docks; and Sidonia Brown, a cook for a private family. All the families living at these addresses at the time of the 1920 and 1930 census were members of New Orleans's African American urban working class.

Race, Ethnicity, and Working-Class Consumer Culture

At first glance, the three assemblages described here seem to have little direct basis for comparison. They were produced by individuals and/or families of different ethnic and racial backgrounds, and, in the case of the Bruenns, even a different religious and socioeconomic background. If one thinks of each of these assemblages as evoking the particular decade in which it was deposited, then the material record appears to read as a linear narrative, one with the parameters already set by the historical record. In this view, we could see the material evidence from the earliest privy as reflecting the middle-class aspirations of a first- or second-generation immigrant, and that from the privy of the Bruenns as demonstrating the negotiation of ethnic and religious identities for those seeking acceptance into the city's upper class. The outdated ceramics from the privy of the cottage row would demonstrate a more complex reaction to a racist society on the part of Black residents, even as they were increasingly locked into the bottom tier of a two-tiered racial hierarchy. Seen in conjunction with the demographic data of the census, this interpretation as a whole would fit with the narrative of urban neighborhoods abandoned by white residents and by the middle class, a desertion to be followed shortly by city services and by economic investment. From this perspective, the neighborhood was on an inexorable path to slumdom, with the roughly quarter century in which the white-only St. Thomas Housing Project reclaimed the neighborhood as white space simply an anomaly on the path of decline, one that many people in the contemporary city have entirely forgotten because of its apparent inconsequentiality in the present-day landscape.

The identification of the St. Thomas Street area as a slum was a disciplinary intervention, characterizing its social heterogeneity as an ill that could be cured through clearance. And yet what endangered the racial hierarchy of the city was not just this heterogeneity but its transformative and culturally productive potential, particularly considered across lines of race and class. This productivity is expressed materially, even when it shows itself only haltingly in documents, and it presents us with a different story than inevitable decline and abandonment. During the first decades of the twentieth century, the St. Thomas area had developed into a multiethnic and multiracial neighborhood formed around an urban working class that shared many common experiences. Households in the area were often headed by women, and, as often as not, women worked outside the home to supplement families' incomes. Many families adopted living arrangements at odds with the idealized conception of a single nuclear family in a single home; they incorporated roomers and lodgers, extended families, and associates from their workplaces into households, sometimes in conditions that would have allowed very little private space. Many also drew on the informal networks thus formed for access to goods outside of regular markets. Finally, even while later accounts often seek to highlight the Irish immigrant background of neighborhood residents, social life in the area incorporated many ethnic groups by the end of the nineteenth century, and all the cultural traditions that they brought to the city shaped daily practices within it.

While those racially identified as Black were being increasingly consigned to the service sector, many male laborers in the St. Thomas neighborhood shared backgrounds in the shipping industry, particularly in the rail yards and docks, and it is tempting to see this occupation as the essential commonality in the development of the neighborhood. Riverfront commerce, particularly as related to the timely shipping of cotton, was the cornerstone of New Orleans's economy during the nineteenth and early twentieth centuries. During times of prosperity (when there was plenty of work on the docks), the cotton screwmen, longshoremen, teamsters, draymen, and other dockworkers, Black and white, enjoyed an unprecedented degree of cooperation, as was best expressed in the Cotton Men's Executive Council of the 1880s and the Dock and

Cotton Council of the early 1900s. On rare but significant occasions, these biracial unions could wield power even outside of the docks, as when they joined brewery workers in a major 1907 strike.[42] However, while the riverfront could be a crucible of interracial working-class cooperation, racial tensions were also consistently used to divide workers, and the achievements of biracial cooperation on the docks were crippled both by the unwillingness of white labor unions to recognize equality for their Black union counterparts and by their members' own racist attitudes to questions of African American social equality. In times of economic stress, union jobs were disproportionately reserved for white workers, and not surprisingly, employers played on this tension to undercut wages and convince African American laborers to leave unions that treated them unequally. The situation of Black laborers became even more precarious during periodic outbreaks of racist violence, such as the dock riots of 1894 and 1895 or the riots that were sparked in 1900 by the Robert Charles incident.[43] The area encompassed by St. Thomas, with its proximity to the wharfs, racially mixed demographics, and large population of dockworkers, is often mentioned in historical accounts of labor activities of the period, and tense encounters between white and Black residents were a fact of life.

While the St. Thomas area was no working-class racial utopia, it still posed a very real danger to the dominant system of racial and class hierarchy. This threat was enacted at the level of the everyday, where shared experiences, both of conflict and of community, formed the basis for questioning the hegemonic conventions of white supremacy in the Jim Crow South. Even as racial integration was less and less tolerated by city and state authorities, the fact that cross-racial and cross-ethnic interaction was unavoidable in daily practice in neighborhoods like that which became St. Thomas continued to push the boundaries of tolerated norms. Moreover, given similarities in social class on the part of Black and white residents, the continuities between the daily experiences of each group could not easily be denied. In this sense, some of the similarities in assemblages from the privies associated with Irish and African American laborers are worth noting. Despite the difference of some thirty years in their depositions, the two assemblages share a number of similar motifs on their ceramic wares, among them identical flow black transfer-printed patterns of a sailing ship and Rockingham patterns featuring a molded tulip. A variety of ceramic wares characterized by unmatched and outdated vessels has previously been noted in other urban assemblages associated with African American families in the postemancipation period, and it has been suggested that such a pattern results from thrift, expressed through intentional curation and acquisition of secondhand wares.[44] In this case, the similarities suggest the beginnings of a working-class aesthetic in

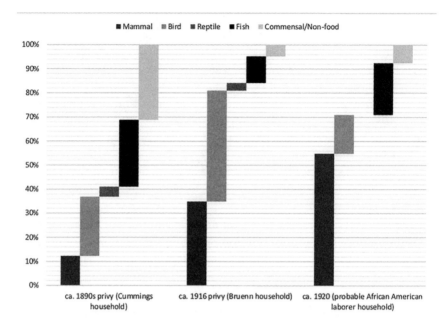

Figure 3.7. Comparison of minimum number of individuals (MNI) by taxa from three primary residential components investigated at City Square 70. (D. Ryan Gray)

the neighborhood, one characterized by this very diversity. Both of the assemblages likewise contain objects that suggest connections to the many fraternal and benevolent societies that helped to provide a social safety net within the community, and it is perhaps in such organizations that one should look for the origins of this shared aesthetic.[45] Even though the faunal assemblage from the African American household demonstrated a much heavier reliance on commercially available meat cuts, both groups supplemented their meat consumption with fish and game that would have likely been either self-provisioned or purchased from street hawkers, outside of traditional or more formal market networks (figure 3.7). Such strategies could have been essential to the survival of the family in times of unemployment or other stresses, like the seasonal fluctuations in availability of dock jobs.

It is tempting to see, in the assemblage from the Bruenn household, something of an outlier here. With its more fashionable and up-to-date ceramic and glasswares, it would seem to be a holdover from the more affluent era of the neighborhood. If the assemblage is considered exclusively along the axis of class, this may certainly be the case, and the social position of Bernard Bruenn, a successful lawyer, would seem to support it. However, despite the supposed economic decline of the neighborhood, both Bruenn men chose to remain at the house at 729–731 St. Mary Street until their deaths. This decision may reflect an awareness of the tensions surrounding their own ethnic and religious identity, one that is borne out by seeming contradictions in the material record. The faunal assemblage would seem to indicate some attempts to sustain a kosher diet on the part of one or more residents of the home, and if the fish and egg remains within the privy are indicative of the practice of traditional Jewish mourning rituals on their behalf, it would seem that someone, likely Zachary Bruenn's daughter, recognized the importance of such rituals to the family members involved. However, the presence of items connected to the Catholic faith and evidence of small quantities of nonkosher food items like shellfish suggest that there was at least some acknowledgment of the younger Bruenn's need to fit in with the non-Jewish groups that dominated much of New Orleans's public culture. This need may also be expressed by the *amitie* tumbler in the assemblage, perhaps connected to Bernard's membership in fraternal societies. By occupying what was certainly still a nice home in an area otherwise becoming marginalized, the Bruenns could take advantage of the relative anonymity that the neighborhood offered them in their daily life.

Incorporating this perspective on the Bruenn assemblage, I suggest that another fundamental aspect of the neighborhood that made it a threat to the social order of the Jim Crow city was an increased though implicit awareness of the instrumental nature of ethnicity in such a social world. Many individual products from all three assemblages were either produced internationally or emphasized a connection to specific ethnicities through naming or packaging. The prevalence of snuff bottles and of products associated with German manufacture in the Bruenn assemblage has already been noted. But what, then, about items that would appear to express the multiplicity of ethnic heritage in the neighborhood? Items suggesting the Francophone heritage of the city are particularly abundant, from pipes manufactured by Gambier of Paris and the Miraculous Medallion of Saint Catherine Labouré to French perfumes, found in an area characteristically linked with the Anglo-Irish heritage of the city. Such consumer choices indicate the possibilities for contesting and negotiating identities in a complex multiethnic environment. Rather than falling into sharply delimited patterns of consumption that reinforced one *particular* identity, the households represented by the assemblages at 721 St. Mary and at the cottage row actively experimented with products and, presumably, with the expressive capabilities of these items. By exploiting the ambiguities— the conceived disorder—of the urban environment, the families of Square 70 could begin to define a material basis for a working-class identity that crossed

lines of ethnicity or race. Whether consciously or unconsciously, by expos-
ing the doxic nature—the essential arbitrariness—of supposed ethnic markers, the families could find the material basis for new forms of community.[46]

Conclusion: The Materiality of Slum Life in St. Thomas

In fall 1907, union representative and white longshoreman Harry Keegan addressed New Orleans mayor Martin Behrman in his office before a general
levee strike. He stated that the Black and white unions, despite attempts to
divide them, "are standing together for mutual protection, and are going to
see that they get justice."[47] Unfortunately, in the face of pressure from racist
political and business interests, this stand for justice could not last during
these troubled decades. In subsequent years, biracial cooperation rapidly dis-
solved among waterfront workers, and the legend of the socially and racially
homogeneous Irish Channel coalesced. Since 1947, this legend has been actualized through the Irish Channel St. Patrick's Day parade with which this
chapter began, a symbolic appropriation of the area that has increasingly incorporated a racial subtext since St. Thomas was integrated at the end of the
1960s. This integration, too, was a source of violent resistance on the part of
white supremacist segregationists, who firebombed the homes of Black families that moved into the vicinity of St. Thomas during the decade.[48]

Struggles over space and its meanings are fairly common in an urban environment, but when such struggles are conveyed as symbolic of deeper, un-
changing categories of difference or of irreconcilable competing claims, they
become the grounds for narratives that exclude and divide. The story of the
neighborhood that became St. Thomas is one of both cooperation *and* conflict, a history as prone to periods of harmonious coexistence as to outbreaks
of racial or interethnic violence. To just tell the story as one of difference is
to reproduce the official accounts, the public transcripts, that the segregated
housing projects were meant to make seem incontrovertible. While some residents of the neighborhood like the Bruenn family were undoubtedly wealth-
ier than their counterparts down the street, many of these same households
were connected in their struggle to maintain a place and an identity within a
society from which they were sometimes marginalized. The identification of
the area as a slum was meant to reconceptualize the very order thus formed
as disorder, a sign of abnormality. While such disorder could sometimes be
tolerated in environmentally marginal or undesirable lands away from the
city center, when it co-occurred with a desirable resource—here, well-drained
property along the natural levee of the city—it became a threat to the existing power structure.

In the following chapter, I turn to the segregated counterpart of St. Thomas, the Magnolia Housing Project, which was constructed to replace the Belmont neighborhood near the modern Central City area. By the time that Magnolia was constructed, Belmont was thought to be home almost exclusively to an impoverished population racially defined as Black. If Belmont were this racially and socially homogeneous, the area could hardly seem be the fount of a cross-racial and cross-ethnic working-class subjectivity. What then were the motivations for selecting it as the location of the Magnolia Housing Project? What were the characteristics that made it so disorderly in the eyes of reformers, and what can material remains tell us about the work of cultural production within the area prior to clearance? The threat to the established order of Jim Crow materialized by the Belmont neighborhood was different from that at St. Thomas, but the end results were the same: Belmont was a slum and thus had to be erased from the urban landscape.

4
Magnolia

Creating Order in Belmont

On July 27, 1900, a group of New Orleans policemen aided by armed vigilantes (estimated in number at over a thousand) finally succeeded in forcing a man named Robert Charles from his hiding place in the rear annex of a home on South Saratoga Street. The building had been surrounded and riddled with bullets, but Charles emerged only after a fire was set. He was killed, and his body was dragged through the street, kicked, stomped, and shot repeatedly. This story might sound like a typical mob lynching, taken from any one of many decades of racial violence in American history, were it not for one important fact: Charles, an African American man from Mississippi who had advocated for migration to Africa for Black Americans, had shot twenty-seven white people, killing seven of them, including four policemen. The encounter was triggered by an episode of the sort of routinely humiliating harassment that characterized African American life in many southern cities in the years after Reconstruction. Charles and a friend, waiting on the street at night in an interracial neighborhood, were confronted by police as suspicious, and this incident escalated into an altercation in which Charles shot and injured one policeman. Before and after Charles was killed, mobs searched the streets, both for supposed accomplices and for scapegoats, assaulting and murdering Black men and setting fire to the Thomy Lafon School, an African American school near the area that would become the Magnolia Housing Project. Although some men were charged in connection with these riots, the charges against them were later dropped with little fanfare. While embarrassing to those responsible for administering the law in the city, the possibility for such widespread violence was a natural outgrowth of a system of sustained racial inequality rooted in violence, a consequence that was tolerated so long as it was asymmetrical.[1]

The story of Robert Charles was troubling to white residents and city authorities for a number of reasons. Not only did the incident mark a visible challenge to white supremacy, but it also suggested troubling facts about the resentment of the city's African American residents in the face of the rising stringency of Jim Crow segregation. This population was increasing rapidly in these years, and the backswamp neighborhoods where Charles had lived in the years prior to July 1900 were becoming more and more exclusively Black space. One thing that had been particularly shocking to white residents had been the ability of Charles to conceal himself in the urban environment, even as hundreds, and eventually thousands, of people were searching for him. Suspicion was widespread among city authorities that residents of the areas through which Charles habitually moved were all too happy to assist him in hiding. As the city's newspapers dissected the details of Charles's life in New Orleans, it seemed that the only white man who had regularly interacted with him in the city, a clothing store salesman named Hyman Levy, had only ever known him by an alias.[2] From the perspective of authorities with a vested interest in white supremacy, if Charles, this violent, murderous Black separatist, could maneuver through the city undetected by them, what angers could be roiling behind the seemingly impenetrable façades of the urban slum, waiting only for a spark to make them explode to the surface?

In this chapter, I examine the origins of the Magnolia Street/C. J. Peete Housing Project, constructed concurrently with the St. Thomas Housing Project in 1939–40 and intended to be its Black counterpart. The neighborhood that the Magnolia Project replaced, sometimes referred to as Belmont after a street within it (figure 4.1), followed a very different developmental trajectory from that charted for St. Thomas in the previous chapter. The Belmont neighborhood was in a low-lying zone at the rear of the Mississippi River's natural levee, peripheral to urban development until the massive public drainage projects of the late 1800s and early 1900s opened it to subdivision. African American migrants flooded into the city in these years, leaving oppressive labor conditions on rural plantations and searching for new social and economic opportunities. Decent housing was in short supply, and construction in such areas, both planned and unplanned, proliferated. By the early part of the 1900s, these former backswamp areas were becoming exclusively Black spaces.[3] As was made apparent in the Charles case, they also became opaque, difficult to police or regulate, and impossible for an outsider to read. Conceived in this way, they were places where spatial disorder potentially disrupted a social order predicated on the tangibility of lines of color and class. The only potential remedy for the disorder of this kind of slum life was the housing project: ordered, visible, legible, and isolatable.

Of course, the Magnolia Street Housing Project has since become a site of redevelopment itself. The area has been rebranded as Harmony Oaks, a mixed-income community along the lines of those that replaced other hous-

Figure 4.1. Aerial view of Belmont area before clearance for Magnolia Housing Project, ca. 1939. (From the 1940 *Report of the Housing Authority of New Orleans*)

ing projects in the city.[4] As at St. Thomas, the demolition and new construction provided an opportunity to look into the area's archaeology and history prior to Magnolia's opening in 1940. The discussion here draws on a developmental history of these blocks, examined by linking maps with detailed census records, which are connected in turn to archaeological evidence derived from excavations conducted by ESI. This material demonstrates the extent to which the density of construction in the Belmont area both clouded and obscured the nature of the social relations within it. While this opacity contributed to the perception of the Belmont neighborhood as a slum, the neighborhood's portrayal as such conceals a much more complex history. Contrary to this external view, Belmont was a space where the seeming impenetrability of the physical and social world offered a measure of protection for residents from the racist violence at the heart of the city. Spaces of "insurgent citizenship" like this become crucial in the formation of new cultural forms for marginalized populations, even as the material record also demonstrates the expanding social and class inequalities behind this marginalization.[5]

The archaeological and historical evidence discussed in this chapter follows and maps these processes for the Belmont neighborhood's residents before the opening of the Magnolia Street Housing Project in 1940. This event seemed to hold a great deal of promise for the urban poor, even if it was conceived within the separate and unequal system of Jim Crow. Magnolia was located in proximity to both the new Thomy Lafon School, replacing the one burned in the Charles riots, and the Flint-Goodridge Hospital, the primary medical facility for the city's African American population and an anchor for the Black middle class. Despite these beginnings, Magnolia and the area around it declined rapidly in the post–World War II years, even as the project was expanded and renamed C. J. Peete, in honor of a long-time site manager. The future of the current Peete/Harmony Oaks redevelopment is still uncertain, but some of the controversies surrounding this contemporary remaking of urban space can be seen crystallized in the former site of the Lafon School. These two blocks at the heart of the Harmony Oaks redevelopment are now vacant, as the Lafon School was built—twice, in fact—on the former location of the Locust Grove Cemetery, where thousands of bodies of the city's poor were buried in the nineteenth century. Past inequalities continue to haunt the city, even as archaeology provides a tool to see the ways in which those inequalities are made to seem an inevitable part of the urban landscape.

Backswamp/Belmont/Magnolia

The area in which the Magnolia/C. J. Peete Housing Project was located is a low-lying, poorly drained, and prone-to-flooding environmental zone, positioned to the rear of the higher natural levee along the Mississippi River. Such marginal areas generally form a belt that follows the curving shape of the river, interrupted only by lower natural levees along relict bayou channels. If the land on which New Orleans is situated is indeed shaped like a bowl, as was repeatedly stated after Hurricane Katrina, such areas often form the bottom of that bowl. This is especially the case in the Uptown portion of the city (including the Magnolia area), where a bend in the river forms a zone in which the lowest land is bounded on three sides by the natural levee, naturally exacerbating an already tenuous drainage situation.[6] How well an area like that which became the Magnolia Project fits into Peirce F. Lewis's superblock system, in which radial avenues with more affluent residents surround poorer, lower-lying interior blocks, is debatable. The housing project was constructed in two stages and falls within an area bounded by present-day Louisiana Avenue, South Claiborne Avenue, Washington Avenue, and La Salle Street. Louisiana Avenue is certainly an example of one of Lewis's radial boulevards, and Claiborne an example of a circumferential boulevard. Washington and La Salle, while also major thoroughfares, do not as clearly correspond to the superblock pattern and vary considerably in degree of commercial and residential uses along their length.[7]

There is little evidence for any residential use of the Magnolia area during the colonial or antebellum periods, when riverfront high ground was divided into plantation tracts that were later subdivided for urban use. Because of the peculiar geography of New Orleans, lands at the rear of tracts were often disputed, as the radial boulevards that formed their boundaries converged and crossed in these zones, obscuring ownership prior to subdivision. The Magnolia area, for instance, occurred where three different former plantation faubourgs (Livaudais, Delassize, and Plaisance) met.[8] Nineteenth-century maps frequently depict the city's idealized street grid extending into these back-swamp areas, as with the 1863 *Department of the Gulf: Map No. 5, Approaches to New Orleans*, prepared at the instigation of Union general Nathaniel Banks to show fortifications and transportation networks in the city. This map shows the Magnolia area at the fringe of the street grid, on the edge of vacant land labeled as "Cypress Swamp; Timber Mostly Felled." By 1878, at the time of the production of T. S. Hardee's *Topographical and Drainage Map of New Orleans and Surroundings*, scattered buildings are shown through the area, predominantly grouped along Washington Avenue and La Salle, then referred to as St. George Street.[9]

Despite the apparent paucity of development of the area during the second half of the nineteenth century, the city council had already begun to devote some attention to it, establishing the Locust Grove Cemetery No. 1 on the block bounded by Freret, Sixth, Locust, and Seventh Streets as early as 1859. This cemetery was primarily intended for the indigent, most of them also Black.[10] An account of Locust Grove is responsible for one of the more macabre descriptions in an expansive genre of exoticizing accounts of New Orleans cemeteries. It is taken from an 1875 newspaper and quoted in *Gumbo Ya-Ya*, a book of New Orleans folklore compiled during the WPA era by the Louisiana Writers' Project: "On the left of the central path, it was evident that friends had cared for many of the graves, but on the right the picture was a sad one indeed. Here in a pile some five feet in height were some fifty babies untenanted. After the weary little bodies had wasted away, they were heaped carelessly together like so much old lumber, one upon the other, and the sacrilegious flies seemed to be feasting upon the sickening odor hanging over them. Scattered about them lay coffins of all sizes. . . . Coffin lids were used in many places to mend the fences, and so many were the uses they were put to, the whole place breathed of destruction and pestilence."[11] In the same year that the cemetery was established, another nearby square was designated a public park, a measure that would presumably only be necessary if the surrounding blocks were filling. Contemporary accounts from the period of Reconstruction and just after suggested that freedmen and freedwomen flowing into New Orleans from former plantations gravitated to the fringes of the city, and the shantytowns and impermanent dwellings springing up in such areas were considered to be a serious problem by officials of the Freedmen's Bureau and the city.[12]

Little appreciable trace of this sort of informal development appears in cartographic sources. The blocks of the Magnolia/Belmont area are omitted from the 1885–87 Sanborn map series, the detailed plans of American cities produced to aid in fire insurance assessments—apparently as housing structures, they were either too sporadic or too impermanent to merit consideration. Sanborn maps from 1895 include merely a group of blocks fronting on Washington Avenue, and only in 1909 are all the blocks within what would become the Magnolia area depicted in detail. By this date, many of the blocks were developed almost completely with a mixture of residences, mainly cottages and shotgun-style frame doubles, and businesses, including a soap factory, a wood yard, a druggist's warehouse, and various corner stores and groceries. The Locust Grove Cemetery, by then expanded to two full city squares, was closed in 1879, and the blocks were subsequently used as a neighborhood dump. The increasingly residential character of the neighborhood was eventually marked by the construction of the new Thomy Lafon School within the blocks formerly occupied by the cemetery.[13]

By 1933, again according to the available Sanborn maps, open space had filled dramatically in the blocks that became Magnolia. Some house lots, though intended for single residences, were built with multiple layers of housing stock arranged back from the street frontage, and sometimes as many as three small cottages occupied a single narrow lot. The centers of blocks were developed with closely packed double cottages or buildings labeled as "Tenements" and "Negro Tenements." These long, typically two-story buildings consisted of a series of apartments (most probably one or two rooms) opening out onto a side gallery that ran the length of the building, a floorplan that is now familiar from inexpensive hotels. Square 340 (figure 4.2) is typical of the trend. The lot at 2428 Washington Avenue contained only a single-frame shotgun residence in 1909, with a small detached two-story frame shed at the rear, probably housing both a kitchen and outhouse facilities, and a large, open side yard. By the time of the 1933 update to the map, the structure behind 2428 was a separate domicile, and the side yard was filled by two separate shotgun cottages, both of them doubles. The interior of the block became even more densely developed: replacing the commercial space of open sheds and barns associated with the Irwin Brothers Contractors' Storage Yard was a series of double cottages forming thirteen separate rental units,[14] along with a two-story Negro tenement. Frontages of other blocks were developed with continuous rows of small cottages, each sharing a wall with its neighbor, forming a solid barrier to block interiors. In still other blocks, small courts comprising cottages facing inward formed new informal alley frontages on what had previously been yard space. In the case of Belmont Street, which gave the neighborhood its name, this arrangement was eventually formalized, even

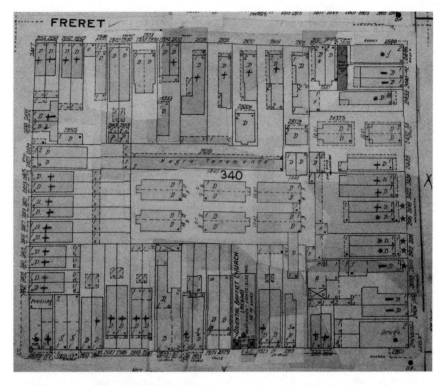

Figure 4.2. Update to Sanborn map of Square 340, 1933 (Vol. 4, Sheet 306). (Courtesy of Southeastern Architectural Archive, Tulane University)

though it did not conform to the original street grid. By the time that land acquisition began for the Magnolia Street Housing Project, the Thomy Lafon School and yard at the area's center and the 1931 Flint-Goodridge Hospital at its periphery (the city's only hospital designated for Black residents) formed the only exceptions to the maze-like housing of the area.

In a material sense, the history of the Belmont/Magnolia neighborhood can be seen in starkly economic terms as a story of predatory capitalist speculation on property in a market of scarcity. It also provides a concrete example of the ways that Jim Crow segregation, by restricting Black residential opportunities in urban areas, artificially created shortages of housing that could be exploited. Most of the residents in the area were renters, particularly by the 1930s, and rents throughout the Belmont area were exorbitantly high for the amount of space involved. This situation provided an incentive for absentee property owners to further subdivide properties, thereby producing the "obsolete, squalid, and dilapidated" slum conditions cited as a reason for Belmont's redevelopment.[15] Of course, in the discourse surrounding slums in the first half of the twentieth century (and even still), these conditions were not attributed to economics. Instead they were blamed on the moral shortcomings of the undeserving poor, with the physical aspects of slum life attributed to a "culture of poverty" that becomes embedded in the urban fabric.[16] In the case of the Magnolia/Belmont area, Black migrants to the city thus became caught in a vicious cycle of exploitation, one that at least some reformers saw as resolvable by the construction of large-scale regulated government housing.

Economic models may help describe what is driving the urban housing market in such situations, but they tell us little about the lived experiences of the people who occupied those areas characterized as slums, nor do they tell us about these sites as more than just static fields, stages where unequal relations are reproduced. These sites are also spaces of cultural production and innovation, places where dominant ideas about class, gender, race, and the family are contested and reconfigured. The challenge for contemporary researchers is not to fall into the same trap as authorities and reformers of the era, who only saw slum dwellers in terms of social disorganization and pathology. Archaeology, and the record of the prosaic elements of daily life in such neighborhoods that it produces, offers some possibilities for pushing back against slum characterizations, but the material record too has its pitfalls in this regard.

(Not) Seeing Like a State: Demography and Visibility in Belmont

In 1934, the Tulane School of Social Work prepared "A Housing Study of the Flint-Goodridge Hospital Area," which presented a social study of 523 African American households in the Belmont neighborhood, out of "a deep concern that the human aspects of rehousing Negro families should not be overlooked in the plans for the construction and maintenance of the federal housing project."[17] Within the context of the national dialogue concerning slum clearance, the area was already identified as a potential candidate for redevelopment, and the proximity of services that could employ and support a Black middle class—the Lafon School and the hospital, in particular—was seen as a positive influence. These more stable social elements were noted in the survey, as were the small family sizes and preponderance of female heads of household in the area, but most residents were described quite differently: "The community, though including a small minority of financially well-situated families, well-educated and well-housed, is a typically underpaid, poorly housed underprivileged group, deficient in education, incompletely employed in the unskilled occupations."[18] According to the survey, many small courts and tenement areas had adopted fanciful names to distinguish themselves within the neighborhood, such as the Pepper, the Yellow Dog, the Lizard, the Ark, the

Buzzards, Bed Bug Row, and the Red Devil.[19] The neighborhood was characterized as having substandard sanitary conditions, with streets consisting of muddy ruts filled with trash, sometimes to a depth of three or four feet. While a number of potential recreational resources were identified in the area, the chief social concern cited in the Tulane survey was the prolific number of lottery houses and informal gambling enterprises run out of private homes. Lottery houses were deemed especially problematic, as they were typically owned by absentee white landlords, who paid local African American residents to operate them.[20]

Surveys like this, while interesting for the information they do record, tend to highlight certain specific conditions (mucky, trash-strewn streets, for instance) and ignore or downplay others (such as social networks built around nontraditional family units), thus formulating a body of supposedly objective knowledge that situates the slum both physically and discursively as subject to curative intervention. These specific configurations of power and knowledge (or *discursive formations*, to use Foucault's term) then begin to set the terms for all future interpretations of social life within the neighborhood, thereby obscuring narratives that do not reinforce the power-laden slum conception. The construction of housing projects like Magnolia represented an outgrowth of the high-modernist ideology that James C. Scott has documented in his work *Seeing like a State*—that is, the construction was a spatial transformation that was overtly intended to imprint legibility on a complex urban landscape and thereby transform social relations within it.[21] In cities like New Orleans, the transformative component of these projects was inevitably racial as well, as the social order dictated by Jim Crow segregation had to be imposed forcefully on a daily life that in practice often defied it.

For St. Thomas, discussed in the previous chapter, the selection and identification of that area as a slum came as a result of its particularity as a space where class interests potentially crossed racial and ethnic lines, and where the urban poor and working class shared a mutually intelligible experience of everyday life that had the potential to challenge the underpinnings of racial hierarchy. At first glance, the Belmont area appears to be much more homogeneous. In the years before Magnolia was constructed, census records suggest that the area was becoming almost exclusively Black space, with the vast majority of those enumerated working either in the service sector or as unskilled or semiskilled labor (figure 4.3).[22] A handful of residences were owner occupied, but renters predominated. Some residential units were spectacularly crowded. In the 1934 Tulane study, for instance, 115 people were counted at the Red Devil tenement, a long, narrow, two-story apartment building at the interior of Square 340. As noted in chapter 1, a surveyor in the same study

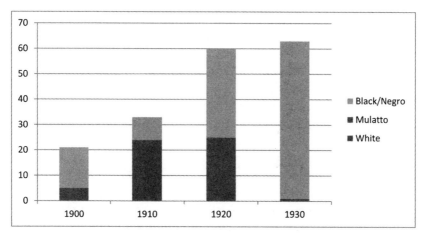

Figure 4.3. Racial composition by head of household according to US Census, City Square 594 in the Belmont neighborhood. (D. Ryan Gray)

purportedly discovered "9 people, 2 dogs, 1 cat, 6 chickens, and a duck" sharing a one-room apartment as illustrative of the state of affairs in the area.[23]

Of course, the census and surveys of population like it are always components of what Foucault terms the *sciences of the individual*, through which the administrative apparatus of a state sees its citizens and their positions in space.[24] But such surveys also produce their subjects: they provide a lens that validates certain criteria of difference and denies others, thus setting the norm in a given time and place. If we rely too heavily on these criteria as our categories of analysis, we only "see" like the state, to again borrow Scott's terminology, and thus we ignore the realities on the ground. Archaeology provides one potential remedy to this, but sometimes the omissions and apparent contradictions in the documentary record may be revealing as well. These productive tensions help to illustrate alternative subjectivities *not* recognized as legitimate by city administrators or advocates of slum clearance. For instance, in surveying census records for the area, we find that nontraditional households, meaning those not having a male head and/or basic nuclear structure, are common, and many of the names are suggestive of connections (kin based or not) between extended social networks. Following a pattern already noted for the St. Thomas area, many households in Belmont consist of multiple generations of families, including widows and widowers, roomers and boarders, and children, often with little obvious connection to the head of household. Occasionally census takers chose to ignore unsanctioned relationships, even when doing so made for awkwardness in the records, as in the case of two unmarried couples residing at the Red Devil (the tenement at 2816 Freret Street) in 1930. Each of these couples was enumerated with an adult male head and a woman of approximately the same age listed as housekeeper in the field for relationship to the head of household. If this living situation were simply an economic arrangement, this role would have presumably been listed as the woman's occupation. Such is not the case: it would instead appear to be an attempt to gloss over an informal relationship, and as such it tells about the inhering bias within these sorts of documents obscuring nontraditional unions like the cohabitation of an unmarried couple. However, proportions of households headed by women do not increase over time in Belmont. In fact, in the blocks for which I recorded information, female-led households actually tend to decrease proportionally over the census years tracked. Square 340, for instance, had a full 43 percent of households headed by women in 1900, versus 30.3 percent in 1930.

In linking census data with individual properties, I also noted that some addresses were omitted, and the fluctuations and other lacunae in the records might be indicative of larger issues pertaining to legibility in the urban environment. The very density of neighborhoods like that of Belmont/Magnolia created opportunities for invisibility to the official apparatus of the state in all its forms, one that African American residents may have used to their advantage. This process may best be understood through a concrete example, again that of the tenement known as the Red Devil. The number of people enumerated at the location fluctuates dramatically, from thirty (in 1910, when it was first listed in the census), to a high of 115 in the 1934 Tulane survey. But interestingly, it is not a linear increase: in 1920, there were ninety residents, but in the intervening US Census in 1930, only thirty residents were recorded at the address. These figures are unlikely to be the result of drastic fluctuations in the actual number of residents; instead, it more probably arose because patterns of residence at the Red Devil were difficult to penetrate for an outsider assigned to take a census of the densely packed buildings in the block interior.

Although the great majority of the Black population of the Belmont neighborhood were renters, Black families could acquire property in the area. In other words, although it is easy to see the increased population density throughout Belmont as part of a linear progression toward slum conditions, the picture that emerges from ownership records is much more complex, as there are many examples of both stability and even what would appear to be upward mobility. For instance, in Square 340, one of the most stable residents was Rodolph Harrison at 2428 Washington Avenue, an upholsterer (and later a railroad porter) whose family owned the property from at least 1900 to 1930. Other working-class Black New Orleanians were still actively acquiring property in Square 340 after 1920: by 1930, William Sherman, a drayman, owned and occupied 2839 La Salle (valued at $1,000), bank porter Everett Franklin had acquired a home at 2828 Freret (valued at $4,000), and minister William McClelland owned and operated his Oriental Baptist Church (valued at $6,500) at 2833 La Salle. Such cases of what would appear to be upward class mobility for Black residents were uncommon but not anomalous in the neighborhood, and they point to a more complex social world than that described by slum reformers.

Archaeology and Consumer Practice at Magnolia

From the standpoint of administrative authorities, the Magnolia area was clearly a slum: it was home to a densely packed, impoverished population, most of it raced as Black, living in unhealthy, crowded conditions physically, and in unconventional arrangements socially. The archaeological record of daily life at Belmont provides a counterpoint to the documentary evidence. It gives us a glimpse of the material conditions in the area uncolored by the preconceptions of early twentieth-century observers. But perhaps more importantly, it allows us to ask other questions about social life in Belmont, ones that the historical documents overlook. For example, it has been suggested that the move to areas away from the center of town allowed African American families to keep gardens and raise livestock for self-provisioning.[25] But is this visible materially, and do we find other strategies designed to increase economic independence reflected in material culture (e.g., evidence of women's household work like sewing and laundry) or architectural features (e.g., self-building and renovations, recycling of building materials)? Some authors have also suggested that the concentration of African American populations in the urban environment may have had the unintended consequence of allowing cultural traditions to flourish, especially ones that emphasized the clustering of extended families or other kinds of social groups.[26] Are there patterns of residential clustering that can relate to the use of in-filled lots by extended families or nontraditional cooperative social groups? If so, how might these patterns be reflected in the material record (e.g., sharing of ceramic sets, food items, and clothing, evidence of group social activities)? Is there any indication in the material record of the public integrative function played by community gathering places (e.g., churches like the Oriental Baptist Church on Square 340, corner groceries, a movie theater on Square 359) as it was expressed in everyday life? Likewise, how do owner-occupied properties differ from those occupied by only renters in these respects?

Considered from documentary sources alone, themselves an attempt to represent populations within categories that allow for only a predefined range of variation, the answers to these questions are necessarily limited. By integrating the material record of the neighborhood, including both that of its built environment and the archaeological remains of day-to-day activities in the area, with detailed spatial information, we can reconsider the active choices that went into the internal semiprivate community side of the Black urban working class. As historian Robin D. G. Kelley has observed, this experience is often neglected in favor of the loci of production in historical accounts, and the archaeological record may provide a much more intimate window into the practices of consumption at the level of individual households.[27] Archaeologists have emphasized the multivalence of objects (or the multiple meanings they carried for consumers) to explore both how the public and private social environments in which they were deployed may affect these meanings, and, as in the work of Paul R. Mullins, how material goods "shaped consumers' understandings of significant social issues, including racial ideology, nationalism, and affluence."[28] Furthermore, as pointed out by Arjun Appadurai, to understand the multiple and active roles played by objects in social life, we must view these objects as commodities, things intended for exchange, rather than simply as products. Although exchange implies commensurability, it does not necessarily mean that the use value ascribed to commodities by different individuals or social groups must be identical or equivalent.[29]

The archaeological effort at the Magnolia Housing Project was initiated with some of these research issues in mind.[30] As at St. Thomas, the testing and excavation at Magnolia were originally undertaken as part of a private mixed-income redevelopment of HANO property, and the work thus fell under the purview of Section 106 of the NHPA. The Magnolia Housing Project itself had been expanded in the 1950s, and the more recent portion of it had already been demolished before Katrina, although this area was rather inexplicably excluded from Section 106 consideration. All blocks that underwent testing were subjected to shovel tests and backhoe trenches, and two of them, Squares 594 and 340, were eventually selected for data recovery based on the presence of well-preserved historical remains. Archaeologists from ESI excavated footings from residences, privies, wells, cisterns, and trash pits, in the process collecting thousands of artifacts, many of them dating back to the decades when this portion of the city was first developed. It was sometimes possible to suggest a specific household associated with a given feature assemblage, yet many addresses had a rapid turnover of occupants in the period of deposition. Therefore, the scale of the analysis in this chapter shifts to seek broad patterns and connections across assemblages, with a few comparable features selected as indicative of the neighborhood as a whole.

At Square 594, intact deposits were concentrated along Freret Street, with the rear yards of a number of the historical lots on the Freret frontage pre-

Figure 4.4. L-shaped privy. Dark area at center is a historical pit excavated into base of privy. (Courtesy of Earth Search, Inc.)

served behind one of the 1939 housing project buildings. A lot at 3323–3325 Freret Street was one focal point of investigations, partially because of the presence there of a distinctive L-shaped privy shaft. According to the 1909 Sanborn map, the lot had been developed with a small one-story double residence, probably of the shotgun variety, set back slightly from the street frontage. By 1920, another double residence was added to the rear of the lot (numbered 3323½ and 3325½). The excavated privy probably served multiple units, though it did not correspond precisely with any structures illustrated on maps. The feature was shallow (less than 60 cm in depth) and lined with brick on the sides, with the base left unlined. On one side of the shaft, a pit had been dug into the soil at the base of the privy and then covered over with corrugated roofing tin (figure 4.4). A particularly rich concentration of material occurred beneath this piece of tin, with large quantities of oyster shell and a number of intact bottles recovered. The feature was likely filled and abandoned around 1920, possibly when the double residence was added to the rear yard. A shifting array of renters, all of whom were identified as Black or Mulatto in the census, resided at the double between 1900 and 1920. For instance, in 1920, Mulatto sisters Victoria and Bessie Jones, both cooks for private families, lived at 3323 Freret with a male roomer who worked as a house painter, while Gertrude Norman, a dressmaker for a private family, lived with three roomers next door, one of whom worked as a longshoreman. In the rear residences were two additional young married couples in which both husbands worked as laborers and both wives tended house. Interestingly, in 1930, there appears to be something of a shift, with a train porter named Overton Holland having purchased the property. He and his wife, a bookkeeper (presumably at the Flint-Goodridge Hospital), would have represented a firmly middle-class family at this time, though the household on the other side of the double had taken in multiple boarders.

The ceramic assemblage from the privy was not very extensive, representing a minimum of thirty-eight vessels, the majority of them tablewares. Porcelain wares make up about a third of the total, and twenty-six of the tableware vessels have some form of decoration, including molded/embossed decoration, overglaze hand-painting, transfer printing, and decals; many of the vessels were manufactured by American potteries from New Jersey and East Liverpool, Ohio. The somewhat larger assemblage of glass containers from the feature (n=64), many of them complete or reconstructed bottles, is dominated by ones with a medicinal function. Many are identified by embossing, including containers from common national brands (like multiple examples of Vaseline jars and of Quina/Laroche dose measuring jars), specific patent medicines (including a bottle of Dr. Thatcher's Liver and Blood Syrup), and only one originating in a local pharmacy, the American Drug Store of New Orleans. Most personal items recovered from the feature were related to clothing (including buttons and shoes) and to children's toys (mostly fragments of porcelain and bisque dolls). One exceptional item recovered was an artificial dental plate with one porcelain tooth and one gold tooth. Very few items overtly associated with work or production-related activities were recovered from the feature, a rare exception being a clothing iron.

A second feature was also excavated in what had been the rear of the 3323–3325 Freret yard. This feature was a large, irregular pit filled as a single deposit in the early twentieth century, including a minimum of fifty ceramic vessels and ninety-one glass containers, many of them complete. An interesting and unique characteristic of the material recovered from this feature was the over-representation of shoe and shoe-related artifacts to the exclusion of almost all other artifacts having to do with clothing and adornment. In all, a total of at least 105 shoe-related artifacts were recovered, including complete shoes (in adult and child sizes), heels, soles, welts, and miscellaneous leather and lining fragments, potentially meant to patch or mend, and this figure excludes a number of other leather fragments that could not be matched up with specific shoe and boot components. In contrast, a total of only ten buttons were recovered, almost all of them of the common Prosser variety.[31] Other typically common personal items—things like smoking pipes or toys—were also comparatively rare in the assemblage.

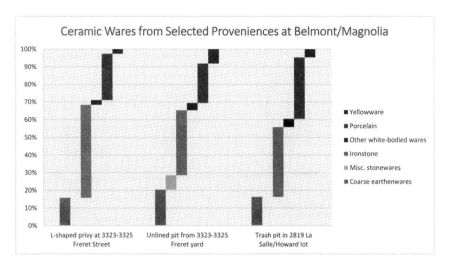

Figure 4.5. Proportions of ceramic wares from three features at Belmont/Magnolia. Bar graph sections correspond to ware types in key vertically from top to bottom. (D. Ryan Gray)

Proportions of ceramic wares in the assemblage from the trash pit were very similar to those from the privy on the same lot (figure 4.5). This was particularly the case with tablewares (n=31), of which porcelain wares made up a similarly large number (35.5 percent, n=11). Again, most of these tablewares were decorated, many with elaborate gilding, overglaze hand-painting, transfer printing, and decals. Marked wares displayed greater variety, both in place of origin and in manufacturing date range. At least some marks represented English potteries, like the Samuel Alcock Company (1891–1910), Clementson Brothers (1865–1916), and Johnson Brothers Limited (post 1900), while others were associated with American firms like Goodwin Brothers, identified by the Pearl White mark dated to 1885–97.[32] There is even one Haviland Limoge–marked porcelain saucer (imported from France) with polychrome decoration, probably dating to the end of the nineteenth century. A number of coarse earthenwares and stoneware storage vessels, including large-sized redware flowerpots, may be related to attempts to utilize the limited space at hand for home gardening. At least a few of the same embossed glass containers are represented in both assemblages, like the Quina/Laroche dose measuring jars. However, the glass assemblage from the trash pit is considerably more diverse in overall composition (figure 4.6), with much less emphasis on bottles and containers with obvious medicinal functions. There are local pharmacies (C. E. Feldner's Gaiennie Street Pharmacy and Abbott's Pharmacy at Felicity and Liberty Streets) and nationally marketed

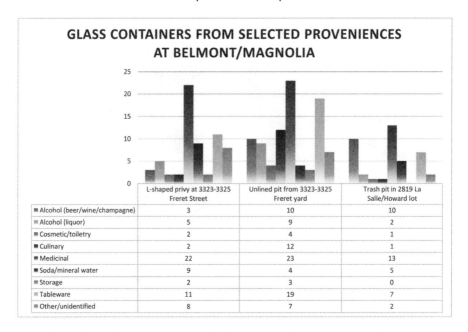

GLASS CONTAINERS FROM SELECTED PROVENIENCES AT BELMONT/MAGNOLIA

	L-shaped privy at 3323-3325 Freret Street	Unlined pit from 3323-3325 Freret yard	Trash pit in 2819 La Salle/Howard lot
■ Alcohol (beer/wine/champagne)	3	10	10
■ Alcohol (liquor)	5	9	2
■ Cosmetic/toiletry	2	4	1
■ Culinary	2	12	1
■ Medicinal	22	23	13
■ Soda/mineral water	9	4	5
■ Storage	2	3	0
■ Tableware	11	19	7
■ Other/unidentified	8	7	2

Figure 4.6. Number of glass containers by function from three assemblages at Belmont/Magnolia. Columns two, three, and four contain listings for all categories of glass containers in the order in which they appear in column one. (D. Ryan Gray)

patent medicines (including at least two bottles of Dr. Kilmer's Swamp Root Kidney, Liver, and Bladder Cure from Binghamton, New York) present, but there are many more embossed examples of culinary and soda/mineral water bottles as well. At least three examples of bottles of Dr. Samuel Brubacher Hartman's popular Peruna cure for catarrh were recovered as well. This product became so notorious for its high alcohol content (reduced from 28 percent to the still quite potent 14 percent after investigation by the newly created Food and Drug Administration in 1906) that it was referred to as the Prohibition Tonic in the 1920s.[33]

Numerous features were also excavated in City Square 340, the block bounded by Howard/La Salle, Washington, Freret, and Sixth Streets. Two in particular were comparable to those at Square 594 in period of deposition, and they provide some additional insight into the neighborhood prior to redevelopment. The first of these was a privy shaft located to the rear of 2816 Freret Street, an L-shaped lot that was the location of the already-mentioned Red Devil tenement. The building located at the street frontage of the address remained fairly consistent over Sanborn years, a two-story frame single with a wraparound gallery and attached two-story kitchen in rear. However, at some time after the preparation of the 1909 Sanborn (and possibly later that year, given the number of residents at the address listed in the 1910 census), a long narrow two-story building was added at the rear bend of the lot, where it extended behind the domiciles at 2820, 2824, 2828, 2832–2834, and 2836–2838 Freret Street. This building, labeled "Negro Tenements" on the 1933 Sanborn update, would have been accessible from the street frontage via the side yard of the residence at the front of 2816, and the location of the excavated privy (presumably representing an aboveground shed) would have further occluded this building from view from Freret. Not only were tenements like this densely occupied, but also the original residence at 2816 had been subdivided into at least four additional rental units at the time of the 1930 census. As noted already, the number of residents increases dramatically by 1920, and there is reason to be suspicious of the accuracy of the 1930 enumeration. The pattern that emerges with the tenement population is one of small family units (often just a husband and wife, or a widow with children), with men employed irregularly and at least some women entering the workforce as laundresses and cooks. Everyone enumerated at the address in these census years is identified racially as nonwhite (i.e., as Black, Mulatto, or Negro, depending on the census year).

The Red Devil privy was undoubtedly filled in the twentieth century, as attested by the prevalence of machine-made bottles and decaled ceramic wares in the assemblage. In fact, deposition may even be as late as the first years of the 1930s, as evinced by the presence of fragments of a record.[34] As with the Square 594 assemblages, porcelain vessels made up a significant portion of the overall ceramic assemblage, composing 32.5 percent of the total minimum number of thirty-seven vessels (39.3 percent of white-bodied tablewares; see figure 4.5). Again, the vast majority of the white-bodied tablewares were decorated, with molding, overglaze decaling, transfer printing, and edging represented. Unlike in the Square 594 privy assemblage, medicinal bottles were not particularly prevalent among the minimum of twenty-nine glass containers identified. Only two of the four examples classified as medicinal were embossed: a Vaseline jar and a bottle of Udolpho Wolfe's Aromatic Schnapps, the latter as popular for its alcohol content as for its medicinal qualities. Only one other bottle could be identified on the basis of embossed lettering, a bottle from the Cosmopolitan Bottling Company of New Orleans. Also noteworthy in the assemblage were an unfired .38-caliber bullet and a plasticoid or celluloid nozzle/applicator from a hygienic syringe.

On the 1909 Sanborn map, the interior of Square 340 had been depicted as largely undeveloped, occupied by a mixture of open stables and small sheds, forming part of the 2422 Washington lot. Its identification on the map as the site of the Irwin Brothers' Contractors Storage Yard was a vestige of light industrial/commercial uses of this land dating to the late nineteenth century, just as the presence next door of the Kirchburg Soft Soap Manufactory attested to the placement of nuisance industries in such areas. By the time of the 1933 Sanborn update, the built environment at the center of the block had changed completely, with the construction of the thirteen rental units aforementioned. These units were associated with the 2819 La Salle/Howard address, and when considered in conjunction with the other buildings on the block, they are almost entirely isolated from view from the surrounding street frontages. According to the 1930 census, fifty adults and eighteen children lived in this complex, all of them listed as Negro. Most of the adult men were employed as laborers, and the women as housemaids or cooks.

At least some features likely associated with the period of the Irwin Brothers' use of the block were located during excavations, including a wood-lined well shaft from which the remains of an entire horse or mule were excavated. A large trash pit, located in between two of the double rental units shown on the 1933 Sanborn update (see figure 4.2), provides some additional data about everyday life in the neighborhood as it became more residential in character. This pit was probably filled no later than 1910, and at first glance, its assemblage bears some notable similarities to the others that have already been described. In particular, porcelain vessels made up a significant proportion of the minimum of forty-three ceramic vessels recovered, some 35 percent of the total (a proportion again even higher if only tablewares are considered). Embossed bottles display no marked preference for any single identifiable brand, with multiple soda water manufacturers, local pharmacies, and national brands of patent medicines represented. However, unlike with the assemblages already described, undecorated wares make up a much greater proportion of white-bodied vessels (mainly ironstone and porcelain wares), accounting for 47 percent of the total recovered. Although the overall assemblage of personal items from the feature was not large, significant quantities of fragments of shoes and shoe leather were also recovered from the area. Very few items relating to leisure activities were identified. For instance, only one smoking-related artifact was recovered from the feature: a fragment of a white ball clay pipe bowl and stem manufactured by the L. Fiolet Company of France, in business until 1920.[35]

In light of the frequency with which renters moved within the project area and of the density of households sharing space within each block, additional excavations were undertaken at Square 340 to gain composite data about daily activities in the area. These excavations took the form of gridded shovel stripping of early twentieth-century sheet midden within interior-block yard areas hidden from view from street frontages by the proliferation of struc-

tures in the period from 1909 to 1933. A total of 3,389 sherds from historical ceramics were recovered during shovel stripping of an area around the
complex of rental units at the center of Square 340. The majority of these
were refined white-bodied wares, predominantly ironstone (55.8 percent of
the total, n=1,893). While porcelain was not quite as prevalent in the assemblage as it was among some of the privy and pit artifacts, it still accounted for
a relatively high proportion of the total (24.6 percent, n=834). Of the white-
bodied wares, 28.2 percent were decorated with a wide variety of techniques,
including gilding, over- and underglaze hand-painting, annular decoration,
transfer printing, and decals. A higher proportion of all porcelain was decorated
(35.6 percent of all porcelain, as compared to 24.9 percent of ironstone). Vessels associated with hygienic functions, particularly chamber pots and wash-
basins, were surprisingly rare in the assemblage. The assemblage of glass
wares was somewhat more difficult to characterize, as functional classification of fragmentary glass is often unclear without reference to full vessels.
A total of 2,624 fragments of glass were recovered during shovel stripping,
representing a similar range of functions to that noted for the privy and pit
assemblages. A number of soda, medicinal, and pharmaceutical bottles with
embossed decoration duplicated examples from excavated features, including Dr. Kilmer's Swamp Root, Udolpho Wolfe's Aromatic Schnapps, Vaseline, and Omega Oil. A few national brands were more unusual, like a patent
medicine from I. C. Kennedy and Co. Proprietors of Pittsburgh, called Seven
Seals or Golden Wonder, referencing the seven seals of the biblical Book of
Revelation. Others harkened to postemancipation ideals of freedom and pa-
triotism as expressed through consumer choices, like a soda bottle embossed
with the figure of the Statue of Liberty and the slogan "Liberty beats them
all / Delicious / Refreshing / Thirst-quenching."

The selection of artifacts besides ceramic vessels and glass containers was
dominated by clothing-related items. Of 241 nonferrous items for which a
function could be identified, 143 were related to clothing. Given the occupations of many of the women in the area as laundresses, seamstresses, and
domestics, such a prevalence would typically be expected to be due to the
presence of large numbers of buttons in the assemblage. Again, in this case,
shoes and shoe leather made up a much greater proportion of clothing artifacts than did buttons (of which forty-three were collected). Despite the relative paucity of buttons, domestic work related to sewing is represented in the
assemblage by two other artifacts, a lace bobbin or needle case and a set of
fine needlework scissors. Otherwise, artifacts identifiably related to household production or to trades and labor were practically nonexistent in the assemblage. Items related to tobacco consumption (i.e., pipe stems and bowls)
were also rare, with only eight examples represented. Despite the increasing

popularity of cigarette smoking during the early 1900s, artifacts associated with pipe smoking still tend to be common in archaeological assemblages throughout the pre–World War II period, so this lack is noteworthy.

Aggregate faunal information was also considered for City Squares 594 and 340.[36] Domesticates like cows, pigs, caprids, turkeys, and chicken were all well represented in the assemblage, typically in common commercially available meat cuts, with chop, steak, ham, and roast cuts identified. While fish bone certainly occurred in some quantities, the variety of species represented was less diverse than in the privy assemblages from St. Thomas Square 70, with only gafftopsail catfish and sheepshead identified to species in the Square 594 privy sample, for example. However, a large amount of unidentifiable fish bone was also recovered, so some of this variation could be due to lack of a sufficient comparative collection for identification. In addition, some of the animal bone recovered seemed to be indicative of species that might have been available through informal networks, or that might potentially be linked to the swampy environment at the fringes of the city. Present were substantial quantities of bone from rabbit and duck, along with opossum, squirrel, turtle, and even one example of an alligator, represented by a single vertebra. These sorts appear to be slightly more numerous in earlier temporal associations, which is to be expected with the increasing urbanization of the area in the first decades of the twentieth century.

Consumption and Identity in the Belmont/Magnolia Slum

The data outlined in the previous section span a considerable range of time and a number of important historical events that certainly affected the material expressions of American consumer practices at the national level: World War I, the enfranchisement of women voters, Prohibition, the Great Depression, and the New Deal, to name some. However, through this time, the *conception* of Belmont as a slum remained essentially unchanged, and it thus marks a constant to be interrogated through the material record of the neighborhood prior to clearance. In tracing national trends in the politics of mass consumption, Lizabeth Cohen has emphasized two separate and sometimes competing conceptions of the consumer in the pre–World War II era, that of the citizen consumer and that of the purchaser consumer. Whereas the citizen consumer was seen as an overtly political force, responsible for driving government policy on the market, the purchaser consumer was seen as a participant in public life primarily through the act of consuming itself.[37] These roles were fraught for African Americans within the Jim Crow South, for whom the range of consumer choices available was often limited by "the same white anxiety about blacks' proper place in racial and class hierarchies that constrained their working and voting."[38]

Paul R. Mullins, in his archaeological and historical studies of African American consumer practice, has confronted the resulting contradictions directly. He emphasizes that even though Black consumers shared in common an experience of a society structured by racism and racial hierarchy, any attempt to universalize a pattern of African American consumption within a politics that "was strategically structured, explicitly articulated, focused on universal goals, or became a philosophy or morals unto itself" will inevitably ignore the complexities of how individuals and groups negotiated this social world. Nevertheless, Mullins identifies some common themes in assemblages from Annapolis, Maryland, shaped around African American consumers' "utopian aspirations" and desire for the privileges offered by full and equal citizenship.[39] The cautions noted by Mullins certainly applied to the heterogeneous African American community of New Orleans, minimally stratified by class, if not also by color, educational opportunities, rural or urban origins, and so forth.

The archaeological deposits associated with the Belmont neighborhood testify to the complexities involved in negotiating consumer space and identity in the Jim Crow South, and they indicate some of the same aspirations for citizenship and equality noted by Mullins but expressed in a manner unique to the local sociopolitics of race in New Orleans. The patterns of African American ceramic tableware consumption in the Belmont/Magnolia neighborhood demonstrate some ways in which Black consumers in New Orleans asserted an identity for themselves that contrasted with the perceptions of slumness ascribed to Belmont/Magnolia. These patterns are marked by a preference for porcelain wares, even in the relatively early period of the neighborhood's dense urban occupation. The differential use of porcelain, typically among the most expensive ceramic ware on the market, suggests a claim on something more than equality in the marketplace, an assertion of affluence in the face of social and economic marginalization. Porcelain usage here was not simply a signifier of middle-class respectability; rather, it designated an identity at odds with that of the dominant norms of white society, increasingly characterized by racist violence and racial hierarchy. Choices in ceramic tablewares may seem an odd way to make such claims, but I suspect that this is just the most tangible material aspect of a much larger pattern of consumption. Monica Miller's work on Black dandyism has emphasized the ways that choices in extravagant fashions were mobilized by Black men in particular to assert political and social ideals, and assemblages like this show that aesthetic suffusing the everyday.[40]

It is one of the deep contradictions at the heart of Jim Crow America that

Black consumers were stigmatized no matter how they behaved. If African American households attempted to purchase conservatively or thriftily, they were characterized as poor, ignorant, or morally degraded, but if they displayed wealth, they were called wasteful and extravagant. As observed by W. E. B. Du Bois at the beginning of the Jim Crow era, Black Americans were aware of these contradictions, and, in the necessity of spanning both white and Black social worlds, found themselves forced to develop what Du Bois termed a *double-consciousness*. In most situations, this consciousness allowed African Americans to see through the veil of race,[41] but, in the material from Belmont/Magnolia, this veil was wrenched aside, as the arbitrariness of racial hierarchy was exposed and confronted. In the area, we see a rejection of the consumer aesthetic of middle-class domesticity within a Jim Crow racial hierarchy, as well as the assertion of a subjectivity and self-consciousness apart from that of white America. This self-consciousness turned inward, reflected in the increasing focus on the interiority of blocks as loci of development and identity. It actively celebrated extravagance, turning the expectations of white society on their head, invoking them just to challenge them, as manifested in the assemblages here through the aesthetic choice of lavishly decorated wares, particularly in the form of expensive, gilded porcelain and decorated tablewares (figure 4.7). This pattern is distinct, both from contemporary assemblages from St. Thomas, and from other late nineteenth- and early twentieth-century assemblages from around the city associated with lower- and middle-class white (both native and European immigrant) households. Here, objects marked a population with revolutionary potential. Perhaps this potential was not couched in the violent resistance of a Robert Charles, but it signified unwillingness to accept a place defined as subordinate to white society.

In New Orleans, between the *Plessy v. Ferguson* decision, which provided the legal basis for Jim Crow segregation, and the modern Civil Rights era, Black political activism is often thought to have fragmented and thus to have been subverted and ineffective.[42] However, Lizabeth Cohen has also noted that during the 1930s, African American consumers turned "familiar strategies of economic self-help and self-sufficiency into a new kind of black mass politics."[43] These attempts at self-sufficiency were matched with an increasing awareness of the economic importance of choices in the marketplace, enacted through the power of the boycott. The assemblages from Magnolia suggest a somewhat more complex picture of this period. Aside from faunal evidence that suggests occasional supplementing of diet through fishing, hunting, and trapping (evidence that is at best ambiguous given the availability of many wild species in local markets), few artifactual remains could be associated with attempts at self-provisioning and self-sufficiency. A lone exception may be the remains of large flowerpots, which are likely connected to attempts to

Figure 4.7. Gilded porcelain teacup recovered from Square
340. (D. Ryan Gray)

maintain backyard gardens, even when there was no longer any cultivatable
yard space left around the house. The paucity of artifacts connected to economic production on the part of women or men, aside from the abundance
of shoe parts, suggests the degree to which local residents found employment in the service industry away from the home. As segregation became
entrenched around the city and urban African American workers resided farther from the homes and businesses of white people by whom they were employed, the opportunities for the economic activities tied to self-sufficiency—
piecework, craft-making, self-provisioning—were constantly lessened. This
pattern is also typified in census records, where employment in the service
sector at the homes and businesses of private families (rather than at the
worker's home) was established as a twentieth-century norm.

The assemblages from the Belmont/Magnolia area do give some indication
of Black residents' awareness of their power as purchaser consumers, even if
they were denied the full privileges of citizenship within the Jim Crow city.

Mullins has observed that, in Annapolis, urban African American residents often chose national brands over locally produced ones, which he sees as a conscious strategy by Black consumers to avoid the everyday impacts of racism.[44] Rather than being forced to rely on personal interactions with racially biased white merchants and local white-owned businesses, African American consumers could be ensured of a consistent measure of quality for the products they used by ordering and purchasing nonlocal brands. A disproportionate reliance on such nationally distributed products (in medicines, culinary products, or soda and mineral water) was not noted for the Belmont/ Magnolia assemblage, but a comparable consumer strategy may be observed by the range of embossed bottles within each of the assemblages. Rather than relying on a single source for products, consumers in the Belmont area diversified, using a wide range of branded goods, even for the same purpose. By exercising their full range of choices as consumers, they could be ensured of a certain standard of quality. While some local businesses obviously catered to Black consumers, some of the embossed bottles represented establishments catering primarily to white customers. Products from such businesses made their way through informal networks of exchange, with those employed in the service sector acting as conduits for the circulation of items that might not be easily accessible to Black consumers.

Over the period between 1910 and 1939, the built environment of the Belmont/ Magnolia area grew rhizomatically.[45] Structures, both residences and ancillary buildings, proliferated, creating informal blocks and courts at the centers of the established city squares. Such areas were hidden from sight and, by their nature, became potential sources of disorder and unruliness. These were spaces where people like Robert Charles could harbor violent resentment and resistance to racial hierarchy and then could be concealed. But they were conceived as disorderly only within a system of domination that defined any social action that contested white supremacy as subject to correction; considered on their own terms, they reflect the everyday support networks and social structures that connected the city's marginalized residents. Overt evidence of everyday resistance to the institutionalized racism and inequalities of Jim Crow segregation is difficult to see archaeologically, but certain idiosyncratic pieces of data may be the best evidence of covert subversion. For instance, was the piece of tin covering the pit in the bottom of the L-shaped privy at Square 594 meant to intentionally conceal its contents? Such might be the case, yet nothing seemed particularly distinctive about the material beneath it, which consisted of a few patent medicine and liquor bottles and large quantities of oyster shell. How should the large proportions of shoes and shoe parts in certain assemblages be interpreted? These could be simply everyday refuse, emblematic of the toil of those working in the service industry, always on their feet. In contrast, they could be signs of individuals creating cottage industries, mending and manufacturing shoes for the local community in an informal market. Within the ideological order of Jim Crow, with the Black working class increasingly consigned to an economic sphere of service in the homes and businesses of white society, such activities, in themselves, could subvert the dominant system.

In the Belmont neighborhood, the dissonance between the supposed American ethos of hard work and equality and the reality of segregation and exploitation within a system of separate and unequal was exposed. In this regard, it is telling that by the 1930s the largest "industry" within the neighborhood was the lottery house. Within a structure of permanent racial subordination, affluence was a dream as much born of luck as born of hard work. The formal space of the Magnolia Housing Project and other housing projects like it across the United States served to further sever the homes of the urban poor from any informal productive capacity that could be maintained within them. By separating such work as illegitimate and illicit, the construction of housing projects would have much broader implications for the subject possibilities of residents. Rather than locating slumness in material conditions like decaying infrastructure and substandard rental housing, early proponents of housing reform discursively linked the slum to the behavior of the racialized poor, making it a permanent feature of the dominant view of Black urban life. This, in turn, set the stage for many of the developments in coming years: unequal policing, a carceral state with its violence disproportionately directed toward African Americans, an imagination of a culture of poverty as an embedded pathology that must be cured.

In the next chapter, I turn to the redevelopment of the Lafitte Housing Project, and to the archaeology of a single household within it. This case, in which the assemblage can be connected to a single household predating Lafitte, gives further insight into the multiple ways that the city's African American residents negotiated the contradictions of class and color in the Jim Crow city.

5
Lafitte

Gender, Race, and Creole Color along Orleans Avenue

In enumerating the household residents at 2024 Orleans Avenue in 1910, a census taker initially listed a Mulatto woman named Julia Metoyer as head of household. Julia was employed as a midwife, and her husband, Hypolite, a laborer doing odd jobs, was listed second in the entry after her, followed by a son who was working as a porter at a drugstore. Later, someone scratched through the designation listing Julia as head and changed the entry to record Hypolite as the more traditional male head of household. Perhaps this bureaucrat lacked the everyday, practical knowledge of this particular urban neighborhood and was unaware that employment as a midwife gave Julia Metoyer considerable status in her family and in the neighborhood more broadly. The person also likely would not have known much about the connections between the work of the midwife and that associated with conjure, rootwork, and African American spirituality in New Orleans, or the traditions of powerful women as spiritual leaders and property owners in the city. This seemingly simple revision in the census is laden with meanings, thick with questions about family roles and norms of race, gender, class, and color in a neighborhood that would be, in about three decades, demolished to make way for the Lafitte Housing Project.[1]

The branch of the Metoyer family mentioned in this census record did not produce a particularly rich record in official administrative sources, despite the fact that Hypolite Metoyer was related to the storied Metoyer Creole of Color family of Natchitoches, Louisiana, northwest of New Orleans. Hypolite and Julia show up in the census and in city directories as renters, moving fairly frequently. We can track important life events such as births, marriages, and deaths in documentary sources. Hypolite, for instance, died in 1917, and Julia never remarried, living at a number of addresses in the city's Fourth and Fifth Wards before moving to California after World War II. She died there in 1963, having reached almost ninety years of age.[2] There are certainly living descendants of the Metoyers, and perhaps they have preserved stories, photographs, or letters that pertain to this family. But lacking these sorts of materials, we must rely on the documents, which leave us with hints and clues that seem to have a certain amount of ambiguity built into any potential interpretation. Perhaps the change to the head of household in the 1910 census entry was a simple mistake, rather than a sign that the structure of the Metoyer family controverted gendered norms. Perhaps Julia Metoyer was "just" a midwife; this is, after all, a rich enough story in itself, particularly in a time when state medical authorities were seeking to regulate and control practices related to health and hygiene. Add to that the complexity of being characterized as Mulatto, a Creole of Color in a city that was being redefined as having a two-tiered racial hierarchy, and there are already enough factors and variables at play in this one moment crystallized in the census as to be dizzyingly confounding.

In the case of the households on the block historically bounded by Orleans, St. Peter, North Johnson, and North Prieur Streets, where the Metoyers lived in 1910, we also have archaeological data that can be brought to bear on some of these complexities, as the square fell into the sixteen-block area that would be replaced by the Lafitte Public Housing Project in 1940. Just as at St. Thomas and Magnolia, compliance with Section 106 of the NHPA required that impacts to the historical and archaeological resources located on the Lafitte property be taken into account before the redevelopment of the Faubourg Lafitte could proceed. After a period of testing and evaluation, specific loci on five city blocks were selected for full-scale excavation, based on their having intact remains and potentially unique research potential. In this chapter, I discuss the historical development of the project at the macroscale, that of the superblock in which the Lafitte Project is located. This area had been well integrated into the city's sewage and drainage infrastructure before the construction of Lafitte, and it was long associated with skilled tradespeople of color, many from a Francophone background, at least some of whom descended from the city's antebellum community of free people of color, who formed its Black Creole elite.[3] And yet it, too, was selected for slum clearance to make way for public housing.

On the larger, neighborhood-level scale, signs of what made Lafitte a slum in the eyes of reformers are noticeable in demographic trends in the census. By the twentieth century, the area contradicted the expectations that were built into the dominant understanding of how the city should be structured in terms of color and class. I review those trends, in which the racial character of the superblock pattern of development was apparently inverted. However, here I am interested chiefly in what this inversion meant at the scale of the intimate and the everyday for families who lived in the neighborhood. I thus shift scale and turn to a detailed assessment of the assemblage produced from the excavation of a single feature, a brick-lined well located at the interior of City Square 252, the same block on which the Metoyers lived in 1910. The artifacts from this feature included a number of items associated with a midwife's work and, potentially, with practices of rootwork, folk magic, and traditional medicine. There is good reason to associate these items directly with Julia Metoyer and her family. I interpret the evidence here in terms of what is known of midwifery and conjure in the Jim Crow South to consider the nature of the social relationships in the Lafitte neighborhood in the era before slum clearance. The Metoyers, like many other families in the area, did not conform to what the census enumerators identified as a normal household. Eventually, considered on both the macro- and the microscale, social spaces like that in what came to be the Lafitte neighborhood would be filled with too many contradictions to sustain in the increasingly racialized environment of the city. It is precisely at this point that they became slums and thus the objects of the projects of clearance and legibility represented by public housing.

Re-Racing Lafitte

The historical development of the area that became the Lafitte Public Housing Project was inextricably connected to the construction of the Carondelet or Old Basin Canal, which forms one boundary for it, along with North Claiborne Avenue, Orleans Avenue, and North Rocheblave Street. Built between 1794 and 1796 and later expanded, the canal provided a convenient commercial linkage between Lake Pontchartrain and the back of the city via Bayou St. John, where cargos could be offloaded and transferred. Access to the canal slowly encouraged the development of businesses associated with woodworking, including cooperages, furniture makers, sawmills, ship builders, and lumber yards, along the Carondelet Walk, the street that fronted it. The location of the canal, draining what was then the swampy margins of the town, also ensured that a racially and socially diverse community was able to settle there and in the nearby Tremé neighborhood. Maintenance of the canal proved to be problematic, and it regularly became clogged with the city's filth. The creation of the deeper New Basin Canal to serve the city's upriver American sector during the antebellum era further contributed to neglect of the Carondelet Canal. Perhaps in part because of this, the area around the Carondelet Walk became a focal point of residential activity for a substantial community of free people of color, many of whom were engaged in skilled building trades as carpenters, bricklayers, plasterers, and cabinetmakers. Residential and small-scale commercial development was further encouraged by the 1822 construction of the Girod Canal for drainage (along the route of modern Orleans Avenue), which lined the area that became Lafitte with waterways on either side. As a result, many individuals listed in city directories from the area throughout the nineteenth century had connections to employment involving shipping or watercraft. By World War I, the Carondelet Canal had declined as a shipping channel, and it was declared unnavigable in 1927 and filled soon thereafter.[4]

As the neighborhood continued to develop in the postemancipation years, it maintained a multiracial character, incorporating both unskilled laborers, especially first-generation immigrants, and skilled tradesmen who formed a more affluent middle class. When sanitary engineer George Waring conducted his surveys of conditions in American cities in the 1870s, the Second District, encompassing both the Lafitte and the Iberville (see chapter 6) Projects, compared quite favorably with much of the rest of the city. Floors and roofs in 99 percent of the over eight thousand premises surveyed were in good condition, as were 61 percent of the privies. This contrasts with the Fourth District, covering much of the Garden District (and the area that became the St. Thomas Project), in which only 32 percent of the privies were in good condition, with the majority classed as either foul or defective. Population was somewhat more densely packed in the Second District, with about 5.6 people per dwelling, versus 4.6 people per dwelling in the Fourth District; when density was calculated based on total number of rooms, it was not appreciably different (see table 3.1).

Although the Tremé/Lafitte areas were already quite racially integrated in the antebellum period, this pattern was not uncommon in the urban South, where the enslaved often lived in proximity to slaveholders. As detailed in chapter 2, after emancipation the racial composition of neighborhoods in New Orleans became quite complex, with at least some following the so-called super-block pattern of large radial boulevards bounding lower multiblock backswamp areas with poor drainage. Typically, more affluent white populations concentrated along the outer portions of these superblocks, and poor first-generation immigrants and/or Black residents, often employed in the service sector, clustered in the interior.[5] This pattern is thought to have broken down in the years after 1900, when the city began large-scale drainage projects powered by an elaborate pumping system and thereby opened previously uninhabitable portions of the city to residential development. In an urban environment characterized by increasingly codified Jim Crow segregation, this process had the consequence of making true residential separation feasible, as African American former residents found themselves pushed into marginal, low-lying properties by de facto and de jure housing discrimination. The newly drained, somewhat higher lakefront neighborhoods excluded Black residents almost across the board, through actions by the state of Louisiana, which approved an act in 1912 that allowed the city to withhold building permits to Black people at-

tempting to build in white neighborhoods, and by the New Orleans City Council, which in 1924 adopted an ordinance that formally prohibited Black people
from establishing residence in white areas. Although such statutes would be
overturned by the Supreme Court in 1927, the patterns of increased segregation persisted, in the form of deed covenants and economic restrictions.[6]

Despite these developments, the sort of Jim Crow separation stipulated
by city and state authorities did not develop in the area eventually to be occupied by the Lafitte Project. In the 1880 census, which lists individual addresses, one can see white, Black, and Mulatto families living alongside one
another, white boarders within Black or Mulatto households, and vice versa.
Most blocks remained a patchwork of residents defined as white and either
Black, Mulatto, or Negro (with specific racial designations changing depending on the census year). A survey of the 1910 census, correlated with street
addresses, shows a remarkable degree of racial diversity within the project
area. Families that identified as Mulatto rather than Black make up the preponderance of people of color in the area for this census year. Many families
also have French-derived surnames, reflecting the descent of many in the area
from the city's antebellum population of free *gens de couleur* tradesmen. Not
only do Black and/or Mulatto families still often reside alongside white families in the 1910 census, but listings also hint at the intricacies of the system
of racial classification. For instance, living on the St. Peter Street side of the
same complex as the Metoyers in 1910 is a widow named Marie Martin. She
and her brother are both identified as Mulatto, but her white mother from
Spain, who was born "at sea," resided with her.

Racial identity was almost impossible to police in such an environment,
even though a concern with the issue of racial purity was becoming prominent in both city and state ideologies.[7] Cross-racial passing was a dramatic
way of contesting the norms of racial segregation, and apparent examples of
this phenomenon can be identified in the area through the census. For instance, a woman in the neighborhood who was listed as a widowed Mulatto
seamstress in 1910 had, by 1920, become a white widow of French parentage.[8] In other examples, antimiscegenation laws forced the census takers into
contradictory conclusions. Frequently, in the handwritten manuscript census, items in the race column are crossed out and changed, and it is easy to
suspect that the census taker strategically overlooked informal arrangements
that deviated from the rules, particularly in the case of cohabiting interracial
couples. While some blocks conformed to the superblock residential pattern,
others had developed in the inverse, with middle-class Black tradesmen occupying the most favorable housing along the periphery of the superblock,
and unskilled first-generation white immigrants settling in the dense housing in its interior. These patterns persist even through the 1930 census, which

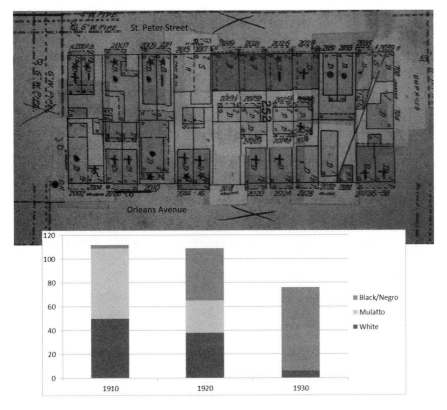

Figure 5.1. Sanborn map of Square 252 in 1909 (Vol. 2, Sheet 151) (courtesy of Southeastern Architectural Archive, Tulane University), with bar graph showing changing racial composition of block residents. (D. Ryan Gray)

still attests to a racially diverse area, although more starkly identifying race as an either/or (white or Negro) category (figure 5.1). Finally, while the majority of families in the neighborhood were renters, there was a higher percentage of home ownership by residents throughout the Lafitte area. For instance, in 1930, in the block bounded by Orleans, North Tonti, St. Peter, and North Rocheblave Streets, of fifteen properties, six were owned by their occupants, with three of those heads of household white and three of them Black.[9]

Given that the neighborhood was racially and socially diverse throughout the period, what were the material conditions in it in the years immediately preceding clearance? Both historical sources and archaeological data provide some evidence for this. As noted, the district compared quite favorably to the rest of the city before 1900, and the proximity of the Carondelet Canal meant that it had been one of the better-drained portions of the city since the beginning of the nineteenth century. Likewise, the Tremé/Lafitte area was one of the first portions of the city with a large African American population to receive service from the Sewerage and Water Board, at least partially because of the presence of a major sewer line along modern Orleans Avenue. Private property owners were required to pay a sewerage connection fee up until 1911, but, judging from the relatively early dates in which many of the privies excavated in the project area were filled with trash and debris, property owners took advantage of the opportunity to connect to the city system relatively early. This fact contrasts to some other archaeologically investigated portions of the city, in which outdoor brick-lined privy shafts and cesspools were sometimes in use into the 1920s and 1930s. The 1938–39 survey undertaken by HANO of conditions in the housing project areas (see table 2.1) further highlights the relatively good condition of housing within the Lafitte area. Of 567 units surveyed by HANO, only 172 had no access to electricity or gas, the lowest proportion of any of the early housing project locations. Additionally, only eighty-one relied on outdoor shared toilets as their primary means of waste disposal, probably reflecting the proximity of the sewerage infrastructure along Orleans Avenue. Here, especially, slumdom would seem to be an imagined category little supported by the material evidence.

Some of these issues will be taken up again in reference to a single block in the Lafitte area, Square 252. However, it is important to note that the construction of Lafitte was not even the first attempt to transform the Tremé area through clearance and urban renewal, and it certainly would not be the last. In the latter part of the 1920s, the city moved to bolster tourism by building a new municipal auditorium in a block just to the rear of Beauregard/Congo Square. While ostensibly a boost to the city's growing culture industry, it remained segregated, with occasional exceptions, for decades. In addition, the footprint occupied by the auditorium steadily grew: in 1955, the city acquired another nine blocks in the surrounding area and razed most of the buildings on them to build a cultural center, with residents forced to relocate with little in the way of compensation or assistance. After years of negotiations and delays because of lack of funds, the area would eventually be turned into the Theater for the Performing Arts/Mahalia Jackson Theater, which opened in 1972–73, and Louis Armstrong Park, which was not officially dedicated until 1980. A number of private development plans for the area foundered in these years, and Armstrong Park remained neglected until very recently. In 1999, the New Orleans Jazz National Historical Park began to maintain the park after leasing it from the city, and in the years since Katrina, Armstrong Park and Congo Square have become a much more active gathering place for public events, many celebrating the city's African American culture.[10]

While redevelopments that were intended to create public space and centers for the performing arts can at least be argued to have potential beneficial long-term effects for the neighborhood, the same could not be said for the other major transformation in urban space affecting the area in the 1960s, when an elevated section of the I-10 Expressway was routed along the course of historic Claiborne Avenue. As segregationist policies excluded Black citizens from the Canal Street retail artery, Claiborne Avenue, with its broad, oak-lined neutral ground (or median), had become a center for the city's African American populations. Lined with late Victorian mansions and offices for insurance companies and funeral parlors, it served as an aspirational center for the downtown Creole of Color community. An initial route proposed for an expansion of the interstate system through New Orleans in the 1960s ran along the city's riverfront, the location of its oldest neighborhoods. If built, it would have devastated the city's French Quarter. When a route along Claiborne was eventually adopted, many of the city's preservationists saw this as a triumph. Instead, the interstate bifurcated the Tremé, creating blight in what had been a thriving space. Despite this imposition, the space is still a gathering point for the city's African American community, hosting festivals, markets, and informal gatherings. Ironically, as the process of gentrification finally makes its way into the areas on either side of Claiborne, there is talk of removing the expressway overpass and restoring the neutral ground. Real estate speculation may ultimately be the greatest threat to the cultural traditions of Black Creole New Orleans.[11]

Investigations at City Square 252

The archaeological excavations in the project area provided a great deal of information about the development of the Lafitte neighborhood, especially during the nineteenth century. Among the loci investigated were the location of an antebellum pleasure garden and the remnants of a pottery kiln operated by a man named Lucien Gex. Gex was a former employee of Bertrand Saloy, the proprietor of the New Orleans Pottery and Porcelain Works, a company that briefly tried to bring the manufacture of hard paste porcelain to the city. Additional excavations were undertaken at the location of the Thomy Lafon Orphan Asylum, which, like the Lafon School discussed in the previous chapter, was part of the legacy of the African American philanthropist of the same name. The Lafon orphanage would eventually be taken over by the Sisters of Charity, who operated it as a Catechism Preparatory School for Black students. A privy at the location was filled with debris connected to institutional life, from ink bottles and slate pencils to toys and medicinal products. These materials will provide valuable data for years to come for those researching the development of New Orleans.

A particularly promising residential locus at Lafitte occurred in what would have been City Square 252, the block historically bounded by North Johnson, St. Peter, Orleans, and North Prieur Streets.[12] Here, between the footprints of two housing project buildings, the archaeological remains of a row of two-story brick townhouses facing St. Peter Street and their two-story service structures were uncovered. These structures backed up to another row of service buildings or dependencies, which served frame cottages facing on Orleans Avenue and built in the classic Creole cottage style. Among these cottages was the one in which the Metoyer family resided in 1910. The St. Peter and Orleans residences were probably constructed around 1851, when they appear in a watercolor of properties being offered for sale that is preserved in the New Orleans Notarial Archives (figure 5.2). By 1893, Sanborn maps indicate that many of the rear service structures had been converted into small apartments. The complex remained essentially unchanged until the 1930s, with residents typifying the largely integrated racial patterns of the neighborhood in the years after Reconstruction. For instance, in 1880, three households were identified at 2019 St. Peter: that of Marie Mulet, a thirty-six-year-old widowed white woman from France (with her six children), and those of the Labostrie and Hill families, both of whom were identified as Mulatto. Felix Labostrie was a shoemaker, and both Henry Hill and his wife were employed, as a laborer and a laundress, respectively. Living with the Hills were Mrs. J. B. and Juanita Lopez, white teachers of Spanish and Italian parentage. Twenty years later, in 1900, one could find a similar pattern on the Orleans side of the complex: Mary Meade, an Irish widow, owned and resided at 2018 Orleans, and Joseph Daunois, a barber identified as Black, along with his wife, daughter, and niece, also resided at the address.[13]

Excavations documented well-constructed brick foundations and chain walls from these buildings, as well as a rich artifactual record from the households that resided there in the late nineteenth and early twentieth centuries. Domestic debris from the service buildings was particularly abundant, much of it appearing to relate to use of the structures as detached kitchens for the main properties prior to having been converted to apartments in the 1880s. Excavated privies in the complex appeared to have been cleaned frequently, and all the associated buildings were probably connected to city water in the 1890s. One of the most intriguing features that was excavated in Square 252 was a brick-lined well or subsurface cistern with a dome-shaped top. It was located near the rear property lines of the homes that fronted Orleans and St. Peter Streets. Preservation was exceptionally good due to the inundated soils within the feature, with complete wooden buckets, numerous items of brass hardware, tools with wooden handles still intact, items relating to clothing and ornament, toys, religious medallions and figurines, and at least one

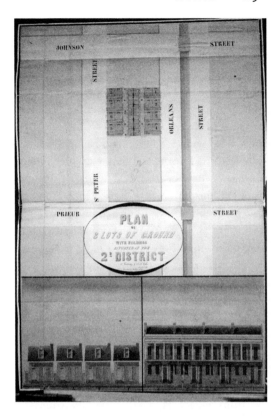

Figure 5.2. St. Peter and Orleans residences on Square 252, depicted in *Plan of 8 Lots of Ground with Buildings Situated in the 2D District*, A. Castaing and G.A. Celles, Architects, 1851 (NONA 044.077). (From the New Orleans Notarial Archives, courtesy of Chelsey Richard Napoleon, Clerk of Civil District Court, Parish of Orleans)

artifact that immediately hinted at a linkage to the census records that had been compiled for the block: a cranial perforator used in performing fetal extractions. This item seemed to offer a direct connection to the midwife Julia Metoyer and her family discussed in the beginning of this chapter, who were enumerated on this block in 1910.

The presence of the Metoyer family itself was certainly intriguing. The Metoyers of Natchitoches are famous locally as one of the most prominent families in the Cane River's Creole of Color community. The family traces a lineage back to the town's founding generation in the second half of the eighteenth century, when Louis Juchereau de St. Denis leased an enslaved woman named Marie Thérèse Coincoin to a local French merchant named Claude Metoyer. Over the next two decades, Metoyer fathered ten children with Coincoin, eventually purchasing and manumitting her and some of those children. Marie and her sons established a series of plantations and landholdings along the Cane River, including, in 1796, what is now known as Melrose Plantation.[14] Hypolite Vincent Metoyer, who appeared in the census, was born in Natchitoches, Louisiana, in 1867, to Hypolite Metoyer Sr. and a woman named

Julia Chevalier. By 1870, this branch of the Metoyers had moved from Natchi-toches to New Orleans, where they lived with Julia Chevalier's mother, Anna, and Hypolite Sr. worked as a barber. He died soon thereafter, and Julia remar-ried to Francis Prevost, also a barber. The younger Hypolite married Julienne Sophia Cummings (most commonly referred to as Julia in later documents, but also sometimes as Juliane, and even sometimes by her middle name) on June 30, 1889, when she was eighteen. By 1900, Hypolite and Julienne re-sided at 221 North Johnson Street with Hypolite's mother and stepfather. The 1910 census found the now-widowed Julia Prevost residing with Julia/Juliane and Hypolite on Square 252 (the site of the dig) at 2024 Orleans. By the time of the 1920 census, the Metoyers had moved again. Julia Metoyer, now wid-owed, was living at 809 North Roman Street, with her daughter, two sons, and the family of one of those sons; another son and his family lived at 2425 St. Peter Street, with his grandmother, Julia Prevost, now eighty-six.[15] Julia Metoyer moved frequently during her later years as a practicing midwife. She was at the North Roman address only briefly before a short stay at 1225 North Prieur and then a longer residence at 1609–1611 Dumaine. This movement suggests some instability in her life. Her son William appears in a number of newspaper articles from the 1920s in trouble with the law for various rea-sons, from passing bad checks to bootlegging. In fact, at one point, the 1611 Dumaine address is the location of a raid that uncovered a still and liquor, though without an owner identified.[16]

When the excavated features from Square 252 were integrated with map overlays, the well in question was located in the backyard of the residences at 2019–2021 St. Peter, thus near but not within the 2024 Orleans lot. Further research showed that the Metoyers spent a short time at the St. Peter Street address, as Julia/Juliane, listed as a midwife in all but 1911, appears in New Orleans city directories at 2021 St. Peter Street from 1911 to 1914. Perhaps this change in address is a sign of the success of Julia's career as a midwife, reflected in the move from the modest cottages fronting Orleans to the larger brick townhouses on St. Peter. It also suggests that the assemblage may be linked to a fairly short span of occupation, perhaps deposited at the time that the Metoyers departed the address. This event would coincide with a period in which these residences would have begun to have access to city water, elimi-nating the need for the antiquated and unhygienic brick-lined well.

Throughout the period for which we have good documentary evidence, Julia Metoyer seems to be at the forefront of the economic life of her household, de-fying the gendered norms of Victorian domesticity. Husband Hypolite, when listed in city directories at all, seems to be drifting between jobs. He shows up as a cooper in the 1910 directory, in the same year that he is listed in the census as a laborer, but in subsequent years he also appears as a clerk, the sort of occupation often associated with young, single men in these years. In contrast, Hypolite's brother Rene Metoyer became a prominent lawyer and church official, who was even recognized in a special column on progressive leaders of the city's African American community.[17] How did Julienne Cummings, eighteen at the time of her marriage to Hypolite, with only the equivalent of a sixth-grade education, become the head of household? What sort of material differences did this inversion of gendered roles entail in the everyday life of the family? And how might those differences be implicated in the perception of the neighborhood as a slum of the sort that the Lafitte Project was meant to normalize and erase? To address these questions, we can return to the material record itself, an assemblage from the household of an African American midwife, deposited in a short span of time around 1914.

Material Culture, Midwifery, and Conjure

Laurie Wilkie has done the most thorough treatment of the material record of African American midwifery in the postemancipation South to date, in an analysis of the contents of a well associated with the home of Lucrecia Perryman of Mobile, Alabama. Perryman apparently took up midwifery after the death of her husband in 1885 and continued her practice into the first decade of the 1900s. The feature was filled in the early 1900s (probably just after 1909, when Perryman retired from her work), and it thus corresponds quite closely in date with the example from Square 252, providing a comparative sample against which the Lafitte well can be assessed. The Perryman well contained a variety of materials that Wilkie has associated with a midwife and nurse's roles, including pharmaceutical and extract bottles, many of them cathartics like castor and cod liver oil, presumably meant to help speed labor and delivery, and lubricants, particularly Vaseline, that would have been used both during delivery and after birth to coat the infant. Wilkie also related the presence of perfumes and skin creams in the assemblage to fussing, a period after the onset of contractions and before delivery when midwives would provide perfumes, oils, and lotions to the woman in labor as a source of comfort. Though this practice was discouraged in the twentieth century when birth was increasingly medicalized, it has gained renewed favor with contemporary midwives and many medical professionals, who see it as a useful way of relaxing the expectant mother. Without prior knowledge that the assemblage was related to the Perryman household, we would have more difficulty connecting other artifacts to a midwife's work: the presence of six blue mineral water bottles is linked by Wilkie to the practice of having a woman blow into a blue glass bottle to help release a retained placenta, and the presence of pocket knives in the deposit was suggested to be related to the folk tradition of placing sharp objects under the mattress or bed of the woman giving birth to "cut" the labor pains. The picture that emerges from the Perryman assemblage is that of a woman informed by both traditional knowledge and the latest medical science, who used the best resources available to her to provide care and comfort to the mother and child before, during, and after labor.[18]

The assemblage from the well at Square 252 was large but not atypical by urban standards. At first glance, the ceramic assemblage of forty-six vessels was not especially remarkable, with a mixture of white-bodied tablewares (in whiteware, ironstone, and porcelain) and utilitarian redwares and stonewares. Included in this latter group were at least seven bisque redware flower pots and three salt-glazed stoneware bottles with impressed marks indicating contents. Two of these had contained orange curacao from Amsterdam, while the other was marked Emser Kraenches Wasser, a German mineral water (figure 5.3). Dating of vessels varied widely, with some clearly dating after the 1890s, as indicated by tablewares with marks from the Lamberton Pottery Works of New Jersey and the Knowles, Taylor, and Knowles firm of East Liverpool, Ohio. Others showed considerable lag between manufacture and deposition; for instance, a marked ironstone plate from Powell and Bishop likely dated to between 1866 and 1878, and another from T. and R. Boote was manufactured between 1842 and 1871.[19]

The approximately three thousand fragments of glass from the well fill included many complete and near-complete glass containers, and there were many products with connections to the work of a midwife. For instance, multiple bottles of Fairchild Brothers and Foster Peptogenic Milk Powder, a late nineteenth-century commercial milk additive, were recovered. It was marketed to medical practitioners for the purpose of making cow's milk more like mother's milk, but it was also sold as an antidote for childhood diarrhea (which could easily be fatal in the period), among its other ostensibly beneficial effects.[20] The most numerous embossed bottles were ones that held soda, mineral, and tonic waters, most from local bottlers like Pablo and Company on Royal Street; the Crescent City Soda and Mineral Water Factory (also on Royal; the Pablo facility later became Crescent City); Keaveny, Buckley, and Company on South Liberty and later Bienville Streets; and the Consumers Soda and Mineral Water Manufacturing Company. The most unusual one of these was a seltzer bottle with a metal pump nozzle and an acid-etched label from George Schweitzer and Company's Hope Soda and Mineral Water Manufactory at 472 and 474 Burgundy Street. Most of these bottles date to the period from the 1880s through the beginning of the 1900s. Other embossed bottles had medicinal functions, including bottles of Reed's Bitters, Cantrell and Cochrane Belfast and Dublin Medicated Aerated Waters, Elixir de Guilie and Dupony, Old Sachem Bitters and Wigwam Tonic, and Hazel-

Figure 5.3. Stoneware bottle from well at Square 252, with detail showing mark on shoulder. (D. Ryan Gray)

tine and Company's Piso's Cure. Other marked bottles included specialty liquors such as chartreuse, vermouth, and multiple bottles of pernod. Multiple bottles of perfumes were also present, including Vinaigre Aromatique de Violet, but the assemblage was also distinguished by the almost complete lack of embossed proprietary bottles from local pharmacies (table 5.1).

There was a dizzying array of other materials in the well assemblage, much of it consisting of objects not typically preserved in the archaeological record. Particularly notable was a profusion of tools, like a mason's trowel and a hatchet, still with their wooden handles intact, a hand saw, a wrench, and numerous axe heads of various sizes and shapes; Hypolite's occasional work as a cooper seemed to have had at least some impact on the assemblage. Also present were items of door and window hardware, like strap hinges, escutcheons, latch hooks, bolts, and braces, and a significant quantity of the sort of miscellaneous items that dominate assemblages of small finds: buttons, pipe

Table 5.1. Bottles and Containers with Identifiable Markings/Brands from a Well at Square 252

Color/Ware	Shape	Function/Type
amber	cylindrical	culinary bottle
aquamarine	cylindrical	soda / mineral water bottle
Aquamarine / green	rectangular with flat chamfered corners	medicine bottle
aquamarine	cylindrical	soda / mineral water bottle
olive	tapered	wine / champagne bottle
olive	champagne shoulder	pernod / absinthe bottle
olive	ovoid seal	liquor bottle
colorless	tapered	mustard jar
colorless	cylindrical	perfume bottle
colorless	short cylinder	ink bottle
colorless	cylindrical	siphon (seltzer) bottle
amber	cylindrical	bitters bottle
aquamarine	cylindrical	condiment bottle
aquamarine	cylindrical	soda / mineral water bottle
aquamarine	cylindrical	soda / mineral water bottle
olive	cylindrical	bitters bottle
amber	cylindrical body, rounded shoulder	beer / ale / soda bottle

Table 5.1. *continued*

Embossing	MNI
embossed "MILK POWDER / PEPTOGENIC" on shoulder; "FAIRCHILD BROTHERS & FOSTER / NEW YORK" on base	Min. 2; possibly 3
embossed "CONSUMERS / S. & M. W. MFG CO. LTD. / N.O., L.A. / THIS BOTTLE NOT TO BE SOLD" and "C" on base	Min. 2
embossed "[H]AZELTINE [& CO.]" (presumably this is a Piso's Cure bottle)	
embossed "KEAVENY & BUCKLEY / CITY / BOTTLING HOUSE / Nᵒˢ 67 TO 71 / S. LIBERTY ST. / NEW ORLEANS, LA" on body, star on base	Min. 3
embossed "BREMEN. H. HEYE."	
embossed "E. PERNOD / COUVET" around cross motif on ring-shaped seal	Min. 2
"VERMOUTH SOPRAFINO [arched] / MARTINI SOLAEC / TORINO [rocker]" embossed on seal	Min. 2
embossed "JAMES GINART / CREOLE / MUSTARD / N. O."	
embossed "MANN'S / PERFUMES" with M monogram	
embossed "EMPIRE"; large ribs with constricted center	
acid etched "HOPE S. & M. W. MANUFACTORY / GEO. SCHWEITZER & Co. / 472 & 474 BURGUNDY ST. N. O. LA." and mark of upside-down anchor; acid etched on base: "MATTHEWS N. Y." with image of a man and a bear making glass	
embossed "REED'S / BITTERS / REED'S BITTERS"	
embossed "WORCESTERSHIRE SAUCE / LEA & PERRINS / J 4D / S"	
embossed "J. B. JUNQUA / NEW ORLEANS"	
embossed "C. C. S. & M. FACTORY / 270 AND 272 ROYAL ST / NEW ORLEANS / GINGER ALE / & / TONIC BEER / THIS BOTTLE IS NEVER TO BE SOLD McC"	
embossed "SAXLEHNERS / HUNYADI JANOS / BITTERQUELLE" on base	
embossed "BECK PHILLIPS & CO. PITTS, PA" around base	

Continued on the next page

Table 5.1. *continued*

Color/Ware	Shape	Function/Type
olive	cylindrical	wine / champagne bottle
olive	tapered cylinder	medicinal
colorless	square base, straight body, cylindrical neck	very small medicine bottle
aquamarine-blue	tapered up body, sloped shoulders, circular base	mineral water bottle
aquamarine	cylindrical body	soda / mineral water bottle
amber	barrel	bitters / tonic bottle
aquamarine	barrel	condiment / preserve jar
colorless	square with flat chamfered corners	extract / toiletries bottle
colorless	unidentified	unidentified
colorless	round with flat sides	small bottle
aquamarine	cylindrical body, tapered neck, rounded shoulder	club sauce bottle
olive	bulged neck, rounded shoulder	wine / liquor bottle
olive	cylindrical	possible liquor / ale bottle
stoneware bottle	cylindrical	mineral water
stoneware bottle	cylindrical	alcohol

Note: MNI is the minimum number of individuals.
Source: Raw data courtesy of Earth Search, Inc.

Table 5.1. *continued*

Embossing	MNI
embossed "FRIEDRICHSHALL-COPPEL & CO" around circumference of base	
large mamelon, embossed shoulder seal "ELIXIR / DE / GUILIE / & / DUPONY" blob seal	
flat chamfered corners, embossed ". . . ICKE / . . . TAFEL" body	
embossed body "PABLO & Co / 270 & 272 / ROYAL STREET / N. O. / MINERAL WATER [arched] / FACTORY"	Min. 2
embossed body "CANTRELL & COCHRANE / BELFAST & / DUBLIN / MEDICATED / AERATED / WATERS"	
embossed "OLD SACHEM [arched] / BITTERS / AND / WIGWAM TONIC [rocker]" on center of body	
3 rings around shoulder, 3 rings on lower body, embossed circum base "G. C. G. / N. Y."	
embossed "VINAIGRE AROMATIQUE/...DE VIOLET" on body	
embossed ". . . Z / . . . AUD . . ." vertical mold seam	
embossed body "...MAGI... / NEW ORLEANS"	
embossed "ENGLISH CLUB-SAUCE" on shoulder, "GILCHREST BROS." on body	
embossed ". . . CHARTREUSE" around shoulder with symbol inside border	
embossed "CLARK & WHITE / C / NEW YORK / [symbol]"	
impressed "ESMER KRAENCHES WASSER"	
impressed "CORACAO / DUBB ORANGE AMSTERDAM"	Min. 2

bowl and stem fragments, marbles, fragments of porcelain dolls, buckles, items of cutlery, shoe leather, thimbles, and so on. In the following discussion, I focus specifically on those unique or distinctive items likely related to the work of Julia Metoyer as a midwife. As will be discussed further, some of the items recovered archaeologically are notable for their uses not just in midwifery but also in practices related to folk magic and African American conjure and rootwork. Almost all these items have common, everyday uses as well, so some of the interpretations are speculative, but they are grounded in both ethnohistoric research and in previous archaeological work.

The historical evidence, while sparse, suggests that Julia Metoyer was concerned with professional recognition and training for her career as a midwife. Louisiana had begun cracking down on unsanctioned medical practices by the end of the nineteenth century. The 1894 Louisiana Medical Practice Act had required that practitioners be licensed by a state board, and the City of New Orleans followed with a number of ordinances directly aimed at those who used magico-religious practices, like hoodoo, Voodoo, and conjure. Midwives initially operated somewhat beneath the radar in this regard, but attention turned in subsequent years to controlling the work of "Irregulars," like homeopaths and root doctors. By the 1920s, the American Medical Association itself began to campaign against home births attended by midwives as unsanitary and unsafe, and the category of Irregulars was extended to include midwives. In the South, many African American women were instead encouraged to enter nursing schools, even as the work of traditional healers and unsanctioned medical workers was criminalized.[21] Metoyer would have been aware of this trend, and, according to a short blurb in the *Daily Picayune* of May 30, 1920, she was one of twelve women (and one of only five Black women) who received a certificate as a midwife from the Louisiana State Board of Medical Examiners. Such official sanction was still rare in this period.[22]

From the presence of the cranial perforator in the assemblage, we may infer that at least one of the services that Metoyer offered involved the extraction of the fetus. The particular type of perforator recovered (figure 5.4), with a long scissors-type handle and a head that comes to an arrow-like shape, with sharpened edges on the outside, is similar to the variety known as a Smellie perforator, introduced by an eighteenth-century British obstetrician named William Smellie. Various improvements or alterations in design were offered during the nineteenth century, even as the basic function remained unchanged. While such tools could have been used in performing abortions, both doctors and midwives of the era would more commonly have used drugs and rubber catheters to induce miscarriages. Perforators were mainly used in case of emergencies, where the life of the mother was threatened by a difficult labor or stillbirth. As historian Leslie Reagan has emphasized, despite

Figure 5.4. Cranial perforator from well at Square 252. (Courtesy of Earth Search, Inc.)

the increasing criminalization of abortion after the late nineteenth century, the practice of ending unwanted pregnancies through a variety of means and for a variety of reasons remained among women from all social classes, with midwives rather than physicians more often serving working-class and immigrant women. Reagan's study focused on urban centers in the North, but given the limited range of choices in health care for Black women in the Jim Crow South, African-American midwives likely served a much greater spectrum of the population in these cases. Certainly, it would be reasonable for a midwife in this era to provide such a service, and the presence of glass pipettes in the assemblage, while not having as visceral a connection to fetal extractions as the perforator, may be just as likely to reflect this aspect of her practice.[23]

More frequent in the assemblage were artifacts that have been argued to have specialized functions when recovered in contexts associated with midwifery. For instance, the wide variety of perfume bottles in the assemblage presumably reflects the practice of fussing noted by Wilkie and others, and the aromatic liqueurs like curacao may have also functioned in this regard. Liqueurs in particular served as the base for the preparation of herbal mixtures, which would have been an important part of the midwife's toolkit in this era. It is tempting to see the unusual number of flowerpots found in the assemblage as related to this practice as well. In an urban environment in which useful plants and herbs were not easily gathered in the wild, such home-provisioning could have made Metoyer's practice more self-sufficient. The numerous soda and mineral waters recovered also were likely associated with the care offered by Metoyer. While soda bottles themselves are too ubiquitous in urban assemblages to readily connect to a specialized magical function or traditional practice (as in the case of the soda bottles from the Perryman well), they would have provided a source of clean, effervescent water that would be refreshing and probably considerably more sanitary than other available sources in the birthing process, including the water from the very well where this material was found.

African American midwives provided much more than just care during the process of labor and birth. They also helped take care of women in the time leading up to labor, and they instructed them in the care of infants and children afterward. The wide range of children's toys in the assemblage, particularly marbles and dolls, may reflect this, though they could also indicate the hand of the Metoyer children in the assemblage. Interestingly, the toys are apparently a divergence from the Perryman assemblage. Julia Metoyer, as a younger woman at the time she began her practice, may have maintained a more active role in the lives of the infants she helped deliver. Some of the health-related items (like the peptogenic milk powder mentioned) would have been typically used with babies, further indicating her importance in the aftercare of pregnancies. The Metoyer assemblage also contained tins from exotic foodstuffs, including sardines and French mushrooms. Wilkie has suggested that such items, along with sauces, mustards, and other condiments, may be related to the cravings of expectant mothers during pregnancy. In the relatively small animal bone assemblage at the Perryman household (in which only eighty-five fragments were identifiable), Wilkie noted a disproportionate number that derive from a cow's head or lower limbs, which she connects to the preparation of specialized nutrient-rich foods, like calf's-foot jelly.[24] No similar pattern was noted in the well at Square 252, which contained bone from a variety of cuts of meat from cows, pigs, and caprids, along with chicken, duck, turtle, catfish, and drum.

Other artifacts recovered from the well point more directly to practices that at the very least span the realm between medically informed midwifery and magical practice, and a midwife of this era, Black or white, would likely have drawn on both, if they were even considered distinct. Certainly both would have had meaning to the clientele being seen by the practitioner, and part of the role of the midwife would have been to provide comfort in any form to a woman experiencing childbirth. A characteristic of the assemblage in this regard was the presence of a remarkable number of knives in various forms: common kitchen knives with bone handles, larger butcher knives, and pocketknives, not to mention axe heads and other cutting instruments (figure 5.5). The placement of knives and axes beneath the bed during childbirth is a rather classic form of sympathetic or imitative magic (in which like produces like) meant to cut the pain of labor. This practice seems not to have a particular source in African American culture but rather to be a widespread folk magical tradition. In this case, the high number of such items recovered,

Figure 5.5. Selection of knives from well at Square 252. (D. Ryan Gray)

many of them in good condition, suggests that in the process of usage they lost their magical potency.[25]

In postemancipation African America, the magical practices potentially seen in some of the other material evidence here have been referred to as conjure, hoodoo, and rootwork, as distinct from Voodoo, which is more often used to refer to a New Orleans variant of the Afro-Caribbean Vodun or Voudou religion. Conjure and Voodoo have both taken on considerable importance in debates over the survival of African beliefs, worldviews, and material traditions in African American culture, and they have also picked up considerable baggage in this regard. Pioneering sociologist and scholar W. E. B. Du Bois believed that the distinctive character of the postemancipation African American experience had at least one source in Africa and its cultural traditions, imparted and passed on even through the violence and oppression of slavery. Despite Du Bois's eloquent and insightful statements about the nature of race in classic works like his 1903 *The Souls of Black Folk*, controversies would continue about the degree of and mechanisms for the survival of African cultures in the New World throughout the first half of the twentieth century. Within anthropology and sociology, the dispute over what this controversy meant for African American culture is sometimes referred to as the Herskovits-Frazier debate. In works like *The Myth of the Negro Past*, Melville Herskovits, a student of Franz Boas, argued for the existence of persistent Africanisms throughout those parts of the Americas affected by the slave trade.

These Africanisms were cultural practices that displayed a direct continuity with ones observable in West and Central Africa, and, for Herskovits, this continuity served as proof of the vitality and importance of African culture in America. In contrast, E. Franklin Frazier, an African American sociologist, argued that African culture had been lost entirely within the US context, precisely through the impact of slavery and the Middle Passage. For Frazier, this loss had a positive valence, in that it meant that there were no impediments to the assimilation of Black Americans into the culture of the dominant society, except for the artificial ones imposed by Jim Crow policies.[26]

Both Herskovits and Frazier saw their respective positions as having anti-racist political and social aspects, and both made valuable contributions to the study of African American life. On the one hand, as Frazier observed, Black Americans certainly were equal in all inherent capacities to their white counterparts, and, if given the opportunity, they would have been able to assimilate if they chose to do so. However, on the other hand, the preponderance of cultural linkages between Black people in the New World and the peoples of sub-Saharan Africa made some sort of continuity increasingly undeniable in the post–World War II years. In 1973, in *The Birth of African-American Culture*, anthropologists Sidney Mintz and Richard Price attempted to synthesize these two viewpoints. They argued that, while the conditions of the Middle Passage, in which the enslaved were stripped of belongings and combined into groups without regard for language or background, may have made the survival of particular elements of individual African cultures impossible, a certain substrate of a shared African worldview may have survived in the New World.[27]

While the attempt at a synthesis of these positions was well intended, it did little to satisfy central questions of how and why certain elements of African cultures were maintained over many generations, and others disappeared or were transformed so completely in content as to represent innovations rather than continuities. As a result, rather than being satisfied with historical accounts produced within the dominant culture, recent scholars have emphasized a more nuanced approach to regional variations in the demographics of African America. Detailed analyses of the slave trade and demographic shifts within it have allowed scholars to attempt to trace particular unique manifestations of African American culture to specific points of origin in Africa, and this, by extension, has allowed new insights into the diverse ways that groups maintained their culture in the face of tremendous, often violent, challenges. Other recent trends within anthropological thought have turned to concepts like creolization, hybridity, syncretization, ethnogenesis, and *métissage* as potential explanatory concepts to deal with the new cultural forms produced as a result of the global transformations of the colonial enterprise. Archaeologists have also been a part of these debates, and archaeological and material evidence has been used to bolster arguments for retentions and continuities of West and Central African culture in African American society. Recent research has attempted to move beyond the implicit notion of bounded, static, monolithic cultural units embedded in earlier assumptions about cultural transmission, instead emphasizing what Christopher Fennell has described as "the dynamics of multilinear cultural developments." Fennell in particular has focused on how "core symbols" are transferred, with their uses spanning a continuum from the *emblematic*, those symbols that represent the identity of a group in a public form, to the *instrumental*, the uses of that core symbol in an often-simplified form for specific ends.[28]

An artifact recovered from the well that has some importance in this regard is a brass skirt lifter or dress holder, a mundane enough object in itself (figure 5.6). Such items were hung from the waist of ladies' garments and used to cinch up folds or trains of long dresses, often as part of a chatelaine. They are thought to have become more popular in the latter part of the nineteenth century, as more women adopted outdoor recreations. This one is notable, in that its central element consists of a clenched hand, and it is thus visually similar to a class of items that Fennell has described as "multivalent figures of an enclosing hand." Archaeological examples of items depicting hands and/or fists like this have been found predominantly in African American contexts in the United States, and their potential meanings have been the source of considerable speculation, particularly as to their relationship to religious, magical, or other culturally significant meanings. Clearly, at their simplest, they are decorative, but the popularity of any particular decoration may derive from its deeper significance, whether conscious or unconscious. Since most of the closures and/or ornaments featuring the closed hand motif are products of Western mass-produced consumer culture, and thus potentially are indicative of a Christian worldview, Fennell has traced the possible emblematic symbolism of them to Europe, particularly to representations of the wounds of Christ or Christ's passion. While noting that jewelry designs featuring such closed hands are common in the nineteenth century, Fennell emphasizes instrumental uses of them specific to African American culture, where they also potentially become "expressions of self-determination through individualized ritual invocations."[29]

James Davidson has recently made a detailed accounting of the occurrence of a particular form of these items commonly referenced as "hand charms," small hands or fists in rings that would have formed garment closures when linked. He cites twelve examples recovered archaeologically, all of which, while presumably associated with African American occupations, were recovered from generalized midden contexts. These items have variously been connected

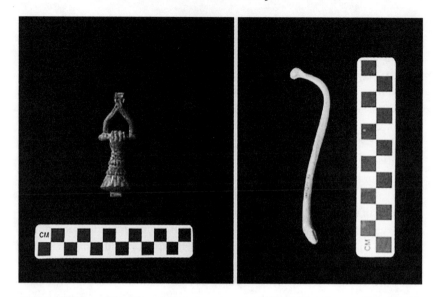

Figure 5.6. Brass skirt lifter (*left*) and raccoon baculum (*right*) from well at Square 252. (D. Ryan Gray)

to Catholic charms known as *figas* or *higas*, to the Islamic Hand of Fatima, or to the use of the term *hand* in African American conjure and traditional magic as a charm. Davidson makes a convincing argument that there is no historical evidence to support the increasingly elaborate interpretations that have been made of these items, in which the fist form is used as a link to the entirety of the uses to which conjure was applied, particularly those involving protections and the exertion of magical potency. At the same time, he acknowledges that mundane objects were often transformed into supernatural paraphernalia in African American conjure, and given the appropriate context, items like these closures certainly could have added significance.[30] Davidson finds that sort of context lacking in the extant examples, but the presence of this item in the Metoyer assemblage adds an element to this discussion. A brass skirt lifter in this form is a relatively rare artifact in the archaeological record, but it is known as a decorative and functional element of late nineteenth-century dress. Its occurrence here evokes both social power and magical potency. While the item may not have been a "hand," in the sense of a charm intended for a specific purpose, it marked Julia Metoyer at multiple levels: it was an unusual and presumably high-status item of dress, even as it potentially identified her as a person with specialized spiritual knowledge, a wielder of hands. Such an allusion to magical power may have served to assure those who used Metoyer's services, even as she herself drew on the most up-to-date training available to her in the medical field. Other items recovered in the assemblage, like silver coins, buttons, and blue beads, have also been connected to conjure and African American cultural traditions, but the link is rather more tenuous in this context.

There are also indications that Julia Metoyer's activities ranged more widely than just services related to childbirth and care, at least in the world of conjure. One of the items recovered with the most overt and direct connection to magical activities and charm use was a raccoon baculum, or penis bone. Baculums are distinctive in appearance, and the one recovered from the Metoyer well was highly polished (see figure 5.6). It was also clearly not part of the conventional faunal assemblage, as no other raccoon bones were recovered from the feature. The raccoon baculum has a considerable reputation that continues to this day for its efficacy as a charm. It is often connected to luck in gambling, but, of perhaps greater importance in this instance, it is used in conjure to cure impotence, particularly when placed under a mattress, whether with or without the knowledge of the man to be affected. Its connection to charms involving love and sexuality extends beyond African America; in the Ozarks, a tradition involves gifts of the raccoon penis bone as a token of love. There have also been suggestions that the special qualities of the raccoon penis bone have origins in Native American traditions in the Midwest, perhaps another example of the resonances between indigenous traditions and the city's communities of color.[31]

Other items in the assemblage speak to conjure work potentially involving love and sex or at least suggest that Metoyer positioned herself as having specialized knowledge connected to these things, a natural enough function for a midwife. Another unusual item in the assemblage was a small badge-like brass object with an eyelet for suspension, which depicted a cherubic couple in an intimate embrace, perhaps representing Cupid and Psyche. The story of Cupid and Psyche in Greek mythology is a tale of love delayed by obstacles that were eventually overcome. While not explicit, the imagery of such an item would have displayed a concern with sexual relationships, even if not having a magical function in itself. In whatever case, Metoyer worked in a Christian, and probably Catholic, vernacular. A number of items in the assemblage had religious origins, including a fragment of a rosary and votive figurines depicting Catholic saints. That many of the practitioners of conjure and rootwork were devoutly Christian, and that they saw their intermediation with the spiritual world as perfectly in keeping with this worldview, is sometimes overlooked in discussions of African influences on magical and religious practice in African America. It is likely that items with Christian symbolism functioned in Metoyer's midwifery just as did ones derived from secular magical traditions.

Gender, Color, and Disorder

While the assemblage associated with the Metoyer family predated the era of slum clearance by some two and a half decades, it provides a window into the everyday lives of the people who would be affected by this effort. It also encourages us to think about what the Lafitte Project was meant to eradicate and to produce. Kodi Roberts has suggested that the development of the magical practices associated with Voodoo in early twentieth-century New Orleans was ultimately about claims on power—social, economic, and personal—in a society that portrayed the dichotomies of race, gender, and class as inviolable. The suite of practices likely incorporated by Metoyer allowed practitioners like her to cross these lines and blur them; for those racialized as Black in the hierarchy of Jim Crow segregation, this crossing of lines became a way of wielding a power that was otherwise inaccessible to them.[32] In the case of Black women, for whom roles in the Victorian-inflected cult of domesticity were further circumscribed by patriarchal social structures and expectations, a specialized occupation that incorporated conjure and spiritual knowledge was a rare but efficacious way to give permanence and stability to that power. Roberts cites the account of Lala Hopkins, a New Orleans Voodoo practitioner interviewed by the Louisiana Writers' Project around 1940, who is described as almost completely dominant over her husband. Roberts sees in the description of their interactions a "gender-based sales pitch" for the power of the worker. By demonstrating her ability to transgress traditional gendered roles, she communicated her wider-reaching powers to exert change on the outside world.[33]

Julia Metoyer's story, like that of Lala Hopkins, is one in a much larger genre: that of women in New Orleans who used spiritual and economic power to defy traditional gendered roles and conventions. Harry Hyatt's multivolume *Hoodoo, Conjuration, Witchcraft, Rootwork* (1970) contains interviews with any number of female and gender-nonconforming practitioners who were contemporaries of Metoyer. Examples include Nahnee, "Boss of Algiers," or the enigmatic informant that Hyatt refers to as Boy-Girl, a transgender or intersex person whom he describes as a "hermaphrodite." One might also see threads of this narrative as much in the Ursuline nuns of the French colonial era as in the Voodoo priestess Marie Laveau, as much in the "bullet-proof" Baroness Pontalba as in Leafy Anderson and Catherine Seal, Mothers of the Spiritual Church movement of the twentieth century. Accounts of powerful women occur in other forms as well. The city's history is filled with women as heads of household and property owners, frequently engaged in the city's business, as well as the special case of the prominent women whose names are associated with Storyville (see chapter 6).[34] Julia Metoyer would have been aware of the structural limitations that she faced as a woman of color, and the material record suggests that, at the very least, she used her position as a midwife and spiritual practitioner to stabilize her family in what were turbulent years.

There is something of a contradiction in the account of Julia Metoyer. Given her prominence in being recognized by the State Board of Health as one of the city's few professional midwives, can one really assume that the often-indirect evidence of conjure-related practices is indicative of her activities? This contradiction may be something of an illusion, implying an either/or choice that was never really so clear cut. If doing something as innocuous as placing a knife under a mattress gave comfort to a woman during childbirth because she expected it to do so, then the question of whether it had any direct physiological effect would have been of little practical consequence. But, seeing that Metoyer drew on a rich body of traditional knowledge in addition to practical medical training, what was the source of her knowledge as a midwife in the first place? Wilkie has emphasized the role of the midwife as a "generational mediator," the source of continuity in both medical and magical knowledge through the apprenticeship with older women.[35] It is at least a possibility that there was a second practitioner in the household, and that this second practitioner was the source of Metoyer's training. Julia Prevost, her mother-in-law and a sometime-member of the Metoyer household, would have been one possible source from whom the younger Julia could have learned such a specialized set of skills. Prevost may have provided the vector for an older body of knowledge derived from conjure and magic to enter the household, even as Metoyer was introduced to a field that was in the process of professionalization and secularization.

A little further investigation into Metoyer's past reveals some other possible sources of this knowledge, even as it raises other questions about her identity. In a place like New Orleans, following individuals through the census can be a tricky process, as there is considerable variation in the transcriptions of names depending on the recorder's familiarity with the linguistic roots involved. Julia Metoyer might also have learned her skills as a midwife from her own mother or a woman in her childhood household rather than from Julia Prevost, so I attempted to track her family back into the nineteenth century. She herself was recorded in the 1880 census as a six-year-old, under her middle name, Sophia, with her mother and father, Louise and Etienne, an older brother named Jerome, and a sister of the same age as her named Marie, perhaps a twin. The family's last name was recorded as Comage, the Cummings spelling apparently an Anglicization of a French surname. Etienne's father was described as French, and Etienne himself was blind. They lived on Basin Street, and everyone in the household was identified as Mulatto. Only Louise was working at the time, as a washer and ironer. Tracing back Etienne and Louise a bit further in time, to the 1870 census, I discovered that both of them, along with infant Jerome, were identified as white, and Etienne, employed as a knife grinder, claimed to have been born in France himself. Perhaps most tantalizingly of all, their next-door neighbor was a woman named Johanna Hassmann, a sixty-five-year-old midwife who was born in Württemburg.

While the presence of cross-race passing from Black or Mulatto to white is something that shows up in both first-person narratives and documents, this case seems to be much more unusual. Apparently in this case, Etienne's Francophone background (and, perhaps, Louise's already mixed-race ancestry) was enough to convince those surrounding the family that they were white. As long as Etienne could present himself as the household's paternal provider, he could conceal the mixed-race composition of the family. But sometime between 1870 and 1880, something happened to cause Etienne to lose his sight. With his wife as the chief earner for the household in 1880, the household took on her racial identity, even her formerly "white" husband. While this situation tells us something about the malleability of racial designations in this era, it also hints at the multiple levels at which gender ideologies could be contested in the everyday. Julia Metoyer, in her youth, would have seen her mother become the de facto head of household after her father's blindness, a strong woman taking on new social roles. Perhaps the family's German midwife neighbor, herself a single woman living alone, taught Julia's mother the specialized skills of midwifery as a way of supplementing her income. This scenario would certainly help to explain the many products from central European sources in the Metoyer assemblage, and it would provide another vector for the entry of folk medical and magical practices into Metoyer's practices: knowledge passed from Johanna Hassmann, to her mother, to her.

The case of Julia Metoyer alone does not explain why the neighborhood in which she occasionally resided was targeted for redevelopment. Considered at a neighborhood-wide scale, the Lafitte area contradicted the imagined racialized templates of urban housing. There were families of color, racialized as Mulatto—a category that ceased to exist in the eyes of the state—and Black, who had deep histories within the neighborhood, both of home ownership and of business. These histories in some cases connected such families to the city's Francophone colonial origins and even allowed some of them to circumvent the color line in their racial ambiguity. This pattern alone was enough to identify the Lafitte area as a potential slum in the eyes of those selecting sites for demolition and redevelopment. However, the story of Julia Metoyer reminds us that the process of normalization represented by the housing projects is also taking place at the level of the individual household, and that it crosscuts race, gender, and class, seeking to bring all these categories into boundaries defined within the dominant ideology. The ways that a woman like Metoyer subverted these categories could easily be obscured if we adhered too closely to the public transcripts produced by the apparatus of the state. After all, her status as head of household at 2024 Orleans could easily be written off as an anomaly: the mistake of a careless recorder of the census. It is here where archaeology serves as a tool to explore the everyday lives of individuals whose actions exposed the arbitrariness of taken-for-granted elements of identity. Metoyer might be an extreme case of this, but she was not actually an exception in this regard. The moments crystallized in documents like the census are an attempt to freeze in time and place an identity that is shifting and negotiated, constructed and reconstructed. That identity constantly presses against and overflows those boundaries that seek to constrain it within a social structure that claims the power to define the normal. Public housing sought to reinscribe those boundaries in the built environment, not just for women like Julia Metoyer who transgressed them at many levels, but for all residents of the neighborhood.

6
Iberville

Desexualizing Space at Storyville

This book began with the story of the redevelopment of the Iberville Housing Project. Well-constructed, little-damaged by Hurricane Katrina, with a substantial resident community that had returned after the storm, Iberville was the last of the city's large-scale housing projects to fall. The history of Iberville, both how it came to be and how it fell, is interwoven with that of Storyville, one of the city's most famous neighborhoods. The Storyville moniker was applied (mostly after the fact) to the space in which the city formalized through ordinance a substantial and highly visible red-light district. The district was only officially sanctioned for just under two decades, from 1898 to 1917, but it is now recognized as the fabled crucible of New Orleans jazz, where performers like Jelly Roll Morton played piano for visitors to luxurious brothels, and where musicians met in late-night jam sessions, helping Black music, developed in the streets of the city, cross the color line to white audiences. Madams such as Josie Arlington and Lulu White are part of the Storyville legend too, and E. J. Bellocq's photographs of the district's women have become one of the most-recognizable visual records of late Victorian sex work. The Storyville name is almost synonymous with the status of New Orleans as the City that Care Forgot, adorning tee-shirt shops, bars, hotels, and other businesses, both in the city and far from it. There is a Storyville Coffee in Seattle, which promotes its mission of ending human trafficking around the world, and across a continent and an ocean, a Storyville Records in Copenhagen, Denmark, devoted to preserving and promoting jazz.[1]

Considering how celebrated the Storyville name has come to be, it comes as a shock to visitors to realize that almost all physical traces of the neighborhood that it occupied have been obliterated. Only three buildings that were once part of Storyville remain standing. Two of them now function as neighborhood corner stores, and at least one has been altered to the point that much of its historical character has been lost (figure 6.1). Occasionally, these architectural

Figure 6.1. Former location of Frank Early's saloon, one of the three remaining buildings from Storyville, during a 1999 event highlighting the archaeology and history of the area. (Courtesy of Earth Search, Inc.)

relics of Storyville are highlighted in local papers, but there has been little attempt at any organized effort to preserve them. All the once-elegant brothels that fronted Basin Street are gone, and the last two cribs—small frame dwellings divided into sparse one- or two-room apartments, which formed the majority of the building stock in Storyville—were demolished in 1999.[2] Until recently, the footprint of the Iberville Housing Project had been almost exactly coterminous with the former location of the district (figure 6.2), and now much of it too has been demolished, making way for a mixed-income redevelopment spearheaded by Historic Restoration, Inc., the local real estate developer also responsible for the St. Thomas/River Gardens Project discussed in chapter 3. Sometimes tour busses pass by, with operators pointing out the location. One tour guide, overheard repeatedly during our archaeological fieldwork at the site in 2012–13, cemented his claim to New Orleans authenticity by stopping to note that, in a back room at a nameless brothel on that very site, one of Storyville's prostitutes gave birth to his grandmother.

Storyville has attracted increasing academic interest in recent years, though surprisingly little scholarly work has been published on it. Up until recently, much of the work that was available came from the field of jazz studies, and the role of Storyville (both the recognized district and its segregated Black-

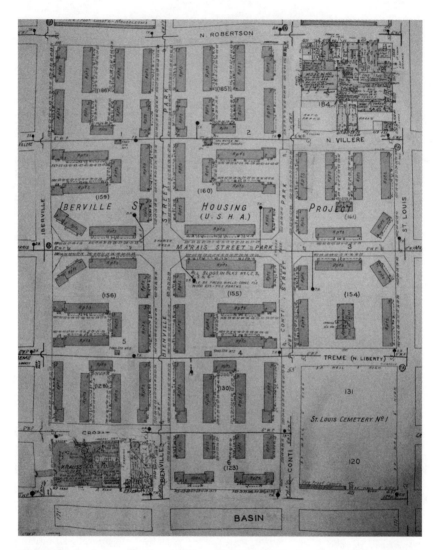

Figure 6.2. Sanborn map showing Iberville Housing Project, 1941 (Vol. 2, Sheet 102). The blocks at the upper right and lower left had been included in the district's boundaries, but the buildings dating from the Storyville period had largely been replaced by later commercial development. The frontage of Iberville (not illustrated) had been included in the original Storyville boundaries as well. (Courtesy of Southeastern Architectural Archive, Tulane University. Reprinted/used with permission from the Sanborn Library, LLC)

only counterpart) in the development of the musical form has been vigor-
ously debated. Was Central and West African music, perhaps filtered through
the Caribbean, the foundation of New Orleans jazz? To what extent did European popular music and folk music influence this distinctly American art
form? How did it use preexisting traditions of marching band and street
music, and how crucial was the space of Storyville itself in bringing seemingly disparate influences together? For much of the research that focuses on
Storyville's musical history, the women and men who made their living from
commercial sex are secondary to this narrative, forming an exotic backdrop
to tales of flamboyant personalities and iconic cultural producers. Some, like
cornetist Buddy Bolden—the man occasionally credited as the originator of
jazz—exist mainly as legend: Bolden died in a mental institution in Mississippi before burial in an unmarked pauper's grave at the city's Holt Cemetery,
with none of his music surviving in recorded form. Others lived to tell their
stories. The reminiscences of pianist Jelly Roll Morton, recorded at length by
Alan Lomax, still form an important source on New Orleans in the period,
even if Morton is not always the most reliable of storytellers. Herbert Asbury, in his popular account of the New Orleans underworld published not
quite twenty years after Storyville was officially shuttered, closes with a nos-
talgic account of the district, though he gives credit for the invention of jazz
to the Spasm Band, a group of white teenagers who played on the streets of
the city. Al Rose, author of the most widely read work on Storyville, did not
trace the origins of jazz to the district, but he does discuss at length its importance as a seminal place in which the music flourished and reached new
audiences, cementing its association with vice. During the 1960s, he also interviewed some women and men who had worked in Storyville, presenting a
selection of their stories (perhaps with considerable creative license; none of
the recordings of the interviews survive) as indicative of different categories
of employment in the district: a madam, a pimp, a crib woman, a working
girl, a trick baby, and a working stiff. Rose's work on Storyville may be loose
in some details and unreliable in others, but it is a valuable resource in understanding the district's structure.[3]

At least a handful of works in recent years address aspects of Storyville that
interrogate the many accounts filtered through a romanticizing male gaze and
that attempt instead to address core issues of gender, race, segregation, and
sexuality at the heart of the district. After all, as historian Alecia P. Long has
observed, the same logics behind the ordinance that created Storyville—that
sexual disorder and immorality could be cordoned off and confined, thereby
protecting "respectable" society—would soon enough be applied to race. In
fact, in Storyville, they already were.[4] I refer to these works, most notably those

by Long and Emily Landau, in my discussion of the archaeology of Storyville. Even though Storyville had been shuttered for two decades when the site for Iberville was selected, it is impossible to ignore how the boundaries of Iberville were so closely matched to those of the district. The material legacy of the district was something that had to be erased; the question considered here is why.

My subject then is the longer history of the area, as seen through an archaeological perspective, including how the neighborhood that became Storyville developed during the nineteenth century and how it was transformed through being selected as the location of the district. This story, integral to why the Iberville area was designated as a slum, requires a consideration of the changing dynamics of race, class, sex, and the color line, and of the ways that the disorderly boundaries of normality were policed in the past and present. Even though Storyville was no longer recognized and sanctioned by the time that Iberville was planned, the contradictions that it had exposed were still very present in the city's imagination. The construction of Iberville marked an attempt to clean up a messy failure of segregation and to permanently erase those contradictions from the landscape.

From City Commons to Storyville

During the first half of the eighteenth century, as the developed areas that would become the heart of New Orleans took shape along the high ground of the riverfront, the land farther back from the river, off the toe of the natural levee, was mostly soon-to-be depleted cypress forest. The land immediately outside the boundaries of the old city on its lakeside (to the north of today's North Rampart Street) had been reserved as the town's military commons, but the unclaimed land just beyond it, used for public grazing and as a source for firewood, was recognized as a city commons. Many years later, in 1852, during a lawsuit over ownership of what had once been undesirable swampland, witnesses attested to the custom of general access to this land, with the city's residents utilizing it "according to their own use, and doing other acts as suited their convenience or necessities."[5] By the latter part of the eighteenth century, some of the land at the edge of the military commons was also used for a chapel and for the town's first Charity Hospital, joined by St. Louis Cemetery No. 1 in 1789, and by St. Louis No. 2 in 1820.

As in the area that became the Lafitte Project, the opening of the Carondelet Canal in 1794 improved drainage and made the city commons more commercially desirable. In 1807, after the Louisiana Purchase, congressional action was required to clarify the extent of the lands held by the city. These were found, with a few exceptions, to extend approximately six hundred yards from the old city walls, corresponding to the area between modern North Rampart Street and Claiborne Avenue. The city had the commons surveyed for subdivision by Jacques Tanesse, with lots sold soon thereafter. Like the adjacent Tremé, the land was developed rapidly after that date, and, as at Lafitte, its proximity to the Carondelet Canal made it an appealing location for people who worked in the skilled building trades, especially those who relied on shipments of wood from the canal: carpenters, cabinetmakers, cistern makers, ship builders, and so on, many of them free people of color. The neighborhood's character was also doubtlessly influenced by the proximity of Congo Square. This land, which became vacant after Fort St. Ferdinand (one of the city's Spanish-era fortifications) was abandoned and demolished in 1804, was initially referred to as Circus Place. It became a site for public gatherings of the enslaved for dances and presumably for worship on Sundays, and the formal designation of Congo Square was eventually noted in the records of the First Municipal Council. These gatherings were a source of both fascination and consternation for residents and visitors to the city, and Congo Square has been cited as a focal point for the emergence of African American culture in New Orleans. In the 1890s, the city would rename this location Beauregard Square after the Confederate Civil War general, an overtly white supremacist move to erase the city's African history from its landscape.[6]

By the period after the Civil War and emancipation, the former city commons was a densely developed urban neighborhood, one of the city's Creole faubourgs with a multiracial population, given a further unique character by boats accessing the Carondelet Canal. Many histories of Storyville trace the district's development to this period. A number of informal tenderloins had developed in the city in the course of the nineteenth century, including one along Gallatin Street near the city's riverfront and another picturesquely referred to as the Swamp at the back edges of what is now the Central Business District. City officials were only rarely concerned with such locales in which vice was concentrated but instead focused on its increasingly visible and pervasive interpenetration elsewhere in the city. In the June 11, 1892, issue of the *Mascot*, a local paper devoted to chronicling vice in the city, an editorial (figure 6.3) opined about the rampant "social evil" in the city, made worse by the fact that disreputable houses could appear overnight in otherwise respectable neighborhoods, with authorities "powerless to interfere as long as the obnoxious people own their house or the landlord of it refuses to eject them."[7] Many issues of the *Mascot* were devoted to advocating for a restricted district, with exposés purporting to document the multitude of ways in which ostensibly legitimate businesses like milliners and dressmakers were becoming fronts for prostitution.

While some businesses within the boundaries of what would become

Figure 6.3. "A Plague of Prostitutes" cartoon on front page of the *Mascot* newspaper, New Orleans, June 11, 1892.

Storyville potentially had a link to commercial sex in the late nineteenth century (like Mary Nott's "house of ill fame" [as it was called in the census] on Square 130, discussed later in this chapter), the largest concentration of sex workers in the period appears to have been in the vicinity of Customhouse/Iberville and Burgundy Streets, within the boundaries of the modern Vieux Carré. The 1880 census identified multiple such "houses of ill fame" in the blocks of Burgundy between Customhouse and Conti Streets, and the 1885 Sanborn maps give further hints as to usage, with addresses near the corner of Customhouse and Burgundy labeled as female boardinghouses, the typical Sanborn euphemism for locations serving as brothels.[8] The census gives some indication of the practicalities of sex work in this very visible area, just a block from Canal Street. Most of these houses appear to have been racially segregated, though ones housing exclusively white women are located alongside ones with Black and Mulatto residents; in fact, in the case of a white couple named Peter and Frances Reese, the keepers of a "house of ill fame" at 59 Burgundy, eighteen-year-old Delphine and the women of color in the adjacent building at 65 Burgundy may have been in their employ. The proximity of the establishments created need for some corollary occupations as well; Chevalley Bonomo, the Mulatto wife of a fruit dealer just down Burgundy Street, is identified in the census as a ladies' doctor.[9] A police ordinance soon after this date required women engaged in sex work within certain boundaries to vacate the ground floors of buildings. Ostensibly, this order forced many of these businesses to relocate to the area across Basin Street.

After traveling abroad and seeing attempts by European cities to regulate commercial sex, alderman Sidney Story, an antiprostitution reformer, proposed the creation of a restricted district in New Orleans. Story was perhaps inspired in part by the work of Parisian reformers like Alexandre Parent-Duchâtelet, who equated the regulation of prostitution with the work of sanitation more broadly. Sex work, like sewage, was thought to be a source of filth and contamination, but one that was unavoidable in an urban environment. It should thus be controlled and made invisible. The city, fearful that it could not legalize prostitution outright, avoided this problem through careful wording of its Ordinance 13032, passed in January 1897 and going into effect late that year. This ordinance made it unlawful for "any public prostitute or woman notoriously abandoned to lewdness" to occupy a premises outside of the boundaries of Basin, North Robertson, Customhouse/Iberville, and St. Louis Streets, even while stating that the ordinance should not be "construed as to authorize" that lewd women could stay in any portion of the city. The city thus formalized a gray area, a place where the application of law was ambiguous and sometimes arbitrary. In 1917, when the secretaries of war and the navy ordered that the district be shuttered, the city would find itself in the odd position of trying to defend something that only existed in the margins of the law.[10]

Alderman Story's name was applied in jest to the new district, apparently to his chagrin, and soon Storyville became anything but invisible. The adjacent rail line along Basin Street and the construction of a new terminal station for it designed by noted Chicago architect Daniel Burnham in 1908 meant that the edge of the district was one of the last sights seen by visitors to the city before they disembarked from the train. Much of the reputation of Storyville to this day stems from the lavish brothels along Basin Street, many of which celebrated their luxurious trappings in advertisements in guides called

Blue Books. These guides to the district listed the women who worked there by name and address, and usually by race, interspersing the more mundane directory-style listings with descriptions of the charms of individual ladies of the tenderloin and with photographs of opulent interiors. The listed sporting houses are associated with the names of famous madams such as Josie Arlington, "Countess" Willie Piazza, Emma Johnson, and Lulu White. At least some of these madams, women of color themselves, catered specifically to white men who sought sex across the color line. They made use of nineteenth-century terms for mixed-race status, such as quadroon and octoroon, to skirt the boundaries of what was tolerated in a district that was intended to be segregated, but that in practice was meant to reserve transgressions of racial boundaries as a privilege of whiteness.[11]

While Storyville may have been best known for the businesses along its high-profile border, the district was riddled with other commercial enterprises as well, especially ones that served the needs of an entertainment district: saloons, beer gardens, pharmacies, corner stores, restaurants, lunch counters, and shooting galleries. Much of the rest of the district consisted of the small houses referred to as cribs, where individual prostitutes would rent rooms and conduct business. Landau describes cribs as "not residences, but bare-bones work sites," where there was little opportunity to do more than rinse off in between each new sexual transaction.[12] This description certainly was true of many of the small shotguns and cottages in the district, though considerable variation in this pattern persisted, and many addresses were still listed with renters not engaged in occupations directly related to servicing the district as late as the 1910 census, the last one conducted before the district was officially closed.

While a comprehensive survey of demographic patterns in Storyville must wait for a future work, the case of Square 159, the block bounded by Bienville, North Villere, Iberville, and North Marais Streets, not far from the geographic center of Storyville, helps to illustrate some of the trends in the neighborhood. In 1900, the census listing of 224–226 North Villere is typical. There, Dixie Wood, a twenty-eight-year-old white woman from Illinois, was enumerated with her "partner," Flossie Livingston; two additional white women in their twenties, both listed as dressmakers; and a Black "house servant" named George Kelz. Dixie and Flossie owned their place, and they are listed as proprietors of the Firm on Villere Street in one of the early Blue Book editions. However, around the corner, the Page family rented rather than owned a place at 1524 Bienville Street; J. S. Page, described as a thirty-nine-year-old Black male, worked as a waiter, presumably at one of the many restaurants in the vicinity, and he lived with his wife, five children ranging in age from one to fifteen, and two older female lodgers, both employed as cooks. By 1910, Dixie Wood was still living on Villere Street, although apparently having lost her house (and mysteriously having actually decreased two years in age over the last decade); she was now enumerated as a boarder in the household of Lillian Young.[13] The 1524 Bienville house had likely shifted over to use for prostitution by this time, with four women (two of them Black, one white, and one Mulatto) residing there, but Mulatto shoemakers lived at both 1526 and 1528 Bienville, as did employees in saloons and a washerwoman. The neighborhood was a patchwork throughout, in terms of both racial composition and occupation, and places like the Union Chapel Methodist Episcopal Church, at 1512 Bienville, would exist throughout the Storyville era.

The creation of vice districts like that envisioned in the Story ordinance was a part of a national trend that sought to create fixed boundaries around particular kinds of bodies. It was only gradually in the twentieth century that the term *segregated district* shifted from primarily denoting a neighborhood set aside for vice to one separated by race, and in many cases these two types of segregated districts were almost co-occurrent. In the case of Storyville, Landau has linked this process to the laws and judicial decisions that institutionalized Jim Crow separation, most notably the 1897 *Plessy* decision, but parallels can be seen in conflicts surrounding vice districts elsewhere. Race riots originating in red-light districts in Atlanta, Georgia, in 1906, and in Springfield, Illinois, in 1908, may have heightened fears about the many ways that the permeability of the color line was flouted in Storyville.[14] The reality on the ground was never as tidy and well regulated as city authorities liked to portray, and the near-constant anxieties over the issue of cross-race contacts betray this fact throughout Storyville's history. As early as 1902, an attempt to police racial divisions in the district had been abandoned as impracticable. Louisiana's 1908 Gay-Shattuck law attempted to criminalize interracial fraternization and concubinage, and, for example, required that permits for saloons designate the race served. Even as the color line was being hardened, cases worked their way through New Orleans courts that emphasized the malleability of racial designations. In a 1910 case that went to the Louisiana Supreme Court, the arrest of a white man named Octave Treadaway for violating the interracial concubinage statute of the 1908 law was overturned because the woman involved was an octoroon, which traditionally meant something other than Black in its usage in the state. The law was later amended so that it applied to any mixing of white and nonwhite. A later city ordinance of 1917, which would finally enforce the full racial segregation of the district, was contested by over twenty nonwhite madams, before the move to close Storyville made the fight unnecessary. Some madams, including both Lulu White and

Willie Piazza, ignored the mandate to shutter the tenderloin even then, living and carrying on business within the old boundaries for years afterward.[15]

In the years after the Story ordinance went into effect, there were additional attempts to regulate contacts across the color line, especially sexual ones, within and outside of the district, including the establishment of a segregated brothel area across Canal Street. The so-called Black Storyville, referred to at the time as the Uptown District, was countenanced in an addendum to the original Storyville ordinance as encompassing the area bounded by Perdido, Gravier, Franklin, and Locust Streets, but officials were apparently initially hesitant or unable to enforce a strict segregation of sex work. Part of the allure of Storyville for white visitors was the promise of illicit sex across the color line, something on which well-known madams like Piazza and White capitalized, and it has been estimated that around a quarter of the women working in the district at any time were identified as Black or Mulatto. Black men were part of the social life of the district too, and even though patronage of Storyville brothels was supposed to be a privilege of whiteness, this prohibition was difficult to police on the ground. Still, businesses related to vice and prostitution became concentrated in the Uptown District too in these years, and it continued in operation as an entertainment district long after 1917. It is finally gaining some recognition in its own right as a locus of cultural production for the city's African American community.[16]

Despite the long-running, often unacknowledged existence of this segregated counterpart, the Storyville district contained its own Black section around North Robertson Street, its lakeside boundary. A description by English visitor Harry Johnston in 1910 purports to give some indication of the racial and ethnic patterning within the district:

> We next entered a district in the vicinity of the great prison and of the police head-quarters: the region under police supervision specially assigned to houses of prostitution. The quarter (besides its special Negro subdivision) was in the arrangements of the police and in the manner of the people, divided into geographical areas: here was the street of Jewish brothels; there two or more streets would be given up to the Italians or the Slavs (generally called Polaks [sic] or Bohemians); and lastly there were the establishments of English-speaking women—Anglo-Saxon Americans, Canadians, English, and Irish. . . . The houses were usually of only two storeys (interspersed with an occasional fine mansion). On the outside of the small dwellings the name of the woman-tenant was painted up in large letters—Nellie Corbet, Lizzie Devant, Sadie Buskin, and so on.

Johnston goes on to discuss the fact that only white clients could visit white women in this district but that many of the establishments were kept by women of color, and, despite the ostensible sexual segregation, white and Black men alike walked through the streets, "looking through the blinds in the long array of mean houses."[17]

Storyville officially closed for business in 1917, with the city providing an ordinance that ended it on October 9, in response to the edict from the secretaries of war and the navy, which stated that open prostitution would not be tolerated within five miles of military installations out of concern for venereal disease in servicemen. There was some drama after this decision, including a rumor that large brothel owners planned to commit arson to collect insurance money for their businesses, but most women who had lived and worked in the district are thought to have moved on gradually over the next couple of months. Although this understanding may be partially true, many other women quietly stayed, and some continued in their previous occupations, though perhaps less visibly. As late as 1930, one could find Willie Piazza back at 317 Basin (now named North Saratoga Street as part of a rechristening process that was apparently meant to cleanse the neighborhood of its past), operating a rooming house with a suspicious number of single female boarders. What is striking about the post-1917 period is just how quickly the blocks that had formerly made up Storyville became almost exclusively Black in racial composition. Square 159, which had been evenly divided between individuals enumerated as Black, Mulatto, and white in 1910, only contained four white residents by 1920, and by 1930 all of them were gone.

By the time that the Iberville area was surveyed, conditions were among the worst that HANO documented. Of the 723 units surveyed in the area, 485 had no lighting facilities (meaning no gas or electricity), and 364 needed major repairs to be livable (see table 2.1). A higher number and proportion of people relied on shared toilets for sanitation that at any of the other four areas discussed in this book, and almost half still shared outdoor privies. A larger percentage than at any other of the original housing project areas had no stove or sink (n=229 of the total), and an even higher number had no bathing facilities (n=476).[18] However, to focus on these conditions ignores an important fact: the Storyville district was created to enforce ideals of sanitation, cleanliness, and control. Many of its brothels were once celebrated for having the latest in amenities, and for Iberville to become a slum like this by the 1930s required an active campaign of forgetting and neglect, one that would culminate in the almost complete erasure of the district from the physical space of the city. It was only in this way that this key property could be reclaimed as white space, in the form of the neatly arranged brick apartment buildings of the segregated Iberville Housing Project, which formed a buffer to the tourist zones of the city until the Civil Rights era. As noted at the opening of this book, many claimed that the recent demolition of Iberville was a blatant attempt to do this once again.

Preparing for the Dig at Iberville

The archaeological possibilities at the Iberville Housing Project had been visible as early as 1999, when renovations along a housing project administration building unintentionally unearthed a great deal of artifactual material, and archaeologists were called in at the time to investigate. A series of dense deposits dating from the Storyville era back to the beginning of the 1800s were located. In fact, at the time, it seemed that the best-preserved materials were from the antebellum era, long before Storyville existed, where a series of brick pavements from the yards of residences on Bienville Street had sealed rich layers of midden and a trash pit containing fragments of numerous wine bottles. These artifacts were interesting in their own right, but only a few hints at the later history of the area could be gleaned from the material evidence. For example, an enameled washbasin of the type that would have been a standard feature of any prostitute's room was found discarded against an abandoned footing (figure 6.4), and many dull-green tin-enameled cosmetic jars or rouge pots (the type known as Marseille monochrome by specialists in French faience) were recovered, scattered through the backdirt. The investigations were confined only to those areas already disturbed by construction, but it seemed very likely that privy shafts, wells, cisterns, and other similar features would also be preserved in the housing project's courtyards and parking lots.[19] At the time, the unique research possibilities of the Storyville material seemed self-evident: large-scale archaeological projects in other cities were looking at the material record of commercial sex and prostitution, and historical archaeology elsewhere had provided a wealth of information about gender, sexuality, work, and daily life in brothels and red-light districts in a way that documentary evidence could not.

Some of these possibilities had also been demonstrated in New Orleans just before Hurricane Katrina, during excavations at 535 Conti Street in the French Quarter. The Historic New Orleans Collection intended to turn a parking garage into a new archival storage facility for some of its extensive holdings. Its façade would replicate that of the Richardson Hotel, a circa 1828 structure documented in an 1853 plan housed at the New Orleans Notarial Archives. The HNOC has been proactive in incorporating archaeological investigations into its building renovation plans for some time, even though, as a private entity, it is not required to do so. This time, the excavations were planned as

Figure 6.4. Excavations in 1999 showing enameled metal washbasin against building footing. (Courtesy of Earth Search, Inc.)

a collaborative effort between Shannon Lee Dawdy at the University of Chicago and ESI. ESI would conduct the bulk of the field investigations, while Dawdy and her students would be primarily responsible for analysis and interpretation of artifacts.[20] The project garnered a great deal of publicity when a routine review of background materials on file in the Vieux Carré Survey revealed that the Richardson Hotel had been built on the site of a hotel and tavern called the Rising Sun Hotel, which had burned to the ground in a dramatic conflagration in 1822. The history of the popular song "House of the Rising Sun" likely goes back much further than the nineteenth century, to traditions of English balladry, and the Rising Sun moniker was frequently applied to taverns, both in New Orleans and elsewhere, so a direct connection was unlikely. However, the possibility that archaeologists could uncover remains from *the* House of the Rising Sun captured the public's imagination, and the interest only increased after a seemingly-disproportionate number of burned and blackened tin-glazed cosmetic jars (the same sort of rouge pots recovered at Iberville in 1999) were recovered from a level associated with the 1822 fire. While excavations were limited in scope—in fact, the parking garage was still in active use while they took place—the rouge pots were certainly evocative. They seemed to be the sort of object that one might find in a nineteenth-century brothel.[21]

Whether the Rising Sun Hotel was a venue that housed commercial sex is unclear from the evidence at hand. Some of the ads for the establishment contain language that today reads suggestively, especially considering the euphemisms that abound in the much-later Blue Books of Storyville. According to an 1821 blurb in the *Louisiana Gazette*, "No pains or expense will be spared by the new proprietors to give general satisfaction, and maintain the character of giving the best entertainment. . . . Gentlemen may here rely upon finding attentive servants."[22] However, such language can be found in descriptions of comparable businesses that had no direct connection to sex work, and, as observed by Dawdy and Richard Weyhing, there are alternative explanations for the prevalence of cosmetic jars in a space that appears to have catered to a male clientele. In this part of the antebellum, makeup and cosmetics were as much the province of male dandies as of women, and so the jars could be indicative of the presence of the sort of sporting men to whom it seemed that the Rising Sun Hotel catered.[23] Moreover, it may even be anachronistic to look for evidence at this time of a brothel in the sense of a house where there was a semipermanent resident category of prostitutes. While there certainly were disorderly houses identified in the antebellum, sex work could also be informal, and places like the Rising Sun Hotel could still have been a locus for it without being designated as a brothel. At the very least, the work at the Rising Sun suggested some directions for a future archaeology of prostitution and sex work in New Orleans, an archaeology that would inevitably need to acknowledge the importance of Storyville in the city's popular history.

Once test excavations by ESI began at Iberville in 2010, they demonstrated rapidly that archaeological mitigation for the redevelopment would be even more complex than at St. Thomas, Magnolia, and Lafitte. Well-preserved historical deposits were found all across the site, spanning the period from when the neighborhood was first subdivided for residential development up through and including the era when Iberville was constructed. That some of these deposits were National Register eligible because of the valuable archaeological data that could be recovered from them was obvious. But what was the appropriate level at which to make that assessment? Individual features? Lots? Blocks? The area as a whole? Even though the presence of remains related to Storyville added a unique aspect of the neighborhood to the consideration, there were also much earlier levels, dating from the late colonial and antebellum eras. Normally these levels might be given higher priority in such an undertaking, but the redevelopment would also effectively destroy most archaeological remnants of the red-light district, erasing the last material remains of what had already disappeared from the visible landscape of the city. On top of that, the Iberville Project was partially surrounded by cemeteries, at least one of which, St. Louis Cemetery No. 1, was shown on historical maps as substantially larger in size. Human remains had been discovered outside the present boundaries of St. Louis No. 1 a number of times over the years,

Figure 6.5. Courtyard used as focal point of University of New Orleans field school excavations, 2012–13. (D. Ryan Gray, courtesy of University of New Orleans Department of Anthropology)

and there was every reason to expect that more graves were preserved underneath part of Iberville.[24]

While the extent of archaeological mitigation was being discussed by the various parties involved (the city and its attorneys, HANO, the State Historic Preservation Office and its Division of Archaeology, and others), UNO volunteered to hold an archaeological field school at the Iberville site.[25] The rationale for doing this was twofold. First, we could provide some additional insight into the quality of preservation on the blocks in Iberville and into the nature of deeply buried remains, especially ones that might be low-density or less visible. Second, we could supplement the data that would eventually be recovered during the excavations mandated by the NHPA by intensively focusing on a single grouping of households, including both their yard areas and the dense pit features associated with them. As UNO's work was not subject to external negotiations or imperatives that might prioritize certain categories of material, we could make the development of Storyville and commercial sex in the city a central component of our research. In 2012–14, UNO conducted a series of summer field schools at the Iberville Housing Project, with some twenty-five students conducting excavations within a single courtyard framed by some of the historical housing project buildings (figure 6.5). The excavations provided insights into the development of the neighborhood, into the everyday lives of the women who worked in Storyville, and into the reasons why this space was stigmatized and selected for clearance to make way for Iberville in 1939–40.[26]

Excavations at City Square 130

The Iberville Project does not conform to the modern street grid, so the housing project buildings cross and truncate multiple historic lots. The area also was crisscrossed with poorly marked utilities associated with those modern buildings. The courtyard area where we focused our efforts was within City Square 130, the block historically bounded by Bienville, North Liberty, Conti, and North Franklin (or Crozat) Streets. The UNO excavations sampled four historic lots, numbered 315–317 and 319 North Franklin and 318–320 and 322 North Liberty, with a particular emphasis on the one at 318–320 North Liberty (figure 6.6). In addition to containing relatively well-preserved deposits in an easily accessible portion of the housing project, these lots seemed to be good candidates to address questions related to the development of Storyville. A frame double residence located at 318–320 North Liberty, for instance, was already designated a "house of ill fame" in the 1880 census, almost twenty years prior to the establishment of Storyville. At the time, Mary Nott, a twenty-nine-year-old white woman of German ancestry, was listed as the head of household there, in a residence with a number of female and male roomers, all of whom were designated as being Black and Mulatto. The neighbor at North Franklin sharing a rear property line with this "house of ill fame" in 1880 was William Boots, a German policeman, living with his Swiss wife and a stepson. The Boots family shared their address with roomers named as Mr. and Mrs. Gregg, described in the census as a Mulatto laborer and a Black cook. Such social and ethnic diversity seems to have characterized the area prior to the establishment of Storyville.

After Storyville was established, it becomes somewhat more difficult to determine who was residing at the lots in question. The addresses occur in census records only intermittently, and it appears that all but one were used for commercial sex. The double at 318–320, for instance, was probably used as a crib, typically rented for short-term occupation, with it maintaining a similar footprint throughout the period documented in Sanborn maps. By 1908, 322 North Liberty was operating as a lunch counter, run by a Mulatto man named Lewis Mumford and his wife. Such small-scale restaurants were common in the district, where they served both low-rent crib customers and the women who worked in them. The empty space on the lot of the Boots home on Franklin was filled after 1898, initially with additional small crib-like residences. Eventually all these were replaced by a larger three-story building used as a brothel, possibly one operated by May Evans and referenced by Al

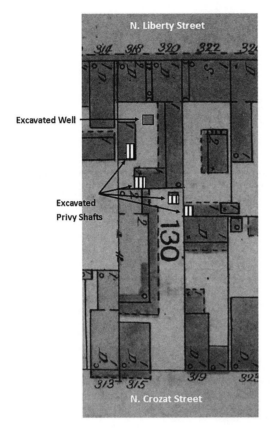

Figure 6.6. Site map showing location of major excavated pit features in Square 130 relative to 1896 Sanborn map (Vol. 1, Sheet 30). (Courtesy of Southeastern Architectural Archive, Tulane University)

Rose. The pattern that emerges is one of intensifying development and density throughout the period, something that continued after the district officially closed. In 1920, the former large brothel had apparently been converted into an apartment building, with twenty-six people enumerated there in five separate households. City Square 130, like much of the rest of the neighborhood that had been Storyville, became more homogeneously Black after 1917, and by the 1930 census, there was only one white family left on the block.

UNO teams hand-excavated some forty-five square meters of surface area within the courtyard overlapping these addresses, with the units divided among a number of distinct locales, uncovering remains that date back to the earliest subdivision of the area through the early twentieth century. These remains include thousands of pieces of ceramic and fragments of glass, pieces of animal bone, building materials, and any range of other items: ceramic doll parts, smoking pipes, marbles, shoes, shell casings and gunflints, beads, hygienic syringes, buttons, watches, and so on. These artifacts are associated with brick-lined privies, wood-lined wells, unlined pits, cistern bases, brick footings, wooden posts, fence lines, and brick pavements, most of which can be linked to specific structures and households shown on historical maps. A portion of what has been recovered so far predates Storyville, but it still helps in understanding why this particular group of blocks was selected for the location of the district, and why it was targeted a second time for redevelopment with the construction of Iberville.

Although documents give us few clues as to who exactly lived on the lots where our excavations took place in the eighteenth century, early artifacts recovered suggest that the city commons was not simply vacant land in this period, but that it attracted people who were socially on the margins in the city, particularly people of color and of mixed heritage. Such people relied on the ability to cross between urban life and the countryside, and the social and cultural worlds of those of African, European, and Native American descent, to make a living. One of the most unusual deposits dating from the early antebellum further illustrates this point: a collection of some 750 blue glass seed beads occurring together, as if they had been strung in a sheet, alongside an inverted bottle base recovered from a unit near the front edge of lots at North Franklin Street. These beads were in a midden related to an early residence on the block, probably constructed soon after the commons was subdivided for development in 1810. Blue beads likely had special significance for people of African descent during the period of the Atlantic slave trade, but these were found in an otherwise undifferentiated deposit, with hundreds of small fragments of English pearlware, other domestic artifacts, and pieces of bone from cuts of meat. It thus seems unlikely that they held any sort of magical or spiritual properties in this kind of context. More likely is that the cache is evidence of informal commerce at the edge of town. Beads were a common currency in the frontier exchange economy of the eighteenth century, and, in the cash-poor New Orleans of the very early antebellum, they may have continued to serve a similar function in economic networks, particularly for the enslaved or those making their living at the margins of the city.[27]

Other portions of the courtyard also produced remains from the antebellum era, including some that hint at the area's later associations with informal economies and wide-ranging trade. For instance, a small section of a wood-lined antebellum privy shaft, preserved beneath a later nineteenth-century brick-lined one, contained an assemblage of artifacts that evoked the far-flung connections of the neighborhood's residents. A copper 80 Réis coin from the reign of Pedro I of Brazil, minted in Rio de Janeiro in 1824, suggests early ties between the ports of the United States and those of that newly independent nation; the United States was, after all, one of the first nations to recognize the new Empire of Brazil in the 1820s. It is tempting to see in the combination of this item with tin-glazed rouge pots and other highly decorated pottery, also recovered from these contexts, a connection to hospitality and entertainment, whether licit or illicit, going far into the antebellum. Of course, given that the enslaved made up some two-thirds of Brazil's population in 1820, probably numbering some two million individuals in total, this coin is also perhaps evidence of some of the networks connecting diasporic populations, even ones across continents, in the broader Atlantic world.[28]

The lot that included this early privy, associated with the 318–320 North Liberty municipal address, became the most intensively investigated of all of those at Square 130, with an emphasis on the period after emancipation, when the developmental history of the block becomes much clearer. At this time the area ostensibly began to gain the reputation that would eventually have it designated as a tenderloin. The contents of a wood-lined box well, excavated during the 2013 season, provided evidence for the changing commercial fortunes of the neighborhood. Initial excavations in the vicinity in 2012 had encountered a brick pavement and chain wall and dense Storyville-era midden deposits associated with a shed or kitchen in the rear yard of the 318 side of the frame double. As these features were followed across the yard, excavators noticed that the strata trailed off and dipped downward to the east, indicating that later soils were constantly slumping into the unconsolidated fill of some sort of pit. As the excavation was expanded, it became clear that later residents at the address had been dealing with this low area in the lot for years, filling it many times over with trash and construction debris. In the feature itself, most likely abandoned just after the mid-nineteenth century, were remains indicative of a number of cottage industries, including what was interpreted as debris from a cigar rolling enterprise. The top of the shaft was capped with fragments of flat white granite, some of which had letters lightly etched into the surface; given the proximity of St. Louis Cemetery No. 1, the stones probably represented practice for an apprentice stonemason.

Archaeologies of Storyville

Storyville was a comparatively brief moment in the overall history of the neighborhood that became Iberville: not quite twenty years in a history that spanned much of the three hundred years since New Orleans's founding. Because it seemed risky to target a single period so heavily in the recovery process, many of the initial research questions for the project were designed to consider the long-term dynamics of the area. Could we identify any signs of what made the area a likely location for the segregated district? Why was it selected, and what could the archaeological record tell us about the intersections of race, class, and gender in everyday life prior to Storyville's founding? Eventually, a rich material record was documented from the period from the

1890s through the early 1900s, allowing us to focus on some of the distinctive aspects of Storyville's history at a variety of scales. Many houses in the block in which we were working had been connected to the city's new water infrastructure in the early 1900s, which typically made older shaft privies obsolete. At the 318–320 North Liberty address, two different brick-lined privies were excavated, one apparently filled after a fire in the 1890s and the other after being abandoned at the time of the addresses' sewerage hook-up in 1913.[29] Another brick-lined privy serving the household on the Franklin side of the block was apparently filled just before the large three-story brothel was built at the location, sometime between 1908 and 1915.

There are some broad patterns that I expect will emerge with the Storyville assemblages, especially when the data from the work conducted by UNO is linked with the broader effort undertaken by ESI in conjunction with the Iberville redevelopment as a whole. Certain markers seem consistent with archaeological excavations from other red-light districts around the urban United States: high proportions of perfume and cosmetic containers; frequent appearances of artifacts relating to feminine hygiene and the treatment of venereal diseases; ceramic tablewares in small sizes, presumed as associated with informal dining, and so on (figure 6.7). Such things have been associated with the archaeology of commercial sex from the East Coast to the West—with the best-known excavations being those at the Five Points in New York, at Mary Ann Hall's brothel in Washington, DC, at various western saloons and brothels, and at a parlor house in Los Angeles.[30] Some recovered material from Square 130 is certainly consistent with this previous research, and although items like glass syringe plungers or nozzles from irrigation syringes are found in all sorts of urban assemblages, their presence is evocative in this context.

Some artifact patterns emerging may be somewhat distinct to the Storyville component. As noted, among the initial objects that seemed to mark the deposits related to commercial sex were rouge pots: tin-enameled galley pots, often in a dull green color, manufactured in the French faience pottery tradition. While such jars held a variety of products historically, including ointments from apothecaries, the frequency of marked examples from parfumiers in France seem to support the association with rouge. As Dawdy has argued, in New Orleans Frenchness was marketed as imparting an aura of sexual indulgence, and this aura seemed to have extended to the level of the everyday within Storyville, with French products recovered in varied forms, from perfumes to smoking pipes. Other items had connections to cosmetic practices for both men and women. For instance, a jar of bear grease was recovered in the Storyville-era component, identifiable by its lid advertising the product with a black-printed image of a bear. Bear grease was initially marketed

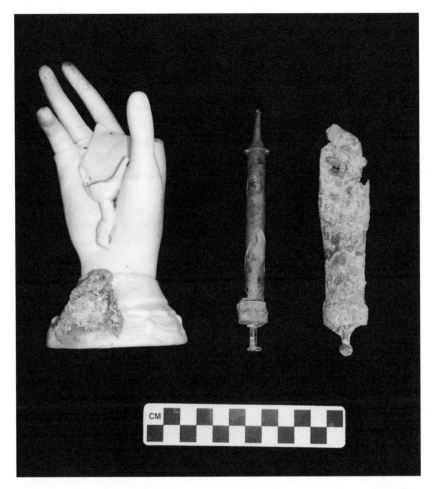

Figure 6.7. Typical Storyville artifacts from excavations at Square 130. *Left to right:* bisque porcelain ring holder, glass syringe, and lead mercury syringe. (D. Ryan Gray, courtesy of University of New Orleans Department of Anthropology)

mainly as a tonic for preventing hair loss, while also maintaining its softness and lushness and restoring its color. By the mid-nineteenth century, real bear grease was hard to come by in the American market, so manufacturers substituted other animal fats, like beef marrow and tallow.[31]

The assemblage of porcelain plates and teacups and fancy glassware deposited in a privy at 317 North Franklin perhaps characterizes a typical Storyville assemblage, at least in a straightforward sense. It probably dates just around the time that the smaller cribs and brothels there were replaced with the massive three-story structure occupying the entirety of the lot, sometime around 1910–14. At first glance relatively stylish, these wares were probably acquired piecemeal, and much of the ceramic tableware was outdated by the time that it entered the archaeological record. Class aspirations were marketed in Storyville, and an assemblage like this demonstrates a concern with Victorian ideologies of class and cleanliness. This privy also included one of the more ubiquitous finds associated with the Storyville component: small colorless vials embossed with the name of the Gray Medicine Company. The catarrh cure that was packaged in these vials contained a considerable amount of cocaine, the sale of which from neighborhood druggists is a frequent subject in literature on the district. Such objects appeal to the public and scholars alike for their seeming illustrative quality relative to the documentary record. In an early presentation on Storyville archaeology, I used the metal washbasin and a liquor bottle recovered in the 1999 excavations to evoke the iconic Bellocq photograph of the woman with striped stockings (figure 6.8), an unnamed Storyville prostitute.[32]

When trying to consider how the material culture of commercial sex in the district relates to the lived experience of women like those in the Bellocq photos, one must inevitably deal with an ambiguity. To what degree does the material reflect their lives, and to what extent does it indicate the habits and proclivities of the male customers who patronized them? Desire itself was commodified within the physical spaces of the brothel, and even the most intimate assemblages there were inflected by the relationship to their function as places for the entertainment of men. There has been a temptation over the years to see in Storyville, especially in some of its fiercely independent and charismatic madams, stories of sexual entrepreneurship, of women exercising choices outside the boundaries of traditional family life and respectability. This narrative falls into a long-standing discussion in histories of prostitution about the relationship between the exploitative structures of gender inequality and sexual violence, in which women were forced to sell sex to survive, and the freedom of women to choose sex work as a means to escape the traditional confines of gendered norms. The two poles here are oversimplifications of these positions, but the material culture of Storyville, and of the era that came before it was established, adds some perspective. By attempting to create and designate a space where prostitution could be legible, where it could be controlled, confined, and isolated, city authorities were allowed to exploit it and profit from it more efficiently than ever before. Private industries profited as well, as establishments like furniture and department stores sold to businesses in the district on credit, and alcohol retailers supplied saloons and brothels. While the sort of hyperconsumption that these economic relationships promoted could certainly present a surface appearance of osten-

Figure 6.8. Storyville woman with striped stockings, ca. 1912, by E. J. Bellocq.

tation in the material record, this was an illusion, a spectacle in which visitors could be immersed.

Historian Emily Landau has noted that "the men who created Storyville were self-styled progressive businessmen; they were white supremacists who believed that prostitutes, people of color, Carnival, excrement, and illicit and interracial sex all constituted pollution, that all contaminated what they touched, literally and figuratively."[33] While these "respectable" businessmen may have been content to profit from Storyville at a discrete distance, not everyone was similarly removed. In the years after 1898, the census indicates the concentration of large numbers of men in boardinghouses around the district's periphery. Perhaps these men were simply attracted by the lure of sexualized entertainment or by cheap housing, but there is something predatory here as well. Pimps were certainly a part of social life in the district, as they receive regular mention in crime reports and newspapers. It was a role that seems to have increased over time, though reliable information on this process is difficult to obtain. Nevertheless, as sex work became constrained and routinized into preexisting gendered power hierarchies, material remains can be expected to reflect this process, perhaps through increasing homogenization or through a decrease in items not directly related to the economic function of the brothel or crib.

In the story of the lot at 318 and 320 North Liberty—the location of Mary Nott's "house of ill fame" in 1880—something of this process can be seen. The material record suggests at least a periodic connection to commercial sex and informal economies throughout much of the lot's history, with fluid social boundaries between the licit and illicit. In the 1880 census, the address may be listed as a "house of ill fame" not only because it was a locus of prostitution but also because the occupants themselves could not be easily characterized by race, ethnicity, class, or familial structure. Storyville attempted to impose order on this situation: to make sexual disorder a category that could be rendered permanent. Of course, the great irony of any such attempt to regulate prostitution historically is that it only deals with one side of a gendered sexual relationship. Storyville may have restricted notorious women (and it did a questionable job of that), but it did not restrict prostitution. Commercial sex was just as intertwined in the lives of those who visited the district, those who profited from renting out rooms at exorbitant rates there, and those who profited from selling the trappings of modernity and elegance to those who worked there. This logic and this deception were at the heart of later attempts at segregation.

Different categories of identity are notoriously difficult to "see" archaeologically, particularly when studying an era when mass-produced objects were widely circulated both nationally and internationally, but at least a few items spoke to the complex social landscape of the neighborhood at the turn of the last century. For instance, in one of the midden deposits at 318–320 North Liberty, a medallion-style badge from the Grand Army of the Republic (GAR), an organization of Union Civil War veterans, was recovered. The stated mission of the GAR was to advance Republican causes in the years after the war, particularly voting rights for Black veterans. This particular variety of medallion is referred to by collectors as the Type 1 or 3BN badge, and it was only issued from 1866 to 1869. If it belonged to one of the African American men who resided at the North Liberty address in 1880, its presence would suggest that he was politically active even before the New Orleans-based Joseph A. Mower Post No. 1 of the GAR was established in 1872. The presence of a GAR branch in Louisiana was certainly significant in itself, but, in addition, a local Colored Veterans Benevolent Association was based at Ramon Urbeso Hall (at 322 Marais Street within the district). As racial divisions in the district became more rigorously enforced, it was forced to move as a nuisance in 1899, as it impinged on the ostensibly more respectable white portion of the district. While the badge could have belonged to one of the residents at the address where it was recovered, it also could have been associated with secondhand clothing or even another resident's activities as a laundress.[34] Indeed, the prevalence of buttons and small finds related to sewing may be the best evidence of some of the additional economies (like laundry and piece-work) that the money flowing into the district supported. By 1910, much of the resident population of the district worked in some capacity related to it, with many of these attendant business opportunities operated by its African American residents. Money itself was manipulated at lunch counters like the one operated on North Liberty Street, as seen in the example of a quartee, a 2½-cent coin, recovered there. These small copper coins were made to serve as change in "2 for 5 cent" lunch specials. Such ad hoc coins would be marked with the initials of the business that issued them, thus guaranteeing a return visit and keeping cash in the neighborhood. Informal economies continued to flourish, even as the city exerted control over sex work.

Rare artifacts offer more personal glimpses behind the façade of Story-ville and capture something of the identities of the women who worked there, while also perhaps showing the impacts of larger structural forces on their lives. Items of jewelry and personal adornment obviously imply something in this regard, as do items denoting religious faith. An intriguing example of this sort of artifact was a badly corroded saint's medal (perhaps with an image of the Virgin Mary) recovered from a circa 1890s privy deposit. While religious medallions themselves are not exceptional, this one was distinguished by its text, which was written in Chinese. It is difficult to surmise a vector for this particular item having entered into the archaeological record, and I have been unable to find analogues from other archaeological sites. Chinese workers had begun arriving in Louisiana after emancipation, when they were briefly promoted as a replacement for the enslaved in plantation agricultural labor. Few of these workers stayed in the oppressive conditions of the sugar parishes, and many relocated to New Orleans, where a small Chinatown had formed near Storyville. Chinese in New Orleans took advantage of the ambiguity of their racial status in the Jim Crow city, even though they technically were subject to the same racial policies of segregation as other nonwhite people. Many Chinese men married women of color in the city and elsewhere in the American South, and the children of these unions would have been considered legally to be nonwhite as well. It is thus entirely possible that a woman enumerated as Black or Mulatto in the census could have had one parent who was Chinese.[35]

Occasionally items with monogrammed names or initials are recovered archaeologically, like an engraved pocket watch with a woman's name from the North Liberty household. However, some more unusual monogrammed

Figure 6.9. Glassware with initials scratched into base.
(D. Ryan Gray, courtesy of University of New Orleans
Department of Anthropology)

items, of which there are now two examples from our excavations, are pieces
of glass tableware with initials crudely scratched in the base of the vessel (figure 6.9). The example seen here, a goblet marked with the inscription "M.C"
is one of two such items; the other was marked with "M S" (or "S W"). They
were found at two different addresses, one likely dating from just before the
Storyville era and the other from early in the twentieth century. One might
assume that the initials are meant to mark personal property in the confines
of a brothel, but to what end? Tableware like this was not especially expensive or rare. Such items belie the supposed extravagance of Storyville. Were
individual prostitutes responsible for keeping track of the furnishings within
their particular rooms? Was this something to which the house held them
to account, with such glasses thus part of an elaborate system of exploitation
comparable to the plantation commissary? The marked objects could also be
none of these things, instead representing attempts to maintain one's personal
identity in an environment that was meant to reduce women to the status of

objects. Many stories demonstrate how the women of Storyville resisted this objectification, and I prefer to see these items as that resistance manifested at the level of the everyday.

Afterlives and Silences

Even as the legacy of Storyville has been memorialized and mythologized, less and less is left to mark the day-to-day experiences of the people who lived and labored there. Documents often indicate names and little more, and many of the names in the district themselves are assumed, fictitious identities that helped women keep the supposed boundaries of the district permeable. Ruth Rosen, in writing about the history of commercial sex in the first part of the twentieth century, has argued that "as Americans investigated the sub-culture of prostitution, they discovered a microcosm of their own daily pros-titution for the almighty dollar."[36] While Rosen may be overstating the degree to which the population at large saw its own relationship to the wages of sex work, this sort of contradiction alone might be enough to make the location of Storyville a lingering source of tension. Such a tension would undoubtedly be heightened by the interpenetration of the economies of Storyville into po-lite or respectable society. The many enterprises with financial stakes in the district have been noted already, and some of the most vocal advocates for the district—and, ironically, against it—profited from speculation on property there. For instance, Santos Oteri, a bank director and businessman, was an early advocate for the elimination of vice outside of Storyville by the enforce-ment of the Story ordinance. Not coincidentally, he also was a major owner of rental properties within it.[37]

The legacy of Storyville echoed in more subtle ways as well. While lines of race and ethnicity in nineteenth century New Orleans were never as clearly demarcated as they were in many American cities, in Storyville these cate-gories were actively performed and manipulated. Moments of this perfor-mance are occasionally crystallized in documents, and even someone as well known as Alabama native Lulu White might claim Jamaican ancestry in the census. Perhaps her neighbor Bertha Golden really was of a mixed Algerian, Armenian, and French background. This seems at least slightly more likely than Josie Black's origins in Arabia, as she told the census taker in 1900. Both these latter women, incidentally, were designated racially as white, and their exotic backgrounds probably served as both a commodity in sexual commerce and a convenient fiction to hide a racially mixed heritage in the increasingly racist environment of post-*Plessy* New Orleans society. While the fluidity of race was exploited in Storyville, it was policed more and more carefully over time. This policing is apparent in the census, as mixed-race households be-come less common between 1900 and 1910 as an absolute, a trend that con-tinued in the neighborhood after the district was closed.[38]

While the lines between Victorian respectability and vice may be presented as clearly drawn in the present, an archaeological analysis of Storyville shows how these distinctions break down. For the urban poor and working class, the line between comfort and survival, relative affluence and impoverishment, was often a fine one, and this was certainly the case with women employed in Storyville. Consider a household at 1418 Conti Street, enumerated in the 1900 census, an apparent boardinghouse operated by thirty-two-year-old Lola Leslie, with two other young single women residing there. Two of the three are widowed, and they might be assumed to work in the sex trade from the house being listed as a female boardinghouse on Sanborn maps and appear-ing in the Storyville Blue Books. But unlike some Storyville prostitutes who listed no employment in the census, the women at 1418 Conti listed other occupations as well: twenty-five-year-old Alice Johnson was listed as an op-era singer, and twenty-year-old Daisy Marlin was a milliner. Perhaps these were aspirations, or perhaps part-time occupations and potential pathways for respectability. For single women of the working class, young widows espe-cially, such lines were fluid, gray areas rather than impermeable boundaries.

The neighborhood that had been Storyville persisted in a kind of limbo for decades as a place in which the impossibility of enforcing segregation through ordinance alone was exposed. It was a source of fascination but also one of revulsion, in which the taint of the past rendered it contaminated, de-spite it being located in commercially advantageous ground alongside major thoroughfares. The construction of Iberville offered a remedy to this. The ar-chitectural remnants of the district would be stripped away, as would the ra-cialized population that had come to reside in those remnants. Such large-scale displacements would become the model for how segregation could be enforced in the urban landscape, not just in New Orleans, but elsewhere in the United States too. Simply designating a district was not sufficient. It had to also be marked and physically isolated. In subsequent years this process would be done through other types of urban renewal. If Storyville marked a first experiment in urban segregation, the construction of large-scale public housing would mark its extension and its eventual perfection.

7
Conclusions

Cities, dynamic and heterogeneous almost by their very nature, are invariably sites of contestation, in which the apparent permanence of the built environment conceals histories of erasures and renewals, both planned and unplanned. The process of what Nancy D. Munn has termed the *becoming-past-of-places* is amplified in contemporary urban settings, where capitalist economies contribute to a fast pace of obsolescence and ruination, leaving behind a complex legacy of presences and absences, material residues, and documentary traces. Recent archaeological work has sought to confront the contemporary city and its ruins to engage with social issues in the present, and to show how cities, often despite the intents of those wielding political authority, provide opportunities for creative action.[1] In the context of American cities, the birth of public housing during the 1930s represented a new kind of intervention into urban space. At its beginning, it was intertwined with the idea of the slum: a space in which the material conditions of urban poverty were linked with moral degradation and social disorder. The housing projects, as tools of slum clearance, were meant to be constitutive of an order defined by segmented, controlled spaces, inhabited by productive families who were also simultaneously docile consumers. Within the ideological structures of Jim Crow America, the order thus formed was also (indeed, *had to be*) racial in nature, defined by hierarchy, division, and the creation of a permanent, dependent underclass. Indeed, American cities were soon to be transformed through many other urban renewal projects wielded as a blunt tool of racial segregation, many of them without the promise of replacement housing. The process of division was exacerbated further by the creation of white flight suburbs and edge cities, linked to urban centers by highways, barred to Black Americans by racial covenants. It took dramatic interventions into the urban fabric, implemented at the level of the everyday, to maintain and reproduce this unequal racial order, with consequences that are still visible throughout urban America today.[2]

It is here that archaeology offers a useful method to interrogate deterministic narratives that downplay the agency of those displaced by different forms of urban renewal. At a surface level, slum clearance was a form of erasure, in which whole neighborhoods and their all-too-messy histories were obliterated from the built environment of the city. Archaeology provides a literal means of excavating and documenting elements of that history, so it is certainly an important tool in that regard. But more importantly, in its focus on materiality, archaeological data allow us to examine the roles of objects in the experiences and everyday lives of residents in those neighborhoods. Rather than just seeing the imagined slum in terms of deprivation and material lack, we can see these spaces as sites that offered viable alternatives to the developing racial and social hierarchies of the city. While those living in densely developed urban neighborhoods faced economic hardships and marginalization, their everyday strategies of survival, subsistence, and spirituality offered physical proof of the inventiveness of those identified as the underclass of the city.[3]

This book has examined the birth of public housing from the material record of what it replaced, with this record as a means of exploring alternative narratives of urban development in the Jim Crow–era city. While New Orleans is often discussed as unique among American cities, it was no exception in this case, and the distinctive aspects of its own experiment in slum clearance help us understand the trajectory of how cities dealt with racial heterogeneity and the perceived disorder that came with it. To conclude, I return to the four cases discussed in this work and consider them in broader historical and geographic perspectives, particularly relative to other working-class and ethnically or racially mixed neighborhoods. Material remains like those derived from archaeology provide a basis for comparison of urban households, and this broader context will help to further interrogate the question of what kind of normality the combined strategies of slum clearance and public housing were meant to produce. This norm was itself a shadow of a ghost, the fiction of an ideology of middle-class domesticity that only ever existed as a distortion of the inhering messiness of urban social life. The failure of public housing to efface heterogeneity and produce an impossible order, as it was meant to do, would quickly become apparent. As a result, the logics of slum clearance and urban renewal turned to practices of containment, isolation, and warehousing in the post–World War II era. Indeed, some American cities adopted this model from the beginning.[4]

Race, Class, and Social Disorder

Urban slums were defined by authorities and reformers as characterized "by an amalgam of dilapidated housing, overcrowding, disease, poverty, and vice," where moral and physical decay were inextricably linked.[5] The addition of racial heterogeneity into this mix had also made them potential targets for clearance, expropriation, or redevelopment even in the nineteenth century. For instance, the mixed-race community of Seneca Village in New York City was seized through eminent domain to make way for the construction of Central Park in the 1850s. While its characterization as a slum served as a justification for its destruction, the site was a refuge for the city's African American middle class, who could find stability and protection from discrimination by moving to a place that had initially been on the city's fringes. Archaeological work at the site has so far emphasized the community's continuities with white Anglo-American middle-class material culture, as distinct from that of the Black working class in the more densely developed part of the city. The material from the site also may indicate the formation of a Black racial consciousness in the period before the community was displaced. The material record of Seneca Village is still too fragmentary to readily compare with that from the New Orleans sites discussed here, though significantly, it shows the same logics of displacement applied to unruly areas on the urban fringes that would later be applied to the city center.[6]

The complexities of race and class are necessarily components in any narrative of the formation of postemancipation urban America. Drawing on a sociological tradition that celebrates the heterogeneity of the Black experience in American cities, even while acknowledging the importance of structural racism in shaping the daily experience of individuals, a number of scholars have explicitly examined identity and class formation in African American communities during the era of segregation. Many of these works suggest that the idea of racial cohesion allowed class differences to be downplayed for political or social gains, even as the notion of a singular racial group, united in its interests, allowed middle-class ideologies to "continually co-opt and divert Black working-class issues."[7] Such historical research has helped develop a more nuanced understanding of the ways that racism impacted African American social and political life in the late nineteenth and twentieth centuries. Furthermore, it has expanded the discussion of the Black working class outside the realm of just organized labor and unions, and into the area of the "sloppy, undetermined, everyday nature of workplace resistance," particularly for those employed outside the industrial sector, like domestic workers.[8] However, such work, centered on public life, has occasionally overlooked the household and the internal domestic sphere, as well as the interconnection of the social and the political at the level of the everyday.

Carol Stack, responding to the concept of the culture of poverty, which locates the supposed decay of the Black family in conditions associated with slum life, recorded the extended cooperative networks that impoverished African American households in a marginalized Midwestern urban community (referred to as "the Flats" in her work) used to survive in situations of "severe economic deprivation."[9] To understand both the kin- and non-kin-based connections through which individuals shared goods and resources, Stack had to reconceptualize the family unit itself, moving away from a definition based on a simple nuclear organization of father, mother, and child. Stack concluded that "the family network is diffused over several kin-based households, and fluctuations in household composition do not significantly affect cooperative familial arrangements. . . . An arbitrary imposition of widely held definitions of the family, the nuclear family, or the matrilocal family blocks the way to understanding how people in the Flats describe and order the world in which they live."[10] Rather than treating urban African American communities as monolithic and comparing them against a homogeneous middle-class ideal, work like that of Stack's suggests that researchers should be careful to recognize social forms and practices that may not correspond to dominant modes or norms but that are just as essential for the survival and cohesion of those communities.

Following Stack, my emphasis is not on the ways that residents of supposed slums aspired to middle-class norms but on the ways that they also subverted them. Racial hierarchy was both implicit and explicit in the ideology that suffused mass-produced consumer culture, and thus material goods, as static markers, constantly seem to reproduce this hierarchy, even as they give some indication of residents' endeavors to improve their material conditions. However, this does not mean that middle-class values were hegemonic, or that slum residents accepted them without question. To treat them as such distorts perceptions of social life in working-class and racially and/or ethnically mixed neighborhoods, valorizing a norm that was the essential claim of the privilege of whiteness itself.

Slum Clearance Beginnings: St. Thomas and Magnolia

The new buildings constructed at sites like St. Thomas, Magnolia, Lafitte, and Iberville were meant to be orderly, low-density units, intended to open the densely developed city squares of the old neighborhoods. Through their architectural form, they also reproduced the middle-class vision of productive domesticity, anchored by an idealized American family: a single, nuclear unit, headed by a man who was employed outside the home, its household needs tended by a woman working within it. Each family would have its own amenities, so that there would be no need to share toilets, bathing facilities, kitchens, bedrooms, or storage. Such a lifestyle would inculcate middle-class values of private ownership, separated work and leisure spheres, patriarchy, and self-reliance, inaugurating "a new way of living" defined by "constructive activity" for families in the projects.[11] The informal networks on which the urban poor had relied to get by—people doing piecework within the home, women working without, extended families pooling resources, households adopting roomers and lodgers for additional income—would no longer be necessary. Many prospective residents were enthusiastic about the opportunity to move into the less crowded, modernized atmosphere of the projects in their early years. It is an irony (and a seeming contradiction) of this era of public housing that access to it was restricted to only those who already outwardly conformed to these norms; interviews separated out the working, upwardly mobile poor and excluded the supposed undeserving and undesirable, reifying a dichotomy that urban reformers had perpetuated since the nineteenth century.[12]

According to census records and other forms of documentary evidence, the St. Thomas neighborhood, prior to clearance, had become an area that was ethnically and racially heterogeneous. While many occupations were represented among its residents, most were part of what would be considered the city's working class, with employment in shipping (both by river and by rail) particularly well represented. Historical accounts of the working class on the riverfront point to both conflict and cooperation. Biracial unions coalesced around workers' issues, but they were also constantly undermined by the divisive influence of business owners, who readily employed racialized ideologies of white supremacy to disrupt common action. Narratives of labor in New Orleans frequently stop during the first decades of the twentieth century, a nadir of race relations in American history, with the abortive attempts at cross-racial solidarity in the city lost and never regained. The material record, however, points to a more complex picture of life and labor in the St. Thomas neighborhood. Black and white residents of the area developed similar strategies for coping with the contingencies of working-class life. Women of both races entered the workforce in large numbers, and substantial numbers of families adopted home piecework as a mechanism of supplementing income. While most households were enmeshed in the market networks of the city, they also apparently adopted informal modes of exchange, developing similar household aesthetics and patterns of consumption, utilizing comparable varieties of ceramic wares, and negotiating the marketplace by buying from a diverse array of consumer products. Based on the heterogeneity of assemblages and the significant lags between manufacture and deposition dates for material recovered archaeologically, many household goods were likely obtained used, through informal exchanges, at secondhand and junk shops, and as hand-me-downs and heirlooms. Finally, in this heterogeneous social environment, residents played with the material markers of ethnicity, drawing freely on consumer products that variously emphasized German, Irish, French, English, and native-born backgrounds. Together, these elements of shared experience provided a potential grounding for a subject position that threatened the racial and class order of the city. The construction of St. Thomas would efface this social heterogeneity in favor of a narrative that focused on the area as exclusively a site of conflict, pitting a mythically white Irish Channel against the encroachment of racial others; perhaps the double irony here is that the story of American immigration is also that of how successive groups like the Irish became white themselves.[13]

The situation with Belmont/Magnolia is in some ways more complex. The area, like Seneca Village in New York, initially appears to have attracted residents because of its environmentally marginal location. Situated in marshy land off of the natural levee, it provided opportunities for land ownership and self-sufficiency for the urban poor. After emancipation it also provided a refuge for former rural Black populations, who moved to the city in large numbers during an era of dislocation and displacement. Shortages of housing for African American migrants were exacerbated by discriminatory policies elsewhere in the city, and the density of development within Belmont/Magnolia was multiplied, sometimes exponentially. Housing lots were subdivided in ways never quite intended, and small homes were further subdivided into tiny rental units, creating a situation in which the integrity of the gridded layout of the city began to break down. Over time, as residential segregation took hold, the neighborhood became increasingly identified with an African American population relegated to the service sector, located in a belt that shadowed more affluent white neighborhoods closer to the river.

The historical record can be read as overtly consistent with the classic narrative of the formation of what was termed a slum: squalid and overcrowded, a danger both to health and to moral sensibilities, with property owners exploiting the needs of the impoverished and the marginalized. As the residential opportunities for African Americans in other parts of the city decreased, absentee landlords in areas like Belmont were able to charge higher and higher rents for less and less living space, and individual households often still took in extended family members and roomers to make ends meet. Such densely developed areas were neglected by city services, and the resulting problems in sanitation and health were blamed on residents, interpreted by racist ideologues as signs of the interlinkage of biological and moral failings. The spending practices of the urban poor also entered into slum discourses, with wastefulness and profligacy seen by reformers and authorities as evinced in the reliance on credit purchases. Even as Black Americans attempted to demonstrate their equality through their purchasing power in the marketplace, they were stigmatized as wasteful, their lack of thrift character-

ized within the racialized system of Jim Crow as evidence of inherent infe-
riority.[14] In this narrative, locked into a cycle of poverty in the most deteriorated, isolated parts of the urban environment, confined to the most menial
of jobs, urban African American poor would naturally experience the social
disorganization long discursively associated with slum life. The material record, in a surface sense, would appear to fit with this reading, with consumers
in the Belmont neighborhood attempting to assert their respectability and ad-
herence to middle-class values through patterns of conspicuous material consumption, expressed through, for example, the use of stylish porcelain tablewares, even as it allowed them to be attacked for their vanity and extravagance.

This interpretation follows the trend already mentioned of seeing consumption as a meaningful practice, one in which a sense of self is created through
the world of objects. Unfortunately, in an era of mass production and mass
consumption, the terms of this meaning seem to be set by the very materiality of consumer goods, with liberatory self-consciousness defined by the as-
piration to consume as an equal within the marketplace, itself a product of a
dominant class-based system. Seen through the mask of ideologies of Victorian domesticity and respectability, practically any collection of mass-produced
goods looks like evidence of striving for that very respectability. Many productive archaeological analyses of working-class neighborhoods have examined household assemblages precisely in terms of how they contest stereo-
typical images of slums, instead showing that residents ascribed to the same
core values as their middle-class neighbors. If that is the case, other aspects
of identity are more likely to impact the distinctive aspects of individual assemblages. For instance, at late nineteenth- and early twentieth-century sites
investigated in San Francisco and West Oakland, California, although some
broad correlation existed between a household's wealth and the occurrence of
expensive and high-status ceramic wares like porcelain, points of divergence
also existed, as in the tendency for unskilled households, the lowest end of
the socioeconomic spectrum, to invest more in serving wares. Likewise, any
individual household could deviate from this pattern based on the personal
histories or attributes of its residents, and the analyst must try to understand
how the multiple vectors of race, gender, class, profession, ethnicity, religion,
and individual biography are responsible for the observed material.[15]

Such diversity characterizes the assemblages here, where many different
contextual factors influence the distribution of artifacts within individual assemblages. Table 7.1 shows a comparison of ware types among some assemblages discussed in this volume. Some points of similarity do emerge. For
instance, the high proportions of porcelain already noted in the Magnolia assemblages are also found in the brothel-related privies in the Iberville area,
despite differing dates of deposition among them. Other distinctive attributes

Table 7.1. Comparisons of Ware Types from Assemblages at St. Thomas, Magnolia, Lafitte, and Iberville

Project Area	St. Thomas				Magnolia	
	ca. 1890s wood-lined privy		ca. 1920s brick-lined privy		ca. 1910 trash pit	
Context	Vessel count by MNI	Proportion (%)	Vessel count by MNI	Proportion (%)	Vessel count by MNI	Proportion (%)
brownware	0	0	4	4	3	7
brown/gray stoneware	1	3.5	4	4	2	4
ironstone	17	59	64	66	18	41
porcelain (incl. soft-paste)	3	10	4	4	15	34
porcelaneous stoneware	1	3.5	5	5	1	2
whiteware	1	3.5	2	2	1	2
yellowware (incl. Rockingham)	5	17	13	14	2	5
redware	1	3.5	1	1	2	5
unidentified white-bodied ware	0	0	0	0	0	0
other (English majolica, caneware, Jackfield-type, etc.)	0	0	0	0	0	0

Note: MNI is minimum number of individuals.

of the assemblages become more apparent considered across sites, as in the unusually high number of earthenwares (mostly from flowerpots and storage containers) in the Metoyer assemblage, presumably related to its having been connected to household labor and production. However, with multiple axes of difference that must be accounted for, along with depositional factors (like speed and type of deposition) and broad temporal changes in categories of objects available to consumers, a contextual approach that considers the relationships between multiple categories of objects is essential. While

Table 7.1. *continued*

| Magnolia | | Lafitte | | Iberville | | | |
| ca. 1920 trash pit | | ca. 1914 Metoyer well | | ca. 1890s brothel privy | | ca. 1910 brothel privy | |
Vessel count by MNI	Proportion (%)	Vessel count by MNI	Proportion (%)	Vessel count by MNI	Proportion (%)	Vessel count by MNI	Proportion (%)
5	10	4	9	0	0	0	0
3	6	3	6	1	4	0	0
18	35	7	15	12	46	30	50
11	21	8	17	7	27	16	27
1	2	0	0	0	0	0	0
1	2	11	23	4	15	10	17
4	8	5	11	2	8	2	3
5	10	7	15	0	0	2	3
0	0	2	4	0	0	0	0
3	6	0	0	0	0	0	0

an ever-increasing body of data is becoming available for comparison in the period between emancipation and World War II in New Orleans, a truly exhaustive project of comparison must wait for the systematizing of those data so that some of the previously noted variables can be controlled.[16]

Studies of African American and working-class consumption within the United States have confronted the multiple meanings of objects for consumers by attempting to isolate the variables responsible for the patterning of object assemblages at a broad scale even while acknowledging individual agency at the household level. W. E. B. Du Bois's idea of double-consciousness has been adopted elsewhere in reference to African American consumption in the postemancipation era, and it is particularly relevant for a more nuanced interpretation of the assemblages from Belmont/Magnolia.[17] Whereas the prevalence of, for instance, porcelain tablewares in the earliest assemblages on-site may be related to the attempts by those on the margins of the city to assert their respectability and equality, these meanings shifted (and doubled) as Belmont became closely developed and crowded. The extravagance for which such consumer purchases were criticized was mobilized into an oppositional aesthetic that asserted an independent identity, one initially mirroring that maintained in the social world of the Jim Crow city. The preference for gilded decoration along with the large assemblages of clothing-related artifacts, particularly large quantities of shoes and shoe leather, may suggest parallels with Monica Miller's account of Black dandyism as a particular form of identity that utilized cultural hybridity to gain status, even while negotiating racial oppression through its ambiguity.[18] However, in the case of the Belmont assemblages, these choices were overt, pointed in their challenge to white supremacy. Severed more than ever from access to the tools of production, forced to find employment within the households and businesses of the dominant white society, residents of Belmont developed a shared ethos reflected in similar strategies of consumption and the use of space. Moreover, they developed an awareness of the capacity of the urban environment for maintaining anonymity and for lending itself to obscurity and concealment. Even while working in plain view of their racial oppressors, Black residents of Belmont countenanced a subjectivity that was separate and asserted on its own terms rather than those of the dominant society. This, then, was what made Belmont such a danger. Ironically, by the time that the Magnolia Housing Project was redeveloped beginning in 2007, the same could be said for it.

The significance of marginal areas like Belmont goes beyond the formation of such dual subjectivities. To understand why reformers and city authorities identified Belmont/Magnolia as such a problem, the neighborhood's built environment, the archaeological record, and the modes of subject action for area residents must be considered together. The peripherality of the urban fringe initially fell into the interstices of control and visibility, and the density of the built landscape of the area eventually made this marginality a problem for governance. Ironically, it was an environment created in part by the predatory exploitation of consumers' vulnerability in a system of segregated housing. Courts and alleys formed within blocks, many of them developing their own names and identities; these names and identities in turn became a form of local knowledge that was opaque to governance and administration. Economic structures revolved around alternative sites as well, like lottery houses, social clubs, and informal businesses, which also developed their own sets of spatial and material practices. Historian Robin D. G. Kelley has argued that unregulated social sites in Black neighborhoods became places where attitudes of resistance, hidden transcripts of opposition, could be articulated, and the opacity of a space like Belmont suffused the entire neighborhood, and the entire social body, with this possibility.[19]

Slum Clearance Multiplied: Lafitte, Iberville, and Beyond

St. Thomas and Magnolia were the first housing projects to be opened, and others soon followed. The segregated Iberville and Lafitte Housing Projects also erased problematic areas from the landscape. The Black-only Lafitte Project was built paralleling the location of the old Carondelet Canal, which had been an important commercial locus for New Orleans's antebellum community of free people of color, many of whom had been employed in skilled building and craft trades. Their descendants, who came to be identified as Creoles of Color, formed a ready-made African American upper class after emancipation. In the Lafitte area, their association with material affluence proved too contradictory to the racial hierarchy of Jim Crow, particularly when poor, white immigrants appeared to occupy the lowest rungs of the class structure in the area. Class, gender, *and* color were all complicated things at Lafitte, and, as often as not, none mapped neatly onto the dominant ideological conception of how a "normal" family or neighborhood should be structured. The Metoyer family is one such case, as part of a long line of mixed and racially ambiguous unions, where a woman wielded social and spiritual power in an occupation that was gradually being marginalized in the larger society. It is a particularly cogent example of one of hundreds of microhistories that could be written about those in the area before and after clearance.

In the case of the neighborhood that the white-only Iberville Project replaced, the situation was somewhat different, as the project almost exactly matched the boundaries of Storyville, the city's semilegal prostitution district from 1898 until 1917. At the time that Storyville was established, the area was fairly racially integrated, something that was a concern of Victorian reformers, who tried to also establish a segregated red-light district for Black clientele nearby. After Storyville was closed, it seems to have left a lingering effect on the neighborhood, with respectable New Orleans essentially abandoning the area. Perhaps this disregard was meant to conceal just how closely interwoven the district had been economically with those same respectable elements of the city, but material conditions in the neighborhood appear to have declined considerably, presumably a consequence of abandonment by city services. It also became primarily an African American residential space.

The near-complete razing of Storyville was necessary to reclaim the area as white, a project of reclamation that would be abandoned when Iberville was integrated in the 1960s. Some would say that it has been taken up yet again in post-Katrina redevelopments of the area.

As noted by Daphne Spain, the construction of public housing already had undeniably made New Orleans more segregated, but it also did not remedy the lack of affordable, decent housing available to Black residents of the city.[20] It was a problem that was just as acute in other cities, as urban renewal became synonymous with "Negro removal" in the era after World War II (ca. 1949–68). It is estimated that 425,000 units housing poor and minority populations were demolished in this period, replaced by the construction of only 125,000 new units, at least half of those apartments intended for the more affluent.[21] Public housing and urban renewal were almost inevitably twinned with a slum clearance that targeted African American or racially mixed communities without sufficient provisions for the populations affected. The individual trajectories of the process were often distinct. In Houston, Texas, Freedmen's Town, established by the formerly enslaved after emancipation, became an economic hub for the city's growing Black population. It was targeted by a series of redevelopment projects beginning in the 1930s, including the construction of San Felipe Courts (later known as Allen Parkway Village), a white-only housing project, on land seized through eminent domain. This neighborhood would be targeted again and again over the next decades, and now it is threatened by gentrification. In Atlanta, Georgia, as early as 1935, the white-only Techwood Homes housing project replaced the mixed-race Techwood Flats slum on valuable downtown property adjacent to the Georgia Institute of Technology, spurred on by local business interests. It is a story that was repeated over and over across the United States, with largely the same result: a more segregated city. It is an irony that the archaeological remains of the neighborhoods replaced by public housing decades ago are actually better protected through the provisions of the NHPA than urban housing itself is or ever was.[22]

In a study of the urban housing problem in New Orleans during the 1950s, Forrest LaViolette and Joseph Taylor identified racially mixed blocks as still the fundamental issue informing housing policy in the city, mainly because of the uncertainty that they created about market rates and values for potential buyers and sellers.[23] The racially mixed block was compared unfavorably in this respect with both the private, segregated subdivision and the racially homogeneous housing project, and the best solution to shortages of housing was seen in the controlled development of exclusively Black neighborhoods at the fringes of the city. Such neighborhoods, like Pontchartrain Park, an upper middle-class African American residential enclave constructed around a golf course (itself supposedly built to avoid desegregating white-only courses in the 1950s), were a contrast to the ongoing uncontrolled auto-construction at the urban margins, described thusly by LaViolette and Taylor: "One can see in the houses themselves that individual home seekers have shown great fortitude and initiative and persistence in their quest for housing. Most generally, they have found a piece of land which they would purchase, usually in an undeveloped area, and proceeded to build or have built a home. Unfortunately, the city has been too lenient, if not negligent, in not insisting that the housing be standard. Consequently, though numerous such dwellings have been built since 1950, many of them are woefully below standard. One large area below the Industrial Canal abounds in homes of this type and quickly took on the appearance of a slum area."[24] The fact that the Lower Ninth Ward, that "large area below the Industrial Canal" mentioned by LaViolette and Taylor, and low-lying peripheral areas like it (particularly New Orleans East) represented the best opportunities for African American home ownership was not lost on real estate speculators. Capitalizing on the improved economic circumstances of some Black families in the years after World War II, especially those of veterans, developers drained such areas, connected them to city services, and subdivided them into small lots for sale to first-time home buyers. Development in the Lower Ninth Ward would also be accelerated by expropriations of other Black residences and properties, something that would be largely forgotten by those outside the neighborhood after Hurricane Katrina.[25]

Soon, public housing also became an unsatisfactory solution to the problem of housing the urban African American poor. After World War II, existing projects were expanded, and enormous new projects were opened in isolated and peripheral areas of New Orleans. The Desire Housing Project, for instance, was opened in 1956. Almost from its beginning, it was considered a failure in all of the goals of public housing except for the provision of basic shelter. Shoddily and rapidly built over a dump in an almost inaccessible part of the city, it housed as many as fourteen thousand residents by 1957, despite its undesirability.[26] As the projects became larger in scale, they became sources of potential disorder themselves: difficult to police and govern, associated by authorities with lawlessness and resistance, opaque to outsiders. But as they were neglected and abandoned by city services, they became sources of local identity and local pride, many developing distinctive nicknames and reputations. Desire became a stronghold of the local Black Panther movement in the 1960s, and the projects became focal points of activism (from both within and without) and of community organization.[27] Developments in social welfare policies that had been meant to aid the poor contributed to a new ethos of public housing after World War II as well. New Deal programs had been unequally applied at the local level since their inception, but particularly in the South, those who were found to violate social norms by lacking morals or having a nontraditional family life were removed from the public aid rolls. Black women in particular were targeted, and as a result found themselves pressured into low-wage service work.[28]

After the integration of public housing in the 1960s, housing projects rapidly became almost exclusively Black space in urban areas like New Orleans. The process by which this happened has been argued to be distinct from any formal policy on the part of HANO; for instance, Martha Mahoney, in her study of public housing in New Orleans, states outright that "There was a wall surrounding these projects. It was not of the Housing Authority's making."[29] Michael E. Crutcher Jr., in a recent work on the Tremé area of New Orleans, has illustrated that despite the reputation of New Orleans as largely spared from large-scale post-war urban renewal, significant examples of the sorts of widespread demolitions associated with urban renewal did take place, among them the construction of the elevated interstate highway hub that followed the route of Claiborne Avenue (discussed in chapter 5) and the clearance of land that would become Armstrong Park and its associated cultural center.[30] Such smaller-scale impositions in the name of urban renewal also adopted slum discourse to frame their efforts. Local planners Michael P. Smith and Marlene Keller, for instance, suggested that demolition of a residential gray area to make way for the new civic center associated with Armstrong Park had "successfully exorcized a wretched slum."[31] As in many other American cities, such interventions disproportionately affected poor and Black residents and thus had profound consequences for the subsequent history of the affected neighborhoods. However, slum clearance as a component of urban renewal was distinct from its function as an aspect of public housing, in which it was meant to also act in a productive capacity at the level of the individual family or household.

The contemporary narrative of the relationship of race, class, and space in New Orleans is inextricably accented by the events and systemic failures triggered by the landfall of Hurricane Katrina in August 2005. After more than a decade, the decision by HUD and HANO to replace almost all the projects with private mixed-income developments is still contentious, even if it is all but accomplished. While the administrators of some new developments took considerable pains to reach out to resident councils, these efforts were hampered by the dispersal of the population after Hurricane Katrina. Those without the resources to come back to the city were excluded from decision-making, and many were integrated into the social welfare systems of other cities. Those who did return, reliant on the informal networks developed as coping mechanisms during displacement, sometimes found themselves categorically excluded from the new normal represented by the private mixed-income developments, which still imposed strict conditions on those residents receiving subsidized housing. An answer to the frequently asked question of "Can I have overnight guests?" from the website for the Columbia Parc Redevelopment (which replaced the St. Bernard Housing Project) hints at some of the same suspicions about the intent of the developments: "Yes, you can have guests. You can also have overnight guests up to 14 days annually. Remember that each resident is responsible for the conduct and actions of their guests. Therefore, it is your responsibility to explain the property's rules and regulations to your guests. Anyone that stays longer than 14 days is considered an occupant and this person needs to be added to your lease agreement."[32] While the website makes clear that former public housing residents are welcome to apply for housing, they also must submit to a criminal background check, be employed, and—in order to not be wait-listed, at least as of 2013—have submitted the appropriate form between July 1 and July 24, 2009. Such conditions in the rules for subsidized low-income housing are common; public housing in all eras has been marked by a concern with managerial control over the everyday lives of residents, from regulations about pets, paint colors, and the storage of "luxury" items like bikes, to plans that provided for small master bedrooms to discourage cosleeping.[33] These conditions are yet another example of how architectural forms, social lives, and everyday materialities are linked to an imposed vision of middle-class normalcy in the urban setting. When further linked to a racial hierarchy that equates this norm with whiteness and its privileges, it has deep implications for considerations of equity in access to housing, ignoring the historical trajectories that structure the form of the city and making those forms appear timeless and unquestionable.

These implications were certainly apparent in the discourse surrounding rebuilding in New Orleans after Hurricane Katrina. The power relationships through which poor, predominantly African American residents came to occupy marginal low-lying land and the processes by which the city sustained a segregated service industry working class at a near-poverty level were not interrogated in themselves. Rather, they were treated as the result of a series of rational choices, with the implication that decisions about rebuilding should operate on a similar risk/reward calculus.[34] In critically examining the context of avowedly benevolent attempts at slum clearance in the first half of the twentieth century, we may provide a counterpoint to this discourse and a genealogy of how it came to be. Slum clearance emerged as a disciplinary technique by which the spatial environment was transformed with the intent to instantiate a two-tiered racial order at the level of the everyday, curtailing possibilities for collective action and rendering the social lives of the urban poor as pathological. An archaeology of those urban neighborhoods identified as

slums may confront the conditions of urban poverty, and of the marginalization and exclusion that accompany it, even as this archaeology helps show alternative strategies of subjectivity and citizenship in those spaces. Narratives
of urban development are all too prone to reproduce a vision of the normal
that is itself a construct of a dominant discourse defined by race and class hierarchy. These narratives materialize those shadows and ghosts, giving them
form and substance. Archaeology may not be able to exorcise those ghosts
alone, but hopefully it can help us imagine different pasts and, ultimately,
different futures.

Notes

Chapter 1

1. Bring New Orleans Back Commission, "Urban Planning Committee: Action Plan for New Orleans: Executive Summary," January 30, 2006, 3. The documents from the Bring New Orleans Back Commission are no longer available through its website but are archived at the website of Columbia University, accessed October 2018, http://www.columbia.edu/itc/journalism/cases/katrina/city_of_new_orleans_bnobc.html.

2. Jedidiah Horne and Brendan Nee, "An Overview of Post-Katrina Planning in New Orleans" (paper, Department of City and Regional Planning, University of California, Berkeley, 2006), http://www.nolaplans.com/research. This website, organized by Horne and Nee, also has many of the post-Katrina rebuilding plans archived. See also Julia Cass and Peter Whoriskey, "New Orleans to Raze Public Housing," *Washington Post*, December 8, 2006; Leslie Eaton, "In New Orleans, Plan to Raze Low-Income Housing Draws Protest," *New York Times*, December 14, 2007; Megan French-Marcelin, "Gentrification's Ground Zero," *Jacobin Magazine*, August 28, 2015, https://www.jacobinmag.com/2015/08/katrina-new-orleans-arne-duncan-charters/; Nora Goddard, "The Destruction of Public Housing in New Orleans," Nola Tour Guy (blog), November 27, 2012, http://www.nolatourguy.com/public-housing/; Roberta Brandes Gratz, "Who Killed Public Housing in New Orleans?" *Nation*, June 2, 2015; and Susan Saulny, "Clamoring to Come Home to New Orleans Projects," *New York Times*, June 6, 2006.

3. Susan J. Popkin et al., *A Decade of HOPE VI: Research Findings and Policy Challenges* (Washington, DC: Urban Institute and Brookings Institution, 2004); and Brod Bagert Jr., "HOPE VI and St. Thomas: Smoke, Mirrors and Urban Mercantilism" (master's thesis, London School of Economics, 2002); cf. Simon Parker, *Urban Theory and the Urban Experience: Encountering the City* (London: Routledge, 2004).

4. Orissa Arend, *Showdown in Desire: The Black Panthers Take a Stand in New Orleans* (Little Rock: University of Arkansas Press, 2009); Kent Germany, *New Orleans after the Promises: Poverty, Citizenship, and the Search for the Great Society* (Athens: University of Georgia Press, 2007); and Rachel Breunlin and Helen A. Regis, "Putting the Ninth Ward on the Map: Race, Place, and Transformation in Desire, New Orleans," *American Anthropologist* 108, no. 4 (2006): 744–64.

5. See, for instance, Constance L. Hays, "For Wal-Mart, New Orleans Is Hardly the Big Easy," *New York Times*, April 27, 2003; Beverly McKenna, "Gentrification Comes to New Orleans," *New Orleans Tribune*, October 2002; C. C. Campbell-Rock, "Hope VI Offers No Hope to Former St. Thomas Residents," *New Orleans Tribune*, October 2002; "St. Thomas Redesign: Super Wal-Mart Brings Economic Hope to New Orleans," *New Orleans Data News Weekly*, October 13, 2001; and Bruce Eggler, "Residents Break Off Talks with Developer," *Times-Picayune*, September 5, 2001.

6. See James Elliott, Kevin Fox Gotham, and Melinda Milligan, "Framing the Urban: Struggles over HOPE VI and New Urbanism in a Historic City," *City and Community* 3, no. 4 (2004): 373–99; and Doug MacCash, "New Orleans: New Urbanism?," *Seattle Times* November 16, 2005; cf. Pete Katz, *The New Urbanism: Toward an Architecture of Community* (New York: McGraw-Hill, 1994). In 2014, Nagin would be convicted of a number of charges related to bribery and sentenced to ten years in prison.

7. Martha Mahoney, "The Changing Nature of Public Housing in New Orleans, 1930–1974" (master's thesis, Tulane University, 1985); and Tulane School of Social Work, "A Housing Study of the Flint-Goodridge Hospital Area" (manuscript on file, Louisiana Collection, Tulane University, New Orleans, 1934).

8. Mahoney, "The Changing Nature of Public Housing," 33.

9. Housing Authority of New Orleans, *Report of the Housing Authority of New Orleans*, 1938 and 1939 vols. (New Orleans: HANO, 1938–39).

10. David Ward, *Poverty, Ethnicity, and the American City, 1840–1925: Changing Conceptions of the Slum and the Ghetto* (New York: Cambridge University Press, 1989), 13–45.

11. Paul Boyer, *Urban Masses and Moral Order in America, 1820–1920* (Cambridge, MA: Harvard University Press, 1978). See also Mel Scott, *American City Planning since 1890* (Berkeley: University of California Press, 1995).

12. For a good overview of the development of urban archaeology in the United States, see Nan Rothschild and Diana diZerega Wall, *The Archaeology of American Cities* (Gainesville: University Press of Florida, 2014).

13. J. Richard Shenkel, *Oak Island Archaeology: Prehistoric Estuarine Adaptations in the Mississippi River Delta* (report on file, Louisiana Division of Archaeology, Baton Rouge, 1981); Shenkel, *The Archaeology of Madame John's Legacy* (report on file, University of New Orleans, Department of Anthropology, 1971); Shenkel, *Archaeological Investigations at the Hermann-Grima House* (report submitted to the Christian Women's Exchange and the Louisiana Division of Archaeology, 1977); and Teresia R. Lamb and Richard C. Beavers, *Archaeology of the Stableyard Complex, Hermann-Grima House, New Orleans, Louisiana* (report submitted to the Christian Women's Exchange and the Louisiana Division of Archaeology, 1983).

14. George J. Castille et al., *Urban Archaeology in Old New Orleans: Historical and Archaeological Investigations within the Greater New Orleans Bridge No. 2 Right-of-Way* (report prepared for the Louisiana Department of Transportation and Development, 1986); and Castille et al., *Archaeological Excavations at Esplanade Avenue and North Rampart Street, New Orleans, Louisiana* (report submitted to the National Park Service, Southwest Region, Santa Fe, 1982); cf. J. Richard Shenkel, Robert Sauder, and E. R. Chatelain, *Archaeology of the Jazz Complex and Beauregard (Congo) Square, Louis Armstrong Park, New Orleans, Louisiana* (report submitted to the City of New Orleans, 1980).

15. R. Christopher Goodwin et al., *New Orleans Is Looking Forward to Its Past* (report submitted to the Louisiana Division of Archaeology, Baton Rouge, 1987); and Jill-Karen Yakubik, "Ceramic Use in Late-Eighteenth-Century and Early-Nineteenth-Century Southeastern Louisiana" (PhD diss., Tulane University, 1990).

16. Shannon Lee Dawdy, *Madame John's Legacy (16OR51) Revisited: A Closer Look at the Archaeology of Colonial New Orleans* (report submitted to Friends of the Cabildo and Louisiana Division of Archaeology, 1996); Shannon Lee Dawdy and Juana Ibáñez, *Beneath the Surface of New Orleans' Warehouse District: Archaeological Investigations at the Maginnis Cotton Mill Site (16OR144)* (report submitted to Cotton Mill Limited Partnership and Historic Restoration, 1997); and Christopher N. Matthews, *Management Report of Excavations at the St. Augustine Site (16OR148)* (report submitted to the Louisiana Division of Archaeology, 1999). Dawdy, now at the University of Chicago, continues to maintain an active research presence in the city.

17. "Bone, Artifact Finds Raise Call for Dig," *Times-Picayune*, June 5, 1999.

18. Lyle Saxon, Edward Dreyer, and Robert Tallant, *Gumbo Ya-Ya: A Collection of Louisiana Folk Tales* (Boston: Houghton Mifflin, 1987), 50–74.

19. John Arena, *Driven from New Orleans: How Nonprofits Betray Public Housing and Promote Privatization* (Minneapolis: University of Minnesota Press, 2012).

20. Rick Fifield and Judy Bethea, *Investigation of St. Thomas Project Area Prior to Construction of LA-1* (report prepared for Historic Restoration, Inc., New Orleans, 1999); and Benjamin Maygarden, *Historical Background and Development Overview for the St. Thomas Housing Project Area* (manuscript on file, Earth Search, Inc., New Orleans, 2001).

21. See D. Ryan Gray, "Incorrigible Vagabonds and Suspicious Spaces in Nineteenth-Century New Orleans," *Historical Archaeology* 45, no. 3 (2011): 55–73; E. Arnesen, *Waterfront Workers of New Orleans: Race, Class, and Politics, 1863–1923* (New York: Oxford University Press, 1994); Daniel Rosenberg, *New Orleans Dockworkers: Race, Labor, and Unionism, 1892–1923* (Albany: State University of New York Press, 1988); Alan Mayne, *The Imagined Slum: Newspaper Representation in Three Cities, 1870–1914* (Leicester, UK: Leicester University Press, 1993); and Alan Mayne and Tim Murray, eds., *The Archaeology of Urban Landscapes: Explorations in Slumland* (Cambridge: Cambridge University Press, 2001).

22. Michel Foucault, *The Order of Things: An Archaeology of the Human Sciences* (New York: Vintage Books, 1970); Foucault, *The Archaeology of Knowledge* (New York: Pantheon Books, 1972); and Foucault, *Discipline and Punish: The Birth of the Prison* (New York: Vintage Books, 1977).

23. João Biehl, Byron Good, and Arthur Kleinman, "Introduction: Rethinking Subjectivity," in *Subjectivity: Ethnographic Investigations*, ed. João Biehl, Byron Good, and Arthur Kleinman (Berkeley: University of California Press, 2007), 13.

24. James C. Scott, *Seeing like a State: How Certain Schemes to Improve the Human Condition Have Failed* (New Haven, CT: Yale University Press, 1998); cf. James Holston, *Insurgent Citizenship: Disjunctions of Democracy and Modernity in Brazil* (Princeton, NJ: Princeton University Press, 2008); and Uğur Ümit Üngör, "Creative Destruction," *Journal of Urban History* 39, no. 2 (2013): 297–314.

25. Loïc Wacquant, *Urban Outcasts: A Comparative Sociology of Advanced Marginality* (Cambridge: Polity, 2008); cf. Gilbert Osofsky, *Harlem: The Making of a Ghetto* (New York: Harper and Row, 1968); Arnold R. Hirsch, *Making the Second Ghetto: Race and Housing in Chicago, 1940–1960* (New York: Cambridge University Press,

1983); Douglas Massey and Nancy Denton, *American Apartheid: Segregation and the Making of the Underclass* (Cambridge, MA: Harvard University Press, 1987); and Michelle Alexander, *The New Jim Crow: Mass Incarceration in the Age of Colorblindness* (New York: New Press, 2010).

26. Foucault, *Discipline and Punish*; cf. Timothy Mitchell, *Colonising Egypt* (Los Angeles: University of California Press, 1991); and Paul Rabinow, *French Modern: Norms and Forms of the Social Environment* (Cambridge: MIT Press, 1989).

27. Wacquant, *Urban Outcasts*, 229–56.

Chapter 2

1. "Bomb Negro Apartments in White Neighborhood," *Negro Star* (Wichita, KS), February 17, 1939; "Bombing on Short Street," *Louisiana Weekly*, February 11, 1939.

2. Arnold R. Hirsch, *Making the Second Ghetto: Race and Housing in Chicago, 1940–1960* (New York: Cambridge University Press, 1983), 40–99; and Peirce F. Lewis, *New Orleans: The Making of an Urban Landscape*, 2nd ed. (Santa Fe, NM: Center for American Places, 2003), 50–52; cf. Virginia R. Domínguez, *White by Definition: Social Classification in Creole Louisiana* (New Brunswick, NJ: Rutgers University Press, 1994); Shirley Elizabeth Thompson, *Exiles at Home: The Struggle to Become American in Creole New Orleans* (Cambridge, MA: Harvard University Press, 2009); and Joseph Logsdon and Carolyn C. Bell, "The Americanization of Black New Orleans, 1850–1900," in *Creole New Orleans: Race and Americanization*, ed. Arnold R. Hirsch and Joseph Logsdon (Baton Rouge: Louisiana State University Press, 1992).

3. Pierre Bourdieu, *Outline of a Theory of Practice* (Cambridge: Cambridge University Press, 1995), 72.

4. Donald E. Hall, *Subjectivity: The New Critical Idiom* (London: Routledge, 2004), 1–16.

5. Louis Althusser, *Lenin and Philosophy, and Other Essays* (New York: Monthly Review Press, 1971), 170–77; Michel Foucault, *The History of Sexuality* (New York: Pantheon Books, 1978), 92–98; cf. Foucault, *The Order of Things: An Archaeology of the Human Sciences* (New York, Vintage Books, 1970); Foucault, *The Archaeology of Knowledge* (New York: Pantheon Books, 1972); and Foucault, *Discipline and Punish: The Birth of the Prison* (New York: Vintage Books, 1977). Foucault explicitly operationalizes his approach to institutions in works like "On Governmentality," *Ideology and Consciousness* 6 (1979): 5–21; for examples of applications, see Paul Rabinow, *French Modern: Norms and Forms of the Social Environment* (Cambridge: MIT Press, 1989); James Ferguson, *The Anti-Politics Machine: "Development," Depoliticization, and Bureaucratic Power in Lesotho* (Minneapolis: University of Minnesota Press, 1994); Donald Moore, *Suffering for Territory: Race, Place, and Power in Zimbabwe* (Durham, NC: Duke University Press, 2005), 21; and William Cunningham Bissell, *Urban Design, Chaos, and Colonial Power in Zanzibar* (Bloomington: Indiana University Press, 2010).

6. Antonio Gramsci, *Selections from the Prison Notebooks of Antonio Gramsci* (New York: International, 1971), 5–14; and Bourdieu, *Outline of a Theory of Practice*, 78, 169. Some examples that utilize Gramsci's distinction between hegemony and ideology in archaeology can be found in Mary C. Beaudry, Lauren J. Cook, and Stephen A. Mrozowski, "Artifacts and Active Voices: Material Culture as Social Discourse," in *The Archaeology of Inequality*, ed. Randall McGuire and Robert Paynter (Oxford:

Blackwell, 1991), 150–91; Timothy R. Pauketat, "A New Tradition in Archaeology," in *The Archaeology of Traditions*, ed. Timothy R. Pauketat (Gainesville: University Press of Florida, 1991), 1–16; Adrian Praetzellis and Mary Praetzellis, "Faces and Facades: Victorian Ideology in Early Sacramento," in *The Art and Mystery of Historical Archaeology: Essays in Honor of James Deetz*, ed. Anne Yentsch and Mary Beaudry (Boca Raton, FL: CRC Press, 1992), 75–100; Donald V. Kurtz and Mary Christopher Nunley, "Ideology and Work at Teotihuacan: A Hermeneutic Interpretation," *Man* n.s., 28, no. 4 (1993): 761–78; Matthew S. Tomaso, Richard F. Veit, Carissa A. DeRooy, and Stanley L. Walling, "Social Status and Landscape in a Nineteenth-Century Planned Alternative Industrial Community: Archaeology and Geography of Feltville, New Jersey," *Historical Archaeology* 40, no. 1 (2006): 20–36; and Cameron Wesson, *Households and Hegemony: Early Creek Prestige Goods, Symbolic Capital, and Social Power* (Lincoln: University of Nebraska Press, 2008). See also John L. Comaroff and Jean Comaroff, *Ethnography and the Historical Imagination* (Boulder, CO: Westview Press, 1992), 28–29; and Jean Comaroff and John L. Comaroff, *Of Revelation and Revolution*, vol. 1, *Christianity, Colonialism, and the Colonization of Consciousness in South Africa* (Chicago: University of Chicago Press, 1991).

7. Henri Lefebvre, *The Production of Space* (Oxford: Blackwell, 1991), 33, 63, 182–83; Edward W. Soja, *Thirdspace: Journeys to Los Angeles and Other Real-and-Imagined Places* (Cambridge, MA: Blackwell, 1996), 66–70; David Harvey, *The Urban Experience* (Baltimore: Johns Hopkins University Press, 1989); and Harvey, "The Political Economy of Public Space," in *The Politics of Public Space*, ed. Setha Low and Neil Smith (New York: Routledge, 2005), 17–34. See also Soja, *Postmodern Geographies: The Reassertion of Space in Critical Social Theory* (London: Verso, 1989); and Rob Shields, *Places on the Margin: Alternative Geographies of Modernity* (London: Routledge, 1991).

8. Fran Tonkiss, *Space, the City and Social Theory: Social Relations and Urban Forms* (Cambridge: Polity, 2005), 114. See also Michel de Certeau, *The Practice of Everyday Life* (Berkeley: University of California Press, 1984), 101–30.

9. Akhil Gupta and James Ferguson, "Beyond 'Culture': Space, Identity, and the Politics of Difference," *Cultural Anthropology* 7, no. 1 (1992): 11.

10. James Holston, *Insurgent Citizenship: Disjunctions of Democracy and Modernity in Brazil* (Princeton, NJ: Princeton University Press, 2008); and Neil Smith, "Spaces of Vulnerability: The Space of Flows and the Politics of Scale," *Critique of Anthropology* 16, no. 1 (1996): 63–77.

11. Bernard S. Cohn, "The Census, Social Structure and Objectification in South Asia," in *An Anthropologist among the Historians and Other Essays* (New York: Oxford University Press, 1990), 224–54; Benedict Anderson, *Imagined Communities: Reflections on the Origin and Spread of Nationalism*, rev. ed. (London: Verso, 1991); David I. Kertzer and Dominique Arel, eds., *Census and Identity: The Politics of Race, Ethnicity, and Language in National Census* (Cambridge: Cambridge University Press, 2002); and James C. Scott, John Tehranian, and Jeremy Mathias, "Government Surnames and Legal Identities," in *National Identification Systems: Essays in Opposition*, ed. Carl Watner and Wendy McElroy (Jefferson, NC: McFarland, 2004), 11–54. Of course, much of this work also draws, explicitly or implicitly, on work by Foucault. Rogers Brubaker and Frederick Cooper provide a useful discussion of the primordialist and constructivist approaches to identity and their use in the social sciences; see "Beyond 'Identity,'" *Theory and Society* 29, no. 1 (2000): 1–47. See also Jennifer

L. Hochschild and Brenna M. Powell, "Racial Reorganization in the United States Census 1850–1930: Mulattoes, Half-Breeds, Mixed Parentage, Hindoos, and the Mexican Race," *Studies in American Political Development* 22, no. 1 (2008): 59–96, on the changing uses of racial designations in the US Census.

12. Stephen Mrozowski, "Landscapes of Inequality," In McGuire and Paynter, *The Archaeology of Inequality*, 80; cf. Diane diZerega Wall, *The Archaeology of Gender: Separating the Spheres in Urban America* (New York: Plenum Press, 1999); and Matthew Johnson, *An Archaeology of Capitalism* (Oxford: Blackwell, 1996).

13. Mark P. Leone, *The Archaeology of Liberty in an American Capital: Excavations in Annapolis* (Berkeley: University of California Press, 2005), 67; cf. Leone, "Interpreting Ideology in Historical Archaeology: Using the Rules of Perspective in the William Paca Garden, Annapolis, Maryland," in *Ideology, Power, and Prehistory*, ed. Daniel Miller and Christopher Tilley (Cambridge: Cambridge University Press, 1984), 25–36.

14. Martin Hall, *Archaeology and the Modern World: Colonial Transcripts in South Africa and the Chesapeake* (London: Routledge, 2000), 97.

15. Praetzellis and Praetzellis, "Faces and Facades," 97, 75. Stephen Mrozowski offers a useful summary of approaches to class in historical archaeology; see *The Archaeology of Class in Urban America* (Cambridge: Cambridge University Press, 2006), 1–18.

16. See Alan Mayne and Tim Murray, eds., *The Archaeology of Urban Landscapes: Explorations in Slumland* (Cambridge: Cambridge University Press, 2001), especially the following chapters: John McCarthy, "Values and Identity in the 'Working Class' Worlds of Late Nineteenth-Century Minneapolis," 145–53; and Rebecca Yamin, "Alternative Narratives: Respectability at New York's Five Points," 154–71. See also Yamin, "Wealthy, Free, and Female: Prostitution in Nineteenth-Century New York," *Historical Archaeology* 39, no. 1 (2005): 4–18; and Robert Fitts, "Becoming American: The Archaeology of an Italian Immigrant," *Historical Archaeology* 36, no. 2 (2002): 1–17.

17. Daniel Miller, *Material Culture and Mass Consumption* (Oxford: Basil Blackwell, 1987), 215.

18. Arjun Appadurai, *The Social Life of Things: Commodities in Cultural Perspective* (Cambridge: Cambridge University Press, 1986), 9–15, 31.

19. Charles E. Orser Jr., *Race and Practice in Archaeological Interpretation* (Philadelphia: University of Pennsylvania Press, 2004); and Orser, *The Archaeology of Race and Racialization in Historic America* (Gainesville: University Press of Florida, 2007); cf. Siân Jones, *The Archaeology of Ethnicity: Constructing Identities in the Past and Present* (New York: Routledge, 1997).

20. Mark S. Warner, "'The Best There Is of Us': Ceramics and Status in African American Annapolis," in *Annapolis Pasts: Historical Archaeology in Annapolis, Maryland*, ed. Paul A. Shackel, Paul R. Mullins, and Mark S. Warner (Knoxville: University of Tennessee Press, 1998), 191.

21. Paul R. Mullins, "Racializing the Parlor: Race and Victorian Bric-a-Brac Consumption," in *Race and the Archaeology of Identity*, ed. Charles E. Orser Jr. (Salt Lake City: University of Utah Press, 2001), 159. See also Mullins, "'A Bold and Gorgeous Front': The Contradictions of African America and Consumer Culture," in *Historical Archaeologies of Capitalism*, ed. Mark P. Leone and Parker B. Potter Jr. (New York:

Kluwer Academic, 1999), 169–93; and Mullins, *Race and Affluence: An Archaeology of African America and Consumer Culture* (New York: Kluwer Academic, 1999).

22. Terrence Epperson, "Beyond Biological Reductionism, Ethnicity, and Vulgar Anti-Essentialism: Critical Perspectives on Race and the Practice of African-American Archaeology," *African Diaspora Archaeology Newsletter* 6, no. 22 (1999): article 4, p. 2. See also articles in the following special issues of *Historical Archaeology*: Carol McDavid and David Babson, eds., "In the Realm of Politics: Prospects for Public Participation in African-American and Plantation Archaeology," *Historical Archaeology* 31, no. 3 (1997); and Maria Franklin and Larry McKee, eds., "Transcending Boundaries, Transforming the Discipline: African Diaspora Archaeologies in the New Millennium," *Historical Archaeology* 38, no. 1 (2004).

23. See, for example, Herbert E. Sterkx, *The Free Negro in Antebellum Louisiana* (Rutherford NJ: Fairleigh Dickinson University Press, 1972); John W. Blassingame, *Black New Orleans, 1860–1880* (Chicago: University of Chicago Press, 1973); Gwendolyn Midlo Hall, *Africans in Colonial Louisiana: The Development of Afro-Creole Culture in the Eighteenth Century* (Baton Rouge: Louisiana State University Press, 1992); Virginia R. Dominguez, *White by Definition: Social Classification in Creole Louisiana* (New Brunswick, NJ: Rutgers University Press, 1994); Caryn Cossé Bell, *Revolution, Romanticism, and the Afro-Creole Protest Tradition in Louisiana, 1718–1868* (Baton Rouge: Louisiana State University Press, 1997); Kimberly S. Hanger, *Bounded Lives, Bounded Places: Free Black Society in Colonial New Orleans, 1769–1803* (Durham, NC: Duke University Press, 1997); Nathalie Dessens, *From Saint-Domingue to New Orleans: Migration and Influences* (Gainesville: University Press of Florida, 2007); Jennifer M. Spear, *Race, Sex, and Social Disorder in Early New Orleans* (Baltimore: Johns Hopkins University Press, 2008); Michael E. Crutcher Jr., *Tremé: Race and Place in a New Orleans Neighborhood* (Athens: University of Georgia Press, 2010); and Marcus Christian, "History of Negroes in Louisiana" (n.d., Marcus Christian Collection, Earl K. Long Library, University of New Orleans).

24. Mathe Allain, "Slave Policies in French Louisiana," *Louisiana History* 21, no. 2 (1980): 127–38; and Carl A. Brasseaux, "The Administration of Slave Regulations in French Louisiana, 1724–1766," *Louisiana History* 21, no. 2 (1980): 139–58.

25. G. M. Hall, *Africans in Colonial Louisiana*; and Thomas N. Ingersoll, "The Slave Trade and the Ethnic Diversity of Louisiana's Slave Community," *Louisiana History* 37, no. 2 (1996): 133–61; cf. Richard Campanella, *Geographies of New Orleans: Urban Fabrics before the Storm* (Lafayette: Center for Louisiana Studies, 2006).

26. D. Ryan Gray, *Rediscovering the "Antiguo Cementerio": Archaeological Excavations and Recovery of Human Remains from the St. Peter Street Cemetery (16OR92), Orleans Parish, Louisiana* (report submitted to the Louisiana Division of Archaeology, Baton Rouge, 2016).

27. Donald Everett, "Free Persons of Color in Colonial Louisiana," *Louisiana History* 7, no. 1 (1966): 21–50; Jerah Johnson, "Colonial New Orleans: A Fragment of the Eighteenth-Century French Ethos," in Hirsch and Logsdon, *Creole New Orleans*, 33–34; and Shannon Lee Dawdy, *Building the Devil's Empire: French Colonial New Orleans* (Chicago: University of Chicago Press, 2008), 154–58.

28. Hanger, *Bounded Lives, Bounded Places*, 17–54; cf. Virginia Meacham Gould, "'A Chaos of Iniquity and Discord': Slave and Free Women of Color in the Spanish Ports of New Orleans, Mobile, and Pensacola," in *The Devil's Lane: Sex and Race in*

the Early South, ed. Catherine Clinton and Michele Gillespie (Oxford: Oxford University Press, 1997), 232–46; and Lawrence Powell, *The Accidental City: Improvising New Orleans* (Cambridge, MA: Harvard University Press, 2013).

29. Campanella, *Geographies of New Orleans*, 9.

30. Dessens, *From Saint-Domingue to New Orleans*; Paul Lachance, "The Foreign French," in Hirsch and Logsdon, *Creole New Orleans*, 101–30.

31. Richard Follett, *The Sugar Masters: Planters and Slaves in Louisiana's Cane World, 1820–1860* (Baton Rouge: Louisiana State University Press, 2007).

32. Nicholas J. Demerath and Harlan Gilmore, "The Ecology of Southern Cities," in *The Urban South*, ed. Rupert Vance and Nicholas J. Demerath (Chapel Hill: University of North Carolina Press, 1954), 155; and Daphne Spain, "Race Relations and Residential Segregation in New Orleans: Two Centuries of Paradox," *Annals of the American Academy of Political and Social Science* 441 (1979): 82–96.

33. Hall, *Africans in Colonial Louisiana*, 343–74; James H. Dormon, "The Persistent Specter: Slave Rebellion in Territorial Louisiana," *Louisiana History* 18, no. 4 (1977): 389–404; Daniel Rasmussen, *American Uprising: The Untold Story of America's Largest Slave Revolt* (New York: Harper Perennial, 2012); and Judith Kelleher Schafer, *Becoming Free, Remaining Free: Manumission and Enslavement in New Orleans, 1846–1862* (Baton Rouge: Louisiana State University Press, 2003).

34. Campanella, *Geographies of New Orleans*, 16–29; James K. Hogue, *Uncivil War: Five New Orleans Street Battles and the Rise and Fall of Radical Reconstruction* (Baton Rouge: Louisiana State University Press, 2006); James Hollandsworth Jr., *An Absolute Massacre: The New Orleans Race Riot of July 30, 1866* (Baton Rouge: Louisiana State University Press, 2001); and Rebecca J. Scott, *Degrees of Freedom: Louisiana and Cuba after Slavery* (Cambridge, MA: Belknap Press of Harvard University Press, 2005); cf. Elizabeth Regosin, *Freedom's Promise: Ex-Slave Families and Citizenship in the Age of Emancipation* (Charlottesville: University Press of Virginia, 2002); and Michael A. Gomez, *Exchanging Our Country Marks: The Transformation of African Identities in the Colonial and Antebellum South* (Chapel Hill: University of North Carolina Press, 1998).

35. See Thompson, *Exiles at Home*; R. J. Scott, *Degrees of Freedom*; Bell, *Revolution*; and Blassingame, *Black New Orleans*.

36. C. Vann Woodward, *The Strange Career of Jim Crow* (New York: Oxford University Press, 1966); W. E. B. Du Bois, *The Philadelphia Negro: A Social Study* (New York: Oxford University Press, 2007); Dominguez, *White by Definition*, 28–29; Rebecca J. Scott, "Public Rights, Social Equality, and the Conceptual Roots of the *Plessy* Challenge," *Michigan Law Review* 106, no. 5 (2008): 777–804; Scott, *Degrees of Freedom*, 155–61, 189–207; Kevin Fox Gotham, *Authentic New Orleans: Tourism, Culture, and Race in the Big Easy* (New York: New York University Press, 2007), 80.

37. Campanella *Geographies of New Orleans*, 13–19.

38. Roger Fischer, "Racial Segregation in Antebellum New Orleans," *American Historical Review* 74 (1969): 926–37; Spain, "Race Relations," 82–96; P. F. Lewis, *New Orleans*, 50–52; and Campanella, *Geographies of New Orleans*, 304.

39. P. F. Lewis, *New Orleans*, 50–52, fig. 18; cf. John Kellogg, "Negro Urban Clusters in the Postbellum South," *Geographical Review* 67, no. 3 (1977): 310–21.

40. Craig E. Colten, *An Unnatural Metropolis: Wresting New Orleans from Nature* (Baton Rouge: Louisiana State University Press, 2005).

41. Spain, "Race Relations," 89; cf. Colten, *An Unnatural Metropolis*, 104.

42. See, for example, John M. Merriman, *The Margins of City Life: Explorations on the French Urban Frontier, 1815–1851* (New York: Oxford University Press, 1991); Kenneth T. Jackson, *Crabgrass Frontier: The Suburbanization of the United States* (New York: Oxford University Press, 1985); and D. Ward, *Poverty, Ethnicity, and the American City.*

43. Antoine Paccoud, "Planning Law, Power, and Practice: Haussmann in Paris (1853–1870)," *Planning Perspectives* 31, no. 3 (2016): 341–61; cf. Howard Saalman, *Haussmann: Paris Transformed* (New York: G. Braziller, 1976).

44. Gwendolyn Wright, *Building the Dream: A Social History of Housing in America* (Cambridge: MIT Press, 1981), 131; and Alan Mayne, *The Imagined Slum: Newspaper Representation in Three Cities, 1870–1914* (Leicester, UK: Leicester University Press, 1993); cf. Robert Roberts, *The Classic Slum: Salford Life in the First Quarter of the Century* (London: Penguin Books, 1971); and Jacob Riis, *How the Other Half Lives: Studies among the Tenements of New York* (1890; Mineola, NY: Dover, 1971). The slum exposé genre goes back considerably further than Riis, of course, particularly in Europe. See, for example, Henry Mayhew, *London Labour and the London Poor* (1865; London: Penguin, 1985). See also Kellow Chesney, *The Victorian Underworld* (Harmonsworth: Penguin Books, 1970); Gareth Stedman Jones, *Outcast London: A Study in the Relationship between Classes in Victorian Society* (Oxford: Peregrine Penguin, 1984); and Dell Upton, "The City as Material Culture," in Yentsch and Beaudry, *The Art and Mystery of Historical Archaeology*, 51–73.

45. See, for example, Thomas Schlereth, "Burnham's Plan and Moody's Manual: City Planning as Progressive Reform," *Journal of the American Planning Association* 47, no. 1 (1981): 70–82; and Carl Smith, *The Plan of Chicago: Daniel Burnham and the Remaking of the American City* (Chicago: University of Chicago Press, 2006).

46. Thomas Lee Philpott, *The Slum and the Ghetto: Neighborhood Deterioration and Middle-Class Reform, Chicago, 1880–1930* (New York: Oxford University Press, 1978); and Devereux Bowly Jr., *The Poorhouse: Subsidized Housing in Chicago, 1895–1976* (Carbondale: Southern Illinois University Press, 1978), 3–16. The slum reform movement is also intertwined with the larger history of public welfare in the United States; see Michael Katz, *In the Shadow of the Poorhouse* (New York: Basic Books, 1986).

47. Robert Fogelson, *Bourgeois Nightmares: Suburbia, 1870–1930* (New Haven, CT: Yale University Press, 2005), 95–101, 203; Leonard Freedman, *Public Housing: The Politics of Poverty* (New York: Holt, Rinehart, and Winston, 1969), 134–35; and Christopher Silver, "The Racial Origins of Zoning in American Cities," in *Urban Planning and the African American Community*, ed. June Manning Thomas and Marsha Ritzdorf (Thousand Oaks, CA: Sage, 1997), 23–42. The general trends are noted in, for example, K. T. Jackson, *Crabgrass Frontier*; and Mel Scott, *American City Planning since 1890* (Berkeley: University of California Press, 1995), 47–182.

48. Kent Germany, *New Orleans after the Promises: Poverty, Citizenship, and the Search for the Great Society* (Athens: University of Georgia Press, 2007), 39; cf. "Community Chest Starts with 50 Charities Listed," *Times-Picayune*, October 2, 1924; Ad, *Times-Picayune*, January 25, 1927; and "Chest Solicitors to Renew Pleas for Funds Today," *Times-Picayune*, November 30, 1931.

49. See T. H. Watkins, *The Great Depression: America in the 1930s* (Boston: Little, Brown, 1993); Robert D. Leighninger Jr., *Building Louisiana: The Legacy of the Public Works Administration* (Jackson: University Press of Mississippi, 2007); and John

Robert Moore, "The New Deal in Louisiana," in *The New Deal: The State and Local Levels*, ed. John Braeman, Robert Hamlet Bremner, and David Brody (Columbus: Ohio State University Press, 1975), 137–65.

50. Qtd. in M. Scott, *American City Planning*, 318.

51. John B. Willman, *The Department of Housing and Urban Development* (New York: Frederick A. Praeger, 1968), 7–10.

52. Bowly, *The Poorhouse*, 17–27; and John F. Bauman, *Public Housing, Race, and Renewal: Urban Planning in Philadelphia, 1920–1974* (Philadelphia: Temple University Press, 1987).

53. For more on the origins of public housing, see: Robert Barrows, "The Local Origins of a New Deal Housing Project: The Case of Lockfield Gardens in Indianapolis," *Indiana Magazine of History* 103, no. 2 (2007): 125–51; Carol Flores, "U.S. Public Housing in the 1930s: The First Projects in Atlanta, Georgia," *Planning Perspectives* 9, no. 4 (2004): 405–30; Kevin Fox Gotham, "Racialization and the State: The Housing Act of 1934 and the Creation of the Federal Housing Administration," *Sociological Perspectives* 43, no. 2 (2000): 291–317; Frank Ruechel, "New Deal Public Housing, Urban Poverty, and Jim Crow: Techwood and University Homes in Atlanta," *Georgia Historical Quarterly* 81, no. 4 (1997): 915–37; Joseph Heathcott, "'In the Nature of a Clinic': The Design of Early Public Housing in St. Louis," *Journal of the Society of Architectural Historians* 70, no. 1 (2011): 82–103; Paul Lusignan, "Public Housing in the United States, 1933–1949," *Cultural Resource Management* 25, no. 1 (2002): 36–37; Peter Marcuse, "The Beginnings of Public Housing in New York," *Journal of Urban History* 12, no. 4 (1986): 353–90; and Richard Pommer, "The Architecture of Urban Housing in the United States during the Early 1930s," *Journal of the Society of Architectural Historians* 37, no. 4 (1978): 235–64.

54. M. Scott, *American City Planning*, 327–29.

55. Freedman, *Public Housing*, 38–57.

56. Freedman, 38–57; cf. Frances Fox Piven and Richard Cloward, *Regulating the Poor: The Functions of Public Welfare* (New York: Vintage Books, 1971), 76.

57. Housing Authority of New Orleans, *Report of the Housing Authority of New Orleans* (New Orleans: HANO, 1938–39); Sam Carter, *A Report on Survey of Metropolitan New Orleans Land Use, Real Property, and Low Income Housing Area* (Baton Rouge: Louisiana State Department of Public Welfare and HANO, 1941).

58. "Enumerators Begin House Census—to Visit Every Home," *Times-Picayune*, January 15, 1939.

59. Carter, *A Report on Survey*, 91.

60. Carter, 153.

61. Martha Mahoney, "The Changing Nature of Public Housing in New Orleans, 1930–1974" (master's thesis, Tulane University, 1985); Mahoney, "Law and Racial Geography: Public Housing and the Economy in New Orleans," *Stanford Law Review* 42, no. 5 (1990): 1251–90; Margaret C. Gonzalez-Perez, "A House Divided: Public Housing Policy in New Orleans," *Louisiana History* 44, no. 4 (2003): 443–61; and Alecia P. Long, "Poverty Is the New Prostitution: Race, Poverty, and Public Housing in Post-Katrina New Orleans," *Journal of American History* 94, no. 3 (2007): 795–803; cf. Forrest LaViolette and Joseph Taylor, *Negro Housing in New Orleans* (special research report to the Commission on Race and Housing, New Orleans, 1957); and John Arena, *Driven from New Orleans: How Nonprofits Betray Public Housing and Promote Privatization* (Minneapolis: University of Minnesota Press, 2012). See also

Lawrence J. Vale, *Purging the Poorest: Public Housing and the Design Politics of Twice-Cleared Communities* (Chicago: University of Chicago Press, 2013).

62. Williams is quoted in an article about his promotion of the act in the *Times-Picayune*, June 1, 1938. See also Mahoney, "The Changing Nature of Public Housing"; Peggy Lentz, "Public Housing in New Orleans: Public Castles?," in *A Place to Live: Housing in New Orleans*, ed. James Bobo (New Orleans: Urban Studies Institute, University of New Orleans, 1978), 176–211; "Slum Clearance Works Approved in Roosevelt Act," *Times-Picayune*, March 18, 1938.

63. For example, see articles in the *Times-Picayune* from 1938 (August 24, October 23, October 26, October 30, November 1, November 23, etc.). The newspaper emphasized the "exorbitant" amounts being asked by owners. The short account of the case of Dr. Nathan Polmer was typical of the descriptions of condemnation proceedings. Polmer owned 3323 North Robertson in the Magnolia area. HANO offered $2,600 for the property, while Polmer wanted $5,000 for it. A court eventually judged it as worth $3,000, with the whole process apparently taking just less than a month; see *Times-Picayune*, October 30 and November 23, 1938.

64. Housing Authority of New Orleans, *Report of the Housing Authority of New Orleans*, 1939, 1941; e.g., *Louisiana Weekly*, March 18, 1939; *Louisiana Weekly*, February 17, 1940; *Louisiana Weekly*, May 11, 1940; *Louisiana Weekly*, December 21, 1940; and Mahoney, "The Changing Nature of Public Housing," 30.

65. "St. Thomas Buildings Rise; First Tenants in Spring," *Times-Picayune*, December 17, 1939.

Chapter 3

1. See: "Louisiana—Orleans County—Historic Districts," National Register of Historic Places, accessed October 2018, http://www.nationalregisterofhistoricplaces.com/la/Orleans/districts.html; "Historic District Maps & Location Information," Historic District Landmarks Commission, City of New Orleans, accessed October 2018, http://www.nola.gov/hdlc/map/; and "St. Patrick's Day Parade in the Irish Channel Starts at 1 p.m.," *Times-Picayune*, March 17, 2012.

2. The various theories about the location of the Irish Channel have been usefully summarized and discussed in Richard Campanella, *Geographies of New Orleans: Urban Fabrics before the Storm* (Lafayette: Center for Louisiana Studies, 2006), 227–45; see also Lyle Saxon, Edward Dreyer, and Robert Tallant, *Gumbo Ya-Ya: A Collection of Louisiana Folk Tales* (Boston: Houghton Mifflin, 1987), 50–74.

3. On the significance of parade traditions in African American New Orleans, see Rachel Breunlin and Helen A. Regis, "Putting the Ninth Ward on the Map: Race, Place, and Transformation in Desire, New Orleans," *American Anthropologist* 108, no. 4 (2006): 745–65; cf. Aurélie Godet, "'Meet de Boys on the Battlefront': Festive Parades and the Struggle to Reclaim Public Spaces in Post-Katrina New Orleans," *European Journal of American Studies* 10, no. 3 (2015), document 1.9; Roberto E. Barrios, "You Found Us Doing This, This Is Our Way: Criminalizing Second Lines, Super Sunday, and Habitus in Post-Katrina New Orleans," *Identities* 17 (2010): 586–612; and Mark Souther, *New Orleans on Parade: Tourism and the Transformation of the Crescent City* (Baton Rouge: Louisiana State University Press, 2006).

4. "St. Thomas Buildings Rise; First Tenants in Spring," *Times-Picayune*, December 17, 1939.

5. "Added $10,000,000 to Finance More Housing for the City," *Times-Picayune*, June 1, 1938; and "Colonel Williams Receives the Times-Picayune Annual Award for Service to the City," *Times-Picayune*, December 18, 1939.

6. "Three Breslin Brothers Find It Hard to Move after 60 Years in Old Homestead/Brothers See Scattering of Childhood Acquaintances as Federal Housing Project Advances," *Times-Picayune*, May 12, 1939.

7. "St. Thomas Buildings Rise; First Tenants in Spring," *Times-Picayune*, December 17, 1939. Martha Mahoney, "The Changing Nature of Public Housing in New Orleans, 1930–1974" (master's thesis, Tulane University, 1985), 31–32 (for the "poor housekeeping," etc. quotes).

8. Qtd. in John F. Bauman, *Public Housing, Race, and Renewal: Urban Planning in Philadelphia, 1920–1974* (Philadelphia: Temple University Press, 1987), 115–16.

9. Joseph Heathcott, "'In the Nature of a Clinic': The Design of Early Public Housing in St. Louis," *Journal of the Society of Architectural Historians* 70, no. 1 (2011): 86–87; and Michel Foucault, *Discipline and Punish: The Birth of the Prison* (New York: Vintage Books, 1977).

10. Alan Mayne, *The Imagined Slum: Newspaper Representation in Three Cities, 1870–1914* (Leicester, UK: Leicester University Press, 1993), 4, 10; James C. Scott, *Seeing like a State: How Certain Schemes to Improve the Human Condition Have Failed* (New Haven, CT: Yale University Press, 1998); and Dell Upton, *Another City: Urban Life and Urban Spaces in the New American Republic* (New Haven, CT: Yale University Press, 2008).

11. James C. Scott, *Domination and the Arts of Resistance: Hidden Transcripts* (New Haven, CT: Yale University Press, 1990); and Jean Comaroff and John L. Comaroff, *Of Revelation and Revolution*, vol. 1, *Christianity, Colonialism, and the Colonization of Consciousness in South Africa* (Chicago: University of Chicago Press, 1991), 38; cf. Robin D. G. Kelley, "'We Are Not What We Seem': Rethinking Black Working-Class Opposition in the Jim Crow South," in *The New African American Urban History*, ed. Kenneth Goings and Raymond Mohl (Thousand Oaks, CA: Sage, 1996), 187–239; and Martin Hall, *Archaeology and the Modern World: Colonial Transcripts in South Africa and the Chesapeake* (London: Routledge, 2000). Scott's notion of public and hidden transcripts has gained considerable currency among historical archaeologists, even though its text-based epistemology has limitations in this field.

12. The constructivist/instrumentalist approach to ethnicity in anthropology and archaeology has been usefully summarized in Timothy Baumann, "Defining Ethnicity," *SAA Archaeological Record* 4, no. 4 (2004): 12–14; and it is discussed more fully in Siân Jones, *The Archaeology of Ethnicity: Constructing Identities in the Past and Present* (New York: Routledge, 1997). The instrumentalist approach is typically traced to the work of Fredrik Barth. See his introduction to *Ethnic Groups and Boundaries* (Boston: Little, Brown, 1969): 9–38.

13. Samuel Wilson and Bernard Lemann, *New Orleans Architecture*, vol. 1, *The Lower Garden District* (Gretna, LA: Friends of the Cabildo and Pelican, 1998), 1–33; John Churchill Chase, *Frenchmen, Desire, Good Children, and Other Streets of New Orleans* (New York: Collier Books, 2001), 139–52; Benjamin Maygarden, *Historical Background and Development Overview for the St. Thomas Housing Project Area* (manuscript on file, Earth Search, Inc., New Orleans, 2001); and Kathryn Briede, "A History of the City of Lafayette," *Louisiana Historical Quarterly* 20, no. 4 (1937): 895–964.

14. Maygarden, *Historical Background*; and Briede, "A History of the City of Lafayette," 935–54.

15. Campanella, *Geographies of New Orleans*, 231–32.

16. D. Ryan Gray, "Incorrigible Vagabonds and Suspicious Spaces in Nineteenth-Century New Orleans," *Historical Archaeology* 45, no. 3 (2011): 55–73; US Bureau of the Census, *Seventh Census of the United States, 1850* (National Archives, Washington, DC), Ancestry.com; and *New Orleans Annual and Commercial Register* (New Orleans: Michel, 1846).

17. Maygarden, *Historical Background*; Briede, "A History of the City of Lafayette," 945–46; and Sanborn Map Company, *Insurance Maps of New Orleans, Louisiana*, 1885 ed. (New York: Sanborn Map, 1876–1937).

18. George E. Waring Jr., *Report on the Social Statistics of Cities*, 1886–87, 2 vols. (New York: Arno Press, 1970), 281–85.

19. Sanborn Map Company, *Insurance Maps of New Orleans, Louisiana*, 1885, 1895, and 1909 eds.

20. John Ker Towles, "Housing Conditions in the Vicinity of St. Mary's Market, New Orleans" (master's thesis, Tulane University, 1904), 13; Maygarden, *Historical Background*; and Benjamin Maygarden et al., *National Register Evaluation of New Orleans Pumping Stations* (report prepared for New Orleans District, US Army Corps of Engineers, New Orleans, 1999); cf. Craig E. Colten, *An Unnatural Metropolis: Wresting New Orleans from Nature* (Baton Rouge: Louisiana State University Press, 2005).

21. Blair Bordelon, "An Ethnic 'State of Mind': Historical Archaeology of Immigrant Identities in the New Orleans Irish Channel, 1850–1920," *Louisiana Archaeology* 40 (2015): 113–34.

22. Louis Ferleger, "Farm Mechanization in the Southern Sugar Sector after the Civil War," *Louisiana History* 23, no. 1 (1982): 21–34; John A. Heitmann, *The Modernization of the Louisiana Sugar Industry, 1830–1910* (Baton Rouge: Louisiana State University Press, 1987); Charles E. Orser Jr., *The Material Basis of the Postbellum Tenant Plantation* (Athens: University of Georgia Press, 1988); Richard Follett and Rick Halpern, "From Slavery to Freedom in Louisiana's Sugar Country: Changing Labor Systems and Workers' Power," in *Sugar, Slavery, and Society: Perspectives on the Caribbean, Indian, the Mascarenes, and the United States*, ed. Bernard Moitt (Gainesville: University Press of Florida, 2004), 135–56; and Richard Follett, *The Sugar Masters: Planters and Slaves in Louisiana's Cane World, 1820–1860* (Baton Rouge: Louisiana State University Press, 2007).

23. Initial attention was brought to this block by preliminary research on census data and land records conducted in advance of the proposed redevelopment by Rick Fifield and Judy Bethea for the private company involved in its redevelopment. See Fifield and Bethea, *Investigation of St. Thomas Project Area prior to Construction of LA-1* (manuscript prepared for Historic Restoration, Inc., New Orleans, 1999).

24. After 1894, New Orleans completely reconfigured its street address numbering system to try to make it more consistent. Throughout this chapter and upcoming ones, I typically refer to the later address numbers, unless I am specifically referring to documents or sources that cite the earlier address.

25. Housing Authority of New Orleans, *Report of the Housing Authority of New Orleans, 1939* (New Orleans: HANO, 1939); Heathcott, "In the Nature of a Clinic"; Paul Boyer, *Urban Masses and Moral Order in America, 1820–1920* (Cambridge, MA: Harvard University Press, 1978); and David Ward, *Poverty, Ethnicity, and the Ameri-*

can City, 1840–1925: Changing Conceptions of the Slum and the Ghetto (Cambridge, Cambridge University Press, 1989).

26. I refer frequently to census data in this and subsequent chapters. All this information was transcribed from the images of the censuses that have been digitized and made available via Ancestry.com. Source information for census data throughout this work, taken from the 1860, 1870, 1880, 1900, 1910, 1920 and 1930 census, is as follows: US Bureau of the Census, *Eighth Census of the United States, 1860* (National Archives, Washington, DC), Ancestry.com; US Bureau of the Census, *Ninth Census of the United States, 1870* (National Archives, Washington, DC), Ancestry.com; US Bureau of the Census, *Tenth Census of the United States, 1880* (National Archives, Washington, DC), Ancestry.com; US Bureau of the Census, *Twelfth Census of the United States, 1900* (National Archives, Washington, DC), Ancestry.com; US Bureau of the Census, *Thirteenth Census of the United States, 1910* (National Archives, Washington, DC), Ancestry.com; US Bureau of the Census, *Fourteenth Census of the United States, 1920* (National Archives, Washington, DC), Ancestry.com; and US Bureau of the Census, *Fifteenth Census of the United States, 1930* (National Archives, Washington, DC), Ancestry.com. Most of the 1890 census was destroyed in a fire, but city directories provide some information that can substitute for it, as is detailed in later notes.

27. Information compiled from US Census data for 1900 and 1910, along with city directories for available years. In some cases, original directories were consulted, but these directories are typically indexed by name rather than address. New collections of city directory material have been digitized in recent years, and while these are easier to consult by name than by address, there are ways to search them by address. See databases at Ancestry.com: *U.S. City Directories, 1822–1995*; and *New Orleans, Louisiana Directories, 1890–1891*. These directories were cross-referenced with Sanborn Map Company, *Insurance Maps of New Orleans, Louisiana*, 1895 and 1909 eds.

28. See, for example, William Hampton Adams, "Dating Historical Sites: The Importance of Understanding Time Lag in the Acquisition, Curation, Use, and Disposal of Artifacts," *Historical Archaeology* 37, no. 2 (2003): 38–64.

29. Information on Saint Catherine Labouré was derived from Robert J. Billett, "St. Catherine Labouré and the Miraculous Medal," Mary's Touch by Mail, accessed October 2018, http://marys-touch.com/Saints/medal/medal.htm. The motto translates as "O Mary, conceived without sin, pray for us who have recourse to thee."

30. For example, see Claude Jacobs, "Benevolent Societies of New Orleans Blacks during the Late Nineteenth and Early Twentieth Centuries," *Louisiana History* 29, no. 1 (1988): 21–33.

31. All identifications of faunal material from Square 70 were done by Rhonda Smith. Interpretations of the raw data are mine.

32. Alcée Fortier, ed., *Louisiana, Comprising Sketches of Counties, Towns, Events, Institutions, and Persons, Arranged in Cyclopedic Form* (Madison, WI: Century Historical Association, 1914), 3: 72–74.

33. Fifield and Bethea, *Investigation of St. Thomas Project Area*, 15.

34. Housing Authority of New Orleans, *Report of Housing Authority of New Orleans, 1938*.

35. Gil Marks, *Encyclopedia of Jewish Food* (New York: Houghton, Mifflin, Harcourt, 2013); see also Zalman Goldstein, "Seudat Havra'ah: The First Meal," Chabad-

Lubavitch Media Center, accessed October 2018, http://www.chabad.org/library/article_cdo/aid/364293/jewish/The-First-Meal.htm.

36. Bertram Wallace Korn, *The Early Jews of New Orleans* (Waltham, MA: American Jewish Historical Society, 1969); and Irwin Lachoff and Catherine Kahn, *The Jewish Community of New Orleans* (Charleston, SC: Arcadia, 2005).

37. James Gill, *Lords of Misrule: Mardi Gras and the Politics of Race in New Orleans* (Jackson: University Press of Mississippi, 1997).

38. The primary row of cottages extends from 701 to 717 St. Mary. A frame add-on at 719 St. Mary was constructed sometime after the original row of cottages was built but is extant by 1880. It is considered to be part of this row for the purpose of this discussion. The buildings are illustrated in a circa 1850s *Plan of 4 Lots of Ground in the Fourth District* in the collection of the New Orleans Notarial Archives. Census information was compiled as described in chapter 3, notes 26 and 27.

39. The census taker may be presumed to have made some errors here. The grandson relationship would appear to refer to Mary Felea, and the similarity in names between Rosatel and Rosaveldt King suggests that they were siblings. Larry Kimball could be a child from a previous marriage of Rosatel or Marie. However, none of the obvious scenarios explains the relationships adequately.

40. Arnold A. Kowalsky and Dorothy E. Kowalsky, *Encyclopedia of Marks on American, English, and European Earthenware, Ironstone, and Stoneware, 1780–1980* (Atglen, PA: Schiffer Books, 1999), 188–89, 199, 310–11, 355.

41. See Mullins, "'A Bold and Gorgeous Front': The Contradictions of African America and Consumer Culture," in *Historical Archaeologies of Capitalism*, ed. Mark P. Leone and Parker B. Potter Jr. (New York: Kluwer Academic, 1999), 169–93; and Mullins, *Race and Affluence: An Archaeology of African America and Consumer Culture* (New York: Kluwer Academic, 1999).

42. Eric Arnesen, *Waterfront Workers of New Orleans: Race, Class, and Politics, 1863–1923* (New York: Oxford University Press, 1994); Daniel Rosenberg, *New Orleans Dockworkers: Race, Labor, and Unionism, 1892–1923* (Albany: State University of New York Press, 1988); Bernard Cook and James Watson, *Louisiana Labor: From Slavery to "Right-to-Work"* (Lanham, MD: University Press of America, 1985); and David Bennetts, "Black and White Workers: New Orleans, 1880–1900" (PhD diss., University of Illinois at Urbana-Champaign, 1972).

43. The Robert Charles incident, in which Charles, an African American man, shot twenty-seven people, both policemen and members of a lynch mob (all of them white), killing seven of them, is discussed in more detail in chapter 4.

44. See, for example, Mark S. Warner, "'The Best There Is of Us': Ceramics and Status in African American Annapolis," in *Annapolis Pasts: Historical Archaeology in Annapolis, Maryland*, ed. Paul A. Shackel, Paul R. Mullins, and Mark S. Warner (Knoxville: University of Tennessee Press, 1998), 190–224; and Mullins, *Race and Affluence*.

45. Jacobs, "Benevolent Societies"; and William R. Jankowiak, *Black Social Aid and Pleasure Clubs: Marching Associations in New Orleans* (Cultural Resources Management Study, Jean Lafitte National Historical Park and the National Park Service, New Orleans, 1989); cf. Marcus Christian, "History of Negroes in Louisiana" (n.d., Marcus B. Christian Collection, Archives, Earl K. Long Library, University of New Orleans). Of course, the formation of social clubs has also been seen as significant in terms of the development of new American industrial elites. Such was certainly

the case in New Orleans, where a number of racially and socially exclusive clubs formed after the Civil War, many of them with connections to Carnival krewes, as discussed in Gill, *Lords of Misrule*; and Kevin Fox Gotham, *Authentic New Orleans: Tourism, Culture, and Race in the Big Easy* (New York: New York University Press, 2007).

46. The concept of doxa (and its relationship to orthodoxy and heterodoxy) is borrowed from the work of Pierre Bourdieu; Siân Jones and Charles E. Orser Jr., among others, have usefully applied the concept to discussions of race and ethnicity. See Bourdieu, *Outline of a Theory of Practice* (Cambridge: Cambridge University Press, 1995); Jones, *The Archaeology of Ethnicity*; Orser, *Race and Practice in Archaeological Interpretation* (Philadelphia: University of Pennsylvania Press, 2004); and Orser, *The Archaeology of Race and Racialization in Historic America* (Gainesville: University Press of Florida, 2007). The debate over constructivist/instrumentalist versus primordialist positions on ethnicity broadly mirrors that for identity more generally, as discussed in Rogers Brubaker and Frederick Cooper, "Beyond 'Identity,'" *Theory and Society* 29, no. 1 (2000): 1–47.

47. Qtd. in Rosenberg, *New Orleans Dockworkers*, 118.

48. Kent Germany, *New Orleans after the Promises: Poverty, Citizenship, and the Search for the Great Society* (Athens: University of Georgia Press, 2007), 35.

Chapter 4

1. William Ivy Hair, *Carnival of Fury: Robert Charles and the New Orleans Race Riot of 1900* (Baton Rouge: Louisiana State University Press, 1976). See also "Thomy Lafon School Burned to the Ground," *Daily Picayune*, July 28, 1900.

2. Hair, *Carnival of Fury*, 95–96. Even Major Henry Hearsey, the virulently racist editor of the *Daily States* newspaper, grudgingly acknowledged in print the "desperate courage" of Charles in the face of the mob (cited in Hair, 180).

3. Peirce F. Lewis, *New Orleans: The Making of an Urban Experience*, 2nd ed. (Santa Fe, NM: Center for American Places, 2003), 50–52; and Richard Campanella, *Geographies of New Orleans: Urban Fabrics before the Storm* (Lafayette: Center for Louisiana Studies, 2006), 304; cf. John Kellogg, "Negro Urban Clusters in the Postbellum South," *Geographical Review* 67, no. 3 (1977): 310–21.

4. Katy Reckdahl, "New C. J. Peete Complex Is Solid, Shiny—But Not as Social, Some Residents Say," *Times-Picayune*, August 21, 2011.

5. James Holston, *Insurgent Citizenship: Disjunctions of Democracy and Modernity in Brazil* (Princeton, NJ: Princeton University Press, 2008).

6. Campanella, *Geographies of New Orleans*, 33–87, 304. I have not been able to ascertain who first gave this description of the bowl shape of New Orleans geography, but it now seems to be a go-to description in popular media; cf. Lewis, *New Orleans*, 26–29.

7. Lewis, *New Orleans*, fig. 18.

8. John Churchill Chase, *Frenchmen, Desire, Good Children, and Other Streets of New Orleans* (New York: Collier Books, 2001).

9. US War Department, *Department of the Gulf: Map No. 5, Approaches to New Orleans*, prepared by order of Major General N. P. Banks, February 14, 1863 (Washington, DC: Government Printing Office, 1891); and T. S. Hardee, *Topographical and Drainage Map of New Orleans and Surroundings* (New Orleans: Lewis Graham, 1878).

10. Leonard Huber, Peggy McDowell, and Mary Louise Christovich, *New Orleans Architecture*, vol. 3, *The Cemeteries* (Gretna, LA: Pelican, 1997).

11. Lyle Saxon, Edward Dreyer, and Robert Tallant, *Gumbo Ya-Ya: A Collection of Louisiana Folk Tales* (Boston: Houghton Mifflin), 341–42.

12. Campanella, *Geographies of New Orleans*, 300–302; Caryn Cossé Bell, "'Une Chimère': The Freedmen's Bureau in Creole New Orleans," in *The Freedmen's Bureau and Reconstruction: Reconsiderations*, ed. Paul Cimbala and Randall Miller (New York: Fordham University Press, 1999), 140–60.

13. The cartographic data discussed here is taken primarily from insurance maps published by the Sanborn Map Company (1876, 1885, 1895, 1909, and 1937), including the originals with updates available in the New Orleans Public Library. See Sanborn Map Company, *Insurance Maps of New Orleans, Louisiana* (New York: Sanborn Map, 1876–1937); and E. Robinson and R. H. Pidgeon, *Atlas of the City of New Orleans, Louisiana* (New York: E. Robinson, 1883). An additional 1939 survey map was produced by HANO as part of property acquisition for the project. It was made available in digital form by HANO during ESI's research.

14. In an interesting idiosyncrasy, these apartments are numbered 1 through 14, with the number 13 skipped for the purpose of identifying the units. Thirteen was apparently considered unlucky for more than just floors of buildings!

15. Qtd. from an announcement of bid openings for Magnolia, *Louisiana Weekly*, March 4, 1939. The amount that households paid for rent is shown in the 1930 census, though not in earlier ones. My assessment of the inflation of rental rates in the Magnolia area is based on an admittedly unsystematic comparison to other neighborhoods around the city in the census; US Bureau of the Census, *Fifteenth Census of the United States, 1930* (National Archives, Washington, DC), Ancestry.com.

16. Debates over the culture of poverty have a long history in the social sciences, a subject that I take up elsewhere in this work. See, for example, Oscar Lewis, *Five Families: Mexican Case Studies in the Culture of Poverty* (New York: Basic Books, 1959); Lewis, "The Culture of Poverty," *Scientific American* 215, no. 4 (1966): 19–25; and William Julius Wilson, *The Truly Disadvantaged: The Inner City, the Underclass, and Public Policy* (Chicago: University of Chicago Press, 1987); cf. Carol Stack's pointed response to its application to the African American context in Stack, *All Our Kin: Strategies for Survival in a Black Community* (New York: Basic Books, 1974). Stack's approach is the one from which this book takes the most inspiration.

17. Tulane School of Social Work, "A Housing Study of the Flint-Goodridge Hospital Area" (manuscript on file, Louisiana Collection, Tulane University, New Orleans, Louisiana, 1934), 1–2.

18. Tulane School of Social Work, 7–8.

19. Some of these fanciful names are also referenced in "St. Thomas Buildings Rise; First Tenants in Spring," *Times-Picayune*, March 18, 1938.

20. Lottery houses were the quasilegal local answer to the numbers racket known from many other American cities, although many such houses in New Orleans were descended from the notoriously corrupt (but legal) Louisiana Lottery Corporation of the late nineteenth century. See the discussion in John Smith Kendall, *The History of New Orleans* (Chicago: Lewis, 1922). The names of the lottery and keno houses are interesting in themselves, with many examples suggesting competition between them. Among the ones cited are names like the Blue Horse Shoe, the Big Louisiana Eagle and the Little Louisiana Eagle, the Red Orleans and the Blue Or-

leans, the Original Relines and the Relines, Old Howard, the Boat, and the Clover; cf. Tulane School of Social Work, "A Housing Study," 6.

21. See Michel Foucault, *The Archaeology of Knowledge* (New York: Pantheon Books, 1972); and James C. Scott, *Seeing like a State: How Certain Schemes to Improve the Human Condition Have Failed* (New Haven, CT: Yale University Press, 1998).

22. Census data in this section is compiled from US Bureau of the Census, *Twelfth Census of the United States, 1900* (National Archives, Washington, DC), Ancestry.com; US Bureau of the Census, *Thirteenth Census of the United States, 1910* (National Archives, Washington, DC), Ancestry.com; US Bureau of the Census, *Fourteenth Census of the United States, 1920* (National Archives, Washington, DC), Ancestry.com; and US Bureau of the Census, *Fifteenth Census of the United States, 1930*. See chapter 3, note 26, on censuses.

23. Tulane School of Social Work, "A Housing Study"; cf. Martha Mahoney, "The Changing Nature of Public Housing in New Orleans, 1930–1974" (master's thesis, Tulane University, 1985).

24. Michel Foucault, "On Governmentality," *Ideology and Consciousness* 6 (1979): 5–21.

25. Andrew Wiese, *Places of Their Own: African American Suburbanization in the Twentieth Century* (Chicago: University of Chicago Press, 2004), 85.

26. See, for example, Steven L. Jones, "The African-American Tradition in Vernacular Architecture," in *The Archaeology of Slavery and Plantation Life*, ed. Theresa A. Singleton (New York: Academic Press, 1985) 195–214; and J. W. Joseph, "Archaeology and the African-American Experience in the Urban South," in *Archaeology of Southern Urban Landscapes*, ed. Amy Young (Tuscaloosa: University of Alabama Press, 2001), 109–26.

27. Robin D. G. Kelley, "'We Are Not What We Seem': Rethinking Black Working-Class Opposition in the Jim Crow South," in *The New African American Urban History*, ed. Kenneth Goings and Raymond Mohl (Thousand Oaks, CA: Sage, 1996), 191.

28. Paul R. Mullins, "Racializing the Parlor: Race and Victorian Bric-a-Brac Consumption," in *Race and the Archaeology of Identity*, ed. Charles E. Orser Jr. (Salt Lake City: University of Utah Press, 2001), 159; cf. Christopher Tilley, "Interpreting Material Culture," in *The Meaning of Things: Material Culture and Symbolic Expression*, ed. Ian Hodder (London: Unwin Hyman, 1989); and Warren Perry and Robert Paynter, "Artifacts, Ethnicity, and the Archaeology of African Americans," in *"I, Too, Am American": Archaeological Studies of African-American Life*, ed. Theresa Singleton (Charlottesville: University Press of Virginia, 1999), 299–310.

29. Arjun Appadurai, *The Social Life of Things: Commodities in Cultural Perspective* (Cambridge: Cambridge University Press, 1986), 8–9.

30. ESI has so far produced a series of draft reports and management summaries as working documents to structure the data recovery outlined here. The enormous collection of material produced by this work is still under analysis. All the artifact identifications here are mine, although I worked with preliminary tables produced by analysts at ESI to guide my research. Project manager Mike Godzinski made his notes and interpretations of the field investigations available to me as well, for which I am grateful.

31. Roderick Sprague, "China or Prosser Button Identification and Dating," *Historical Archaeology* 36, no. 2 (2002): 111–27.

32. All dates are from Arnold A. Kowalsky and Dorothy E. Kowalsky, *Encyclope-

dia of Marks on American, English, and European Earthenware, Ironstone, and Stone-ware, 1780–1980 (Atglen, PA: Schiffer Books, 1999).

33. Jack Sullivan, "The Peruna Story: Strumming That Old Catarrh," *Bottles and Extras*, May–June 2007.

34. Exact composition used in long-playing records varied considerably through the 1920s, and it is difficult to distinguish between many varieties introduced in the period without chemical compositional analysis.

35. Charles S. Bradley, "Smoking Pipes for the Archaeologist," in *Studies in Material Culture Research*, ed. Karlis Karklins (Tucson, AZ: Society for Historical Archaeology, 2000), 104–33.

36. Preliminary analysis of faunal material was performed by Angele Montana of ESI.

37. Lizabeth Cohen, *A Consumers' Republic: The Politics of Mass Consumption in Postwar America* (New York: Vintage Books, 2004), 18–19.

38. Cohen, 43.

39. Paul R. Mullins, "'A Bold and Gorgeous Front': The Contradictions of African America and Consumer Culture," in *Historical Archaeologies of Capitalism*, ed. Mark P. Leone and Parker B. Potter Jr. (New York: Kluwer Academic, 1999), 187–88; and Mullins, *Race and Affluence: An Archaeology of African America and Consumer Culture* (New York: Kluwer Academic, 1999).

40. See Monica Miller, *Slaves to Fashion: Black Dandyism and the Styling of Black Diasporic Identity* (Durham, NC: Duke University Press, 2009).

41. On double-consciousness and the veil of race, see W. E. B. Du Bois, *The Souls of Black Folk* (1903; Mineola, NY: Dover, 1994).

42. See David Bennetts, "Black and White Workers: New Orleans, 1880–1900" (PhD diss., University of Illinois at Urbana-Champaign); and discussion in chapter 3.

43. Cohen, *A Consumers' Republic*, 52.

44. Mullins, "A Bold and Gorgeous Front," 188.

45. I use the term *rhizomatic* by design here, as my thinking on this was inspired in part by the work of Gilles Deleuze and Felix Guattari, particularly *A Thousand Plateaus* (Minneapolis: University of Minnesota Press, 1987).

Chapter 5

1. Census data in this chapter is compiled from: US Bureau of the Census, *Ninth Census of the United States, 1870* (National Archives, Washington, DC), Ancestry.com; US Bureau of the Census, *Tenth Census of the United States, 1880* (National Archives, Washington, DC), Ancestry.com; US Bureau of the Census, *Twelfth Census of the United States, 1900* (National Archives, Washington, DC), Ancestry.com; US Bureau of the Census, *Thirteenth Census of the United States, 1910* (National Archives, Washington, DC), Ancestry.com; US Bureau of the Census, *Fourteenth Census of the United States, 1920* (National Archives, Washington, DC), Ancestry.com; and US Bureau of the Census, *Fifteenth Census of the United States, 1930*. See chapter 3, note 26, on censuses.

2. Julia Metoyer's death certificate accessed via Ancestry.com database *California, Death Index, 1940–1997*. Hypolite Metoyer death certificate accessed via Ancestry.com database *New Orleans, Louisiana, Death Records Index, 1804–1949*. Record of mar-

riage accessed via Ancestry.com database *New Orleans, Louisiana, Marriage Records Index, 1831–1964.*

3. The term *Creole* is a contentious one in New Orleans, even today, which has only added to confusion stemming from the popularity of creolization as a theoretical paradigm in anthropology and social theory. In New Orleans, the term has gone through at least three cycles of meaning. In the colonial era, it simply referred to anyone born in the colonies, as distinguished from those born in Europe or Africa, while in the antebellum it came to refer to those of French or Spanish background, as opposed to the new Anglophone American population. After emancipation, the meaning shifted again, as it began to have a racial connotation, implying mixed European and African heritage, at least to some. See the discussion in Shannon Dawdy, "Understanding Cultural Change through the Vernacular: Creolization in Louisiana," *Historical Archaeology* 34, no. 3 (2000): 107–23, and the preface from same volume; and Dawdy, "Ethnicity in the Urban Landscape: The Archaeology of Creole New Orleans," in *Archaeology of Southern Urban Landscapes*, ed. Amy Young (Tuscaloosa: University of Alabama Press, 2001), 127–49. See also Stephan Palmié, "Creolization and Its Discontents," *Annual Reviews in Anthropology* 35 (2006): 433–56.

4. Roulhac Toledano and Mary-Louise Christovich, *New Orleans Architecture,* vol. 6, *Faubourg Tremé and the Bayou Road* (Gretna, LA: Pelican, 2003), 3–108; cf. Michael E. Crutcher Jr., *Tremé: Race and Place in a New Orleans Neighborhood* (Athens: University of Georgia Press, 2010); and Gary Van Zante, *New Orleans 1867: Photographs by Theodore Lilienthal* (New York: Merrell, 2008), 80–110.

5. Peirce F. Lewis, *New Orleans: The Making of an Urban Landscape,* 2nd ed. (Santa Fe, NM: Center for American Places), 50–52, fig. 18; cf. John Kellogg, "Negro Urban Clusters in the Postbellum South," *Geographical Review* 67, no. 3 (1977): 310–21.

6. Craig E. Colten, *An Unnatural Metropolis: Wresting New Orleans from Nature* (Baton Rouge: Louisiana State University Press, 2005), 98–99.

7. Virginia R. Domínguez, *White by Definition: Social Classification in Creole Louisiana* (New Brunswick, NJ: Rutgers University Press, 1994).

8. I have not listed the names of individuals who passed over the color line. The consequences of mixed ancestry in a country in which racism and race-based inequalities have remained persistent are still very real.

9. Statistics compiled by author in reference to 1939 HANO survey of properties conducted as part of acquisition process.

10. Toledano and Christovich, *New Orleans Architecture,* 6: 3–108; Freddie Evans, *Congo Square: African Roots of New Orleans* (Lafayette: University of Louisiana at Lafayette, 2011); and Crutcher, *Tremé.*

11. Crutcher, *Tremé*; and Rachel Breunlin, *If Those Bricks Could Talk: A Collaborative Book and Film Devoted to the Lafitte Public Housing Development* (New Orleans: Cornerstones and the Neighborhood Story Project/Center for the Book at the University of New Orleans, 2015); cf. William Borah and Richard Baumbach, *The Second Battle of New Orleans: A History of the Vieux Carre Riverfront Expressway Controversy* (Tuscaloosa: University of Alabama Press, 1980); Mark Souther, *New Orleans on Parade: Tourism and the Transformation of the Crescent City* (Baton Rouge: Louisiana State University Press), 185–220; Laine Kaplan-Levenson, "'The Monster': Claiborne Avenue before and after the Interstate," May 5, 2016, in *TriPod: New Orleans at 300,*

produced by Laine Kaplan-Levenson, podcast, MP3 audio, 10:16, https://www.wwno
.org/post/monster-claiborne-avenue-and-after-interstate. There has been a continued
discussion of the Claiborne freeway overpass, with some planners and community
activists advocating for it to be torn down.

12. Michael Godzinski et al., *Phase I and II Cultural Resources Survey of the Lafitte
Housing Project, New Orleans, Louisiana* (report submitted to Louisiana Division of
Archaeology, Baton Rouge, LA, 2008). ESI generously shared its background research on the Lafitte area; the full technical report was still in progress at the time
of this writing.

13. *Plan of 8 Lots of Ground with Buildings Situated in the 2D District*, A. Castaing and G.A. Celles, Architects, 1851 (NONA 044.077), in the collection of the New
Orleans Notarial Archives.

14. Gary B. Mills, *The Forgotten People: Cane River's Creoles of Color* (Baton Rouge:
Louisiana State University Press, 1977); and Carl A. Brasseaux, Keith P. Fontenot,
and Claude F. Oubre, *Creoles of Color in the Bayou Country* (Jackson: University
Press of Mississippi, 1994). See also: "History," Melrose Plantation, accessed October 2018, http://www.melroseplantation.org/history/; and the Creole Family History Database, a project of the Louisiana Creole Heritage Center, Northwestern State
University, accessed October 2018, https://www.nsula.edu/creole/search.php.

15. Records accessed via Ancestry.com database, *New Orleans, Louisiana, Marriage Records Index, 1831–1964.*

16. New Orleans city directories accessed via Ancestry.com database *U.S. City
Directories, 1822–1995*. For an example of William Metoyer's troubles, see "Policemen
Charge But Negro Is Not," *Times-Picayune*, June 22, 1923.

17. *U.S. City Directories, 1822–1995*, Ancestry.com; and "Fine Progress of the Negro," *Daily Picayune*, December 30, 1913.

18. Laurie A. Wilkie and George Shorter Jr., *Lucrecia's Well: An Archaeological
Glimpse of an African-American Midwife's Household* (Mobile: University of South Ala-
bama, 2001); Laurie Wilkie, *The Archaeology of Mothering: An African-American Mid-
wife's Tale* (New York: Routledge, 2003); and Laurie A. Wilkie, "Expelling Frogs and
Binding Babies: Conception, Gestation, and Birth in Nineteenth-Century African-
American Midwifery," *World Archaeology* 45, no. 2 (2013): 272–84. Some of this work
is informed by both oral history and other research into midwifery. See, for example,
Molly Dougherty, "Southern Midwifery and Organized Health Care: Systems in
Conflict," *Medical Anthropology* 6 (1982): 113–26; Gertrude Fraser, *African-American
Midwifery in the South* (Cambridge: Harvard University Press, 1998); Onnie Logan,
Motherwit: An Alabama Midwife's Story (New York: E. P. Dutton, 1989); and Debra
Ann Susie, *In the Way of Our Grandmothers: A Cultural View of Twentieth-Century
Midwifery in Florida* (Athens: University of Georgia Press, 1988). Discussions of
the role of the midwife and her relationship to the medical profession were going
on internationally as well; see Hilary Marland and Anne Marie Rafferty, eds., *Midwives, Society, and Childbirth: Debates and Controversies in the Modern Period* (London: Routledge, 1997).

19. Arnold A. Kowalsky and Dorothy E. Kowalsky, *Encyclopedia of Marks on American, English, and European Earthenware, Ironstone, and Stoneware, 1780–1980* (Atglen,
PA: Schiffer Books, 1999), 116, 310.

20. For instance, a circa 1884 advertising pamphlet from Fairchild Brothers and
Foster also touts the powder as "the safest and best physiological imitation of moth-

er's milk." See: National Library of Medicine Catalog (NLM ID 101188010), accessed October 2018, https://www.ncbi.nlm.nih.gov/; and *Fairchild's Hand-Book of the Digestive Ferments* (New York: Fairchild Brothers and Foster, 1894).

21. Kodi Roberts has noted that, in forty-one cases of the criminal prosecution of Voodoo workers in Louisiana between 1883 and 1938, the most frequent crimes involved were violations of state medical laws, and six of these cases were initiated by Louisiana's Board of Medical Examiners. See Kodi Roberts, *Voodoo and Power: The Politics of Religion in New Orleans, 1881–1940* (Baton Rouge: Louisiana State Universit Press, 2015), 48, 158–61; cf. Laurie A. Wilkie, "Granny Midwives: Gender and Generational Mediators of the African American Community," in *Engendering African American Archaeology*, ed. Jillian Galle and Amy Young (Knoxville: University of Tennessee Press), 80–81; and Carolyn Morrow Long, *Spiritual Merchants: Religion, Magic, and Commerce* (Knoxville: University of Tennessee Press, 2001).

22. "Medical Examiners," *Daily Picayune*, May 30, 1920.

23. Leslie Reagan, *When Abortion Was a Crime: Women, Medicine, and the Law in the United States, 1867–1973* (Los Angeles: University of California Press, 1997), 54–59. For examples of perforators, see the "Obstetric Instrument Collection," Virtual Medical History Museum, University of Malta, accessed April 2019, http://home.um.edu.mt/med-surg/museum/obstetric.html.

24. Wilkie, "Granny Midwives," 91; and Wilkie, "Expelling Frogs and Binding Babies," 278.

25. The placement of knives under the mattress to cut birth pains (as cited by Wilkie) is widely mentioned as an example of folklore, but I am unaware of the original source. See Barbara Isaacs, "Old Wives' Tales," *Lexington Herald Leader*, August 16, 1999, for a contemporary reference. Julie Webb, in a survey of superstitions among patients and nurses (primarily African American) in Louisiana found, particularly among the nurse, many examples of variations of this practice, involving knives, scissors, and axes. See Julie Yvonne Webb, "Louisiana Voodoo and Superstitions Related to Health," *Health Services and Mental Health Administration Health Reports* 86, no. 4 (1971): 297; and Webb, *Superstitious Influence—Voodoo in Particular—Affecting Health Practices in a Selected Population in Southern Louisiana* (New Orleans: published by author, 1971).

26. W. E. B. Du Bois, *The Souls of Black Folk* (1903; Mineola, NY: Dover, 1994); E. Franklin Frazier, *Race and Culture Contacts in the Modern World* (Boston: Beacon Press, 1957); and Melville Herskovits, *The Myth of the Negro Past* (Boston: Beacon Press, 1941).

27. Sidney Mintz and Richard Price, *The Birth of African-American Culture: An Anthropological Perspective* (Boston: Beacon Press, 1992).

28. Christopher C. Fennell, *Crossroads and Cosmologies: Diasporas and Ethnogenesis in the New World* (Gainesville: University Press of Florida, 2007), 8–9. See also Philip D. Morgan, "The Cultural Implications of the Atlantic Slave Trade: African Regional Origins, American Destinations, and New World Developments," *Slavery and Abolition* 18, no. 1 (1997): 122–45; Palmié, "Creolization and Its Discontents"; and Dawdy, "Understanding Cultural Change."

29. Fennell, *Crossroads and Cosmologies*, 72–77, qtd. material from 72 and 73.

30. James Davidson, "Deconstructing the Myth of the 'Hand Charm': Mundane Clothing Fasteners and Their Curious Transformation into Supernatural Objects," *Historical Archaeology* 48, no. 2 (2014): 18–60.

31. Even though the use of the raccoon baculum as a charm is well known, there seems to be relatively little serious research on the origins and distribution of the beliefs associated with it, with attributions tracing it variously to Appalachia or the Ozarks, or even to Native American traditions. Catherine Yronwode of the Lucky Mojo Curio Company (one of many distributors that sells the item) gives an overview of penis bone use: "Raccoon Penis Bones," Lucky W Amulet Archive, Lucky Mojo Curio Company, accessed October 2018, http://www.luckymojo.com/raccoonpenis .html.

32. Roberts, *Voodoo and Power*, 7–12, 211–12.

33. Roberts, 211–12.

34. Harry Hyatt, *Hoodoo, Conjuration, Witchcraft, Rootwork*, vol. 2 (Hannibal, MO: Western, 1970), 1351–86, 1675–89. See, for example, Emily Clark, *Masterless Mistresses: The New Orleans Ursulines and the Development of a New World Society, 1727–1834* (Chapel Hill: University of North Carolina Press, 2007); Christine Vella, *Intimate Enemies: The Two Worlds of the Baroness Pontalba* (Baton Rouge: Louisiana State University Press, 1997); Martha Ward, *Voodoo Queen: The Spirited Lives of Marie Laveau* (Oxford: University Press of Mississippi, 2004); and Carolyn Morrow Long, *A New Orleans Voudou Priestess: The Legend and Reality of Marie Laveau* (Gainesville: University Press of Florida, 2007).

35. Wilkie, "Granny Midwives," 79.

Chapter 6

1. See, for example, businesses with Storyville in the name in Emily Landau, *Spectacular Wickedness: Sex, Race, and Memory in Storyville, New Orleans* (Baton Rouge: Louisiana State University Press, 2013), 206; and Alecia P. Long, "Poverty Is the New Prostitution: Race, Poverty, and Public Housing in Post-Katrina New Orleans," *Journal of American History* 94, no. 3 (2007): 795–803.

2. "Two Bawdy Reminders of Storyville Razed," *Times-Picayune*, December 28, 1999; and Katy Reckdahl, "Three Buildings Remain from Red Light District," *Advocate New Orleans*, November 10, 2013.

3. Storyville is a point of discussion in oral histories and biographies of a number of jazz musicians, even occasionally ones who are unlikely to have spent substantial time there. See discussion in Matthew Sutton, "Storyville: Discourses in Southern Musicians' Autobiographies" (PhD diss., College of William and Mary, 2012). Jelly Roll Morton discusses Storyville as a birthplace of jazz in Alan Lomax, *Mister Jelly Roll: The Fortunes of Jelly Roll Morton, New Orleans Creole and "Inventor of Jazz"* (Berkeley: University of California Press, 2001); while Buddy Bolden's connections are immortalized in fiction in Michael Ondaatje's *Coming through Slaughter* (Toronto: House of Anansi Press, 1976). See also Herbert Asbury, *The French Quarter: An Informal History of the New Orleans Underworld* (1938; New York: Thunder's Mouth Press, 2003); Al Rose, *Storyville, New Orleans: Being an Authentic, Illustrated Account of the Notorious Red-Light District* (Tuscaloosa: University of Alabama Press, 1979); and Craig Foster, "Tarnished Angels: Prostitution in Storyville, New Orleans, 1900–1910," *Louisiana History* 31, no. 4 (1990): 387–97.

4. Alecia P. Long, *The Great Southern Babylon: Sex, Race, and Respectability in New Orleans* (Baton Rouge: Louisiana State University Press, 2004), 129–38. Landau's *Spectacular Wickedness* remains the most thorough book-length treatment of

the subject, while Pamela Arceneaux has recently examined this aspect of Storyville in great detail in *Guidebooks to Sin: The Blue Books of Storyville, New Orleans* (New Orleans: Historic New Orleans Collection, 2017). A previous and somewhat obscure work, printed under a pseudonym, also focused on the Blue Books while providing some additional information about Storyville; see Semper Idem, *The "Blue Book": A Bibliographical Attempt to Describe the Guide Books to the Houses of Ill Fame in New Orleans*, Heartman's Historical Series no. 50 (N.p.: Privately printed, 1936). Shannon Lee Dawdy's *Patina* (Chicago: University of Chicago Press, 2016) devotes some time to the district as well. My knowledge of Storyville has been enhanced by conversations with local historian Katy Coyle, who has devoted considerable research efforts to the district. On prostitution, commercial sex, and the reputation of New Orleans for licentiousness more generally, see Shannon Lee Dawdy, *Building the Devil's Empire: French Colonial New Orleans* (Chicago: University of Chicago Press, 2008); Mark Souther, *New Orleans on Parade: Tourism and the Transformation of the Crescent City* (Baton Rouge: Louisiana State University Press, 2006); Judith Kelleher Schafer, *Brothels, Depravity, and Abandoned Women: Illegal Sex in Antebellum New Orleans* (Baton Rouge: Louisiana State University Press, 2009); Gary Krist, *Empire of Sin: A Story of Sex, Jazz, Murder, and the Battle for Modern New Orleans* (New York: Crown Press, 2014). Storyville is a subject in many studies of red-light districts and the segregation of prostitution around the country in the Progressive Era. See Ruth Rosen, *The Lost Sisterhood: Prostitution in America, 1900–1918* (Baltimore: John Hopkins University Press, 1983); and Mara Keire, *For Business and Pleasure: Red-Light Districts and the Regulation of Vice in the United States, 1890–1933* (Baltimore: Johns Hopkins University Press, 2010). For prostitution in the Victorian era more generally, see Judith Walkowitz, *Prostitution and Victorian Society: Women, Class, and the State* (Cambridge: Cambridge University Press, 1980).

5. Roulhac Toledano and Mary-Louise Christovich, *New Orleans Architecture*, vol. 6, *Faubourg Tremé and the Bayou Road* (Gretna, LA: Pelican, 2003), 56–57.

6. Toledano and Christovich; cf. Michael E. Crutcher Jr., *Tremé: Race and Place in a New Orleans Neighborhood* (Athens: University of Georgia Press, 2010); and Freddie Evans, *Congo Square: African Roots of New Orleans* (Lafayette: University of Louisiana at Lafayette, 2011).

7. Editorial, *Mascot*, June 11, 1892, cited in Rose, *Storyville*, 37.

8. The Sanborns from the Storyville area in its years of operation show almost all buildings designated with "F. B." to indicate this use.

9. US Bureau of the Census, *Tenth Census of the United States, 1880* (National Archives, Washington, DC), Ancestry.com; and Sanborn Map Company, *Insurance Maps of New Orleans, Louisiana*, 1885 ed. (New York: Sanborn Map, 1876–1937).

10. Landau, *Spectacular Wickedness*, 95, 107; and Rose, *Storyville*, 192–93.

11. See Arceneaux, *Guidebooks to Sin*, for a summary of the state of current knowledge of the Blue Books. I thank ESI, whose historians transcribed the name and address information into spreadsheets by year.

12. Landau, *Spectacular Wickedness*, 23.

13. The age of Lillian Young as listed in the 1910 census matches what Dixie Wood's should have been if she had aged ten years. I think it likely that the census recorder just reversed the names; again, as discussed in this chapter, many of the names and identities used in Storyville were clearly manufactured, so this possibility should not really be a surprise.

14. See Mara Keire, *For Business and Pleasure: Red-Light Districts and the Regulation of Vice in the United States, 1890–1933* (Baltimore: Johns Hopkins University Press, 2010).

15. Long, *The Great Southern Babylon*, 181–82, 191–224; and Landau, *Spectacular Wickedness*, 170–71, 196–97; cf. Virginia R. Domínguez, *White by Definition: Social Classification in Creole Louisiana* (New Brunswick, NJ: Rutgers University Press, 1994).

16. Kim Marie Vaz, *The "Baby Dolls": Breaking the Race and Gender Barriers of the New Orleans Mardi Gras Tradition* (Baton Rouge: Louisiana State University Press, 2013); cf. Foster, "Tarnished Angels"; and Rose, *Storyville*, 177–81.

17. Harry Johnston, *The Negro in the New World* (London: Methuen, 1910), 459.

18. Housing Authority of New Orleans, *Report of the Housing Authority of New Orleans, 1939* (New Orleans: HANO, 1939).

19. "Bone, Artifact Finds Raise Call for Dig," *Times-Picayune*, June 5, 1999; the limited project done at the time is discussed in Eric A. Powell, "Tales from Storyville," *Archaeology Magazine* 55, no. 6 (November/December 2002): 26–31. A manuscript report of those investigations is still on file at ESI and will hopefully be incorporated into the future data recovery reports.

20. I moved from one to the other part of the project during this time: I supervised the excavations for ESI, and I was at the University of Chicago when the analysis and report production were being finished.

21. Shannon Lee Dawdy, D. Ryan Gray, and Jill-Karen Yakubik, *Archaeological Investigations at the Rising Sun Hotel Site (16OR225), New Orleans, Louisiana*, vol. 1 (report prepared for HNOC, 2008).

22. "Rising Sun Hotel," *Louisiana Gazette*, January 29, 1821.

23. Shannon Lee Dawdy and Richard Weyhing, "Beneath the Rising Sun: 'Frenchness' and the Archaeology of Desire," *International Journal of Historical Archaeology* 12, no. 4 (2008): 370–87; property information available in the Collins C. Diboll Vieux Carré Digital Survey, HNOC, accessed October 2018, https://www.hnoc.org/vcs/.

24. Skeleton discoveries were reported in the area almost a century apart; see "25 Skeletons Dug Up by Sewerage Workers," *New Orleans Item*, July 8, 1908; and "Unearthed Bones a Case for Historians," *Times-Picayune* September 18, 1997. Excavations along Basin Street in 1915 had also unearthed human remains. ESI has prepared a number of preliminary reports on its work in the Iberville area. See, for example, Michael Godzinski et al., *Cultural Resource Investigations of Blocks I and F at the Iberville Housing Project, New Orleans, Orleans Parish, Louisiana* (report prepared for HANO, 2013).

25. The first season of UNO excavations at the Iberville Project were directed by me and Andrea White, then the director of the now-defunct Greater New Orleans Archaeology Program, which was also housed at UNO.

26. The UNO students, including undergraduate anthropology majors and graduate students in the Master of Science in Urban Studies program, learned basic excavation techniques and archaeological methods in a hands-on fashion in the field school. Graduate students from other universities, including the University of Florida, Michigan State, and the University of Chicago, joined us as well. While our focus was the era predating the construction of Iberville, the systematic collection of material from the more recent Iberville-era components may allow researchers

to address questions about surveillance, visibility, and the use of space in housing projects. At least one dissertation is in the works that draws on the Iberville data: Grace Krause, doctoral candidate at Michigan State University, is drafting a thesis tentatively titled "Landscape, Food, and the Erotic Commodity Experience in New Orleans." Further, Dutch graphic artist Toon Fibbe of the Deltaworkers artists exchange program made use of this material in a performance piece on the "ghosts of capitalism." This piece was called "New Orleans and the Dark Prince of Finance." For an interview about Fibbe's New Orleans work, see: Toon Fibbe, "Haunted Housing: An Interview with Toon Fibbe," interview by Asher Kaplan, *Pelican Bomb*, June 27, 2016, http://pelicanbomb.com/art-review/2016/haunted-housing-an-interview-with-toon-fibbe.

27. Meanings of blue beads have most often been discussed in reference to Linda Stine, Melanie A. Cabak, and Mark D. Groover, "Blue Beads as African-American Cultural Symbols," *Historical Archaeology* 30, no. 3 (1996): 49–75.

28. Horne, Gerald. *The Deepest South: The United States, Brazil, and the African Slave Trade* (New York: New York University Press, 2007), 3–5.

29. I thank Elizabeth Williams, who did field work with us at UNO as part of the field school and subsequently undertook some of her own research on the Square 130 properties. Williams shared her research from the City Archives at the New Orleans Public Library on sewerage hook-ups in the block. She also presented her research as part of a public "Storyville Uncovered" event in 2013.

30. See, for instance, Rebecca Yamin, "Wealthy, Free, and Female: Prostitution in Nineteenth-Century New York," *Historical Archaeology* 39, no. 1 (2005): 4–18; Michael Foster, John Lindly, and Ronald Ryden, "The Soiled Doves of South Granite Street: The History and Archaeology of a Prescott, Arizona Brothel," *Journal of Southwestern Archaeology and History* 70, no. 4 (2005): 349–74; Robert Schmidt and Barbara Voss, eds., *Archaeologies of Sexuality* (London: Taylor and Francis, 2000); and Donna J. Seifert, "Mrs. Starr's Profession," in *Those of Little Note: Gender, Race and Class in Historical Archaeology*, ed. Elizabeth M. Scott (Tucson: University of Arizona Press, 1994), 149–73.

31. Dawdy, *Patina*, 101–9; Kerry Segrave, *Baldness: A Social History* (Jefferson, NC: McFarland, 1996); Jamie C. Brandon, "Bear Grease in the Bear State and the Power of Artifacts in Context," *Farther Along . . .* (blog), July 10, 2013, https://fartheralong.wordpress.com/2013/07/10/bear-grease-in-the-bear-state-the-power-of-artifacts-in-context/; and John Strachan, *Advertising and Satirical Culture in the Romantic Period* (Cambridge: Cambridge University Press, 2007).

32. Thanks again to Elizabeth Williams and ESI, who have found these bottles from the Gray Medicine Company in abundance in some assemblages. See Jill Jonnes, "Forgotten History of Illegal Drugs," *Baltimore Sun*, February 16, 1995. The product had gained some notoriety already in the early 1900s, being listed in places like the "Report of the Food and Dairy Commissioner to the Governor of Connecticut for the Two Years Ending in 1908" as one of a variety of products containing cocaine.

33. Landau, *Spectacular Wickedness*, 107.

34. Landau, 162. See also Robert Burns Beath, *History of the Grand Army of the Republic* (New York: Bryan, Taylor, 1888); and Grand Army of the Republic, Joseph A. Mower Post No. 1 Records, 1875–1922, Manuscripts Collection 227, Louisiana Research Collection, Tulane University. Thanks to Alexandra Dacy, a student from

my New Orleans archaeology class at UNO, who spent a great deal of time trying to match residents in the vicinity of the address with the GAR membership rolls and Mower Post records housed at Tulane, and to Dean Enderlin, a National GAR Records Officer from the Sons of Union Veterans of the Civil War, who assisted her via email. A number of other students did research projects involving individual objects found in assemblages discussed here, including Brandy Delcazal, Jessica deMelo, and Michael Medina, who researched pine tar oil, bear grease, and Brazilian currency under Pedro I, respectively.

35. Richard Campanella, *Geographies of New Orleans: Urban Fabrics before the Storm* (Lafayette: Center for Louisiana Studies, 2006), 337–55; and D. Ryan Gray, "Identity and the Material Dimensions of Public and Private Practice: Archaeology of a Chinese Laundry in New Orleans" (master's thesis, University of Chicago, 2009); cf. Moon-Ho Jung, *Coolies and Cane: Race, Labor, and Sugar in the Age of Emancipation* (Baltimore: Johns Hopkins University Press, 2006); and Lucy Cohen, *Chinese in the Post–Civil War South: A People without a History* (Baton Rouge: Louisiana State University Press, 1984).

36. Rosen, *The Lost Sisterhood*, 111.

37. Landau, *Spectacular Wickedness*, 100–102.

38. US Bureau of the Census, *Twelfth Census of the United States, 1900* (National Archives, Washington, DC), Ancestry.com; and US Bureau of the Census, *Thirteenth Census of the United States, 1910* (National Archives, Washington, DC), Ancestry.com.

Chapter 7

1. Nancy D. Munn, "The 'Becoming-Past' of Places: Spacetime and Memory in 19th Century, Pre–Civil War New York," *Suomen Antropologi* 29, no. 1 (2004): 2–19; for recent examples, see Laura McAtackney and Krysta Ryzewski, eds., *Contemporary Archaeology and the City: Creativity, Ruination, and Political Action* (New York: Oxford University Press, 2017). Paul R. Mullins's work on urban renewal in Indianapolis particularly matches well with the work discussed here; see his "The Optimism of Absence: An Archaeology of Displacement, Effacement, and Modernity," in McAtackney and Ryzewski, *Contemporary Archaeology and the City*, 244–61. For a good overview of the field more broadly, see Nan Rothschild and Diana diZerega Wall, *The Archaeology of American Cities* (Gainesville: University Press of Florida, 2014).

2. Gilbert Osofsky, *Harlem: The Making of a Ghetto* (New York: Harper and Row, 1968); Arnold R. Hirsch, *Making the Second Ghetto: Race and Housing in Chicago, 1940–1960* (New York: Cambridge University Press, 1983); John F. Bauman, *Public Housing, Race, and Renewal: Urban Planning in Philadelphia, 1920–1974* (Philadelphia: Temple University Press, 1987); David W. Bartelt, "Housing the 'Underclass,'" in *The "Underclass" Debate: Views from History*, ed. Michael Katz (Princeton, NJ: Princeton University Press, 1993); Douglas Massey and Nancy Denton, *American Apartheid: Segregation and the Making of the Underclass* (Cambridge, MA: Harvard University Press, 1987); Steven Gregory, *Black Corona: Race and the Politics of Place in an Urban Community* (Princeton, NJ: Princeton University Press, 1998); James R. Saunders and Renae Shackelford, *Urban Renewal and the End of Black Culture in Charlottesville, Virginia* (Jefferson, NC: McFarland, 1998); Kevin Fox Gotham, *Race, Real Estate, and Uneven Development: The Kansas City Experience, 1900–2000*

(Albany: State University of New York Press, 2002); Lawrence J. Vale, *From the Puritans to the Projects: Public Housing and Public Neighbors* (Cambridge, MA: Harvard University Press, 2000); Vale, *Purging the Poorest: Public Housing and the Design Politics of Twice-Cleared Communities* (Chicago: University of Chicago Press, 2013); Thomas Sugrue, *The Origins of the Urban Crisis: Race and Inequality in Postwar Detroit* (Princeton: Princeton University Press, 2005); Joseph Heathcott, "Black Archipelago: Politics and Civil Life in the Jim Crow City," *Journal of Social History* 38, no. 3 (2005): 705–36; and Loïc Wacquant, *Urban Outcasts: A Comparative Sociology of Advanced Marginality* (Cambridge: Polity, 2008). On the growth of suburbs, see, among others: Kenneth T. Jackson, *Crabgrass Frontier: The Suburbanization of the United States* (New York: Oxford University Press, 1985); Joel Garreau, *Edge City: Life on the New Frontier* (New York: Anchor Books, 1992); and Dolores Hayden, *Building Suburbia: Green Fields and Urban Growth, 1820–2000* (New York: Pantheon Books, 2003).

3. Wacquant, *Urban Outcasts,* 229–56; see the discussion of the application of Oscar Lewis's culture of poverty to inner-city African American neighborhoods in chapter 4 of this volume.

4. Chicago, for instance, was faced with such an acute shortage of housing that this reformist ethos had little opportunity to have a practical effect. See Devereux Bowly Jr., *The Poorhouse: Subsidized Housing in Chicago, 1895–1976* (Carbondale: Southern Illinois University Press, 1978); and Hirsch, *Making the Second Ghetto.*

5. Mike Davis, *Planet of Slums* (London: Verso Books, 2006), 22.

6. Diana diZerega Wall, Nan A. Rothschild, and Cynthia Copeland, "Seneca Village and Little Africa: Two African American Communities in Antebellum New York City," *Historical Archaeology* 42, no. 1 (2008): 97–107; cf. Leslie Harris, *In the Shadow of Slavery: African Americans in New York City, 1626–1863* (Chicago: University of Chicago Press, 2003).

7. Henry Louis Taylor Jr. and Walter Hill, prologue to *Historical Roots of the Urban Crisis: African Americans in the Industrial City, 1900–1950,* ed. Henry Louis Taylor Jr. and Walter Hill (New York: Garland, 2000), 12. See, for example, W. E. B. Du Bois, *The Philadelphia Negro: A Social Study* (New York: Oxford University Press, 2007); and St. Clair Drake and Horace R. Cayton, *Black Metropolis: A Study of Negro Life in a Northern City* (New York: Harcourt, Brace, 1945); cf. John L. Jackson Jr., *Harlemworld: Doing Race and Class in Contemporary Black America* (Chicago: University of Chicago Press, 2001); Joe William Trotter Jr., *Black Milwaukee: The Making of an Industrial Proletariat, 1915–1945* (Urbana: University of Illinois Press, 1985); Trotter, *Coal, Class, and Color: Blacks in Southern West Virginia, 1915–32* (Urbana: University of Illinois Press, 1990); Lizabeth Cohen, *Making a New Deal: Industrial Workers in Chicago, 1919–1939* (Cambridge: Cambridge University Press, 1990); Earl Lewis, *In Their Own Interests: Race, Class, and Power in Twentieth-Century Norfolk, Virginia* (Berkeley: University of California Press, 1991); Robin D. G. Kelley, *Hammer and Hoe: Alabama Communists in the Great Depression* (Durham: University of North Carolina Press, 1990); and Kelley, *Race Rebels: Culture, Politics, and the Black Working Class* (New York: Free Press, 1994).

8. Robin D. G. Kelley, "'We Are Not What We Seem': Rethinking Black Working-Class Opposition in the Jim Crow South," in *The New African American Urban History,* ed. Kenneth Goings and Raymond Mohl (Thousand Oaks, CA: Sage, 1996), 202.

9. Carol Stack, *All Our Kin: Strategies for Survival in a Black Community* (New

York: Basic Books, 1974), 28; cf. Gerald D. Suttles, *The Social Order of the Slums: Ethnicity and Territory in the Inner City* (Chicago: University of Chicago Press, 1968).

10. Stack, *All Our Kin*, 31.

11. Qtd. from "Van of 5000 Local Families Move into Low Rent Project," *Times-Picayune*, January 15, 1941; see also "Magnolia Street Housing Project to Open on Nov. 1," *Times-Picayune* September 22, 1940; cf. Joseph Heathcott, "'In the Nature of a Clinic': The Design of Early Public Housing in St. Louis," *Journal of the Society of Architectural Historians* 70, no. 1 (2011): 82–103; Bauman, *Public Housing*; Gwendolyn Wright, *Building the Dream: A Social History of Housing in America* (Cambridge: MIT Press, 1981); and Richard Pommer, "The Architecture of Urban Housing in the United States during the Early 1930s," *Journal of the Society of Architectural Historians* 37, no. 4 (1978): 235–64.

12. Michael Katz, "The Urban 'Underclass' as a Metaphor for Social Transformation," in Katz, *The "Underclass" Debate*, 3–23; cf. Suzanne Spencer-Wood and Christopher Matthews, "Impoverishment, Criminalization, and the Culture of Poverty," *Historical Archaeology* 45, no. 3 (2011): 2–3.

13. See, for example, David Roediger, *Working toward Whiteness: How America's Immigrants Became White* (New York: Basic Books, 2005).

14. Paul R. Mullins, "'A Bold and Gorgeous Front': The Contradictions of African America and Consumer Culture," in *Historical Archaeologies of Capitalism*, ed. Mark P. Leone and Parker B. Potter Jr. (New York: Kluwer Academic, 1999), 175–76.

15. See, for instance, John McCarthy, "Values and Identity in the 'Working-Class' Worlds of Late Nineteenth-Century Minneapolis," in *The Archaeology of Urban Landscapes: Explorations in Slumland*, ed. Alan Mayne and Tim Murray (Cambridge: Cambridge University Press, 2001), 145–53; and Rebecca Yamin, "Alternative Narratives: Respectability at New York's Five Points," 154–71 in the same volume. Comparisons of assemblages from West Oakland and San Francisco can be found in Mary Praetzellis, ed., *SF-80 Bayshore Viaduct Seismic Retrofit Projects Report on Construction Monitoring, Geoarchaeology, and Technical and Interpretive Studies for Historical Archaeology* (report prepared for the Office of Cultural Resource Studies, California Department of Transportation, 2004), esp. 357–71, 416–24. An invaluable resource for considering the multiplicity of late nineteenth- and early twentieth-century urban assemblages is Mary Praetzellis and Adrian Praetzellis, *Putting the "There" There: Historical Archaeologies of West Oakland: I-880 Cypress Freeway Replacement Project* (report prepared for the California Department of Transportation; Rohnert Park, CA: Anthropological Studies Center, Sonoma State University, 2004); the block technical reports with technical data are available online and were consulted as comparative data in this project.

16. In the era since Katrina, a series of large, well-reported urban investigations have taken place, most of which have scarcely been considered here. See, for instance, R. Christopher Goodwin et al., *Becoming New Orleanian: An Archaeological Perspective on Urbanization and Americanization in Lower Mid-City during the Late 19th and Early 20th Centuries* (report submitted to US Department of Veterans Affairs and Louisiana Division of Archaeology, Baton Rouge, 2016); and Aubra Lee et al., *Cultural Resource Investigations of City Squares 324 (16OR627), 349 (16OR628), 350 (16OR629), 357 (16OR630), 358 (16OR631), and 383 (16OR602) of the William J. Guste Housing Complex, New Orleans, Orleans Parish, Louisiana* (report submitted to HANO and the Louisiana Division of Archaeology, Baton Rouge, 2018).

17. Paul R. Mullins has made effective use of Du Bois's double-consciousness in studies of consumer culture in historical archaeology; see his *Race and Affluence: An Archaeology of African America and Consumer Culture* (New York: Kluwer Academic, 1999).

18. Monica Miller, "W. E. B. Du Bois and the Dandy as Diasporic Race Man," *Callaloo* 26, no. 3 (2003): 738–65; and Miller, *Slaves to Fashion: Black Dandyism and the Styling of Black Diasporic Identity* (Durham, NC: Duke University Press, 2009).

19. Robin D. G. Kelley, "'We Are Not What We Seem': Rethinking Black Working-Class Opposition in the Jim Crow South," in *The New African American Urban History*, ed. Kenneth Goings and Raymond Mohl (Thousand Oaks, CA: Sage, 1996), 187–239.

20. Daphne Spain, "Race Relations and Residential Segregation in New Orleans: Two Centuries of Paradox," *Annas of the American Academy of Political and Social Science* 441 (1979): 90; cf. Anthony Margavio, "Residential Segregation in New Orleans: A Statistical Analysis of Census Data" (PhD diss., Louisiana State University, 1968).

21. Wright, *Building the Dream*, 234.

22. On Freedmen's Town, see Tomiko Meeks, "Freedmen's Town, Texas: A Lesson in the Failure of Historic Preservation," *Houston History* 8, no. 2 (2011): 42–44; see also Eugene Foster and Linda Nance, eds., *Archaeological Investigation Report: Allan Parkway Village, 41HR886, Houston, Harris County, Texas* (report submitted to the Housing Authority of the City of Houston. Austin, TX: PBS&J, 2002). On Techwood Homes, see Irene Hollman, "Techwood Homes," in *New Georgia Encyclopedia*, Georgia Humanities and University of Georgia Press, article published June 20, 2008, last modified May 16, 2018, https://www.georgiaencyclopedia.org/articles/arts-culture/techwood-homes; Frank Ruechel, "New Deal Public Housing, Urban Poverty, and Jim Crow: Techwood and University Homes in Atlanta," *Georgia Historical Quarterly* 81, no. 4 (1997): 915–37; Florence Fleming Corley, "Atlanta's Techwood and University Homes Projects: The Nation's Laboratory for Public Housing," *Atlanta History* 31, no. 4 (1987): 17–36; and Jeffrey W. Gardner et al., *Material Culture and Consumer Choices at Tech Flats: Archaeological and Historical Investigations of the Techwood/Clark Howell Urban Revitalization Tract, Atlanta, Georgia* (Atlanta: Brockington and Associates, 1998).

23. Forrest LaViolette and Joseph Taylor, *Negro Housing in New Orleans* (special research report to the Commission on Race and Houing, New Orleans, 1957), 19–20; and Spain, "Race Relations."

24. LaViolette and Taylor, *Negro Housing in New Orleans*, 53.

25. Juliette Landphair, "'The Forgotten People of New Orleans': Community, Vulnerability, and the Lower Ninth Ward," *Journal of American History* 94, no. 3 (2007): 837–45; Todd Michney, "Black Middle Class Mobility and New Orleans East" (paper, Annual Meeting of the Southern Historical Association, New Orleans, October 2008); and Joyce Jackson, "Declaration of Taking Twice: The Fazendeville Community of the Lower Ninth Ward," *American Anthropologist* 108, no. 4 (2006): 765–80.

26. Ironically, the growth in scale of public housing in New Orleans was considered by some to be a sign of its success. Maurice d'Arlan Needham states that HANO was considered to be one of the four best-run public housing programs in the country, merely by its success in completing so many units; see his *Negro Orleanian: Status and Stake in a City's Economy and Housing* (New Orleans: Tulane,

1962); cf. Martha Mahoney, "The Changing Nature of Public Housing in New Orleans, 1930–1974" (master's thesis, Tulane University, 1985), 61.

27. See, for example, Nine Times Social and Pleasure Club, *Coming Out the Door in the Ninth Ward* (New Orleans: Neighborhood Story Project, 2006); Orissa Arend, *Showdown in Desire: The Black Panthers Take a Stand in New Orleans* (Little Rock: University of Arkansas Press, 2009); and Kent Germany, *New Orleans after the Promises: Poverty, Citizenship, and the Search for the Great Society* (Athens: University of Georgia Press, 2007), 271–95.

28. Frances Fox Piven and Richard Cloward, *Regulating the Poor: The Functions of Public Welfare* (New York: Vintage Books, 1971), 139–41.

29. Mahoney, "The Changing Nature of Public Housing," 6.

30. Michael E. Crutcher Jr., *Tremé: Race and Place in a New Orleans Neighborhood* (Athens: University of Georgia Press, 2010).

31. Michael P. Smith and Marlene Keller, "'Managed Growth' and the Politics of Uneven Development in New Orleans," in *Restructuring the City: The Political Economy of Urban Redevelopment*, ed. Susan Fainstein et al. (New York: Longman, 1983), 135; also cited in Crutcher, *Tremé*, 44–45. For an example of the argument that New Orleans was largely untouched by postwar urban development, see Richard Moe and Carter Wilkie, *Changing Places: Rebuilding Community in the Age of Sprawl* (New York: Henry Holt, 1997), 107.

32. "FAQ," Columbia Parc at the Bayou District, accessed October 2018, http://www.columbiaparc.com/st-bernard/faq.php.

33. Wright, *Building the American Dream*, 231–37.

34. See, for example, Manning Marable and Kristen Clarke, *Seeking Higher Ground: The Hurricane Katrina Crisis, Race, and Public Policy Reader* (New York: Palgrave Macmillan, 2008); Rachel A. Woldoff and Brian J. Gerber, "Protect or Neglect? Social Structure, Decision Making, and the Risk of Living in African American Places in New Orleans," in *Racing the Storm: Racial Implications and Lessons Learned from Hurricane Katrina*, ed. Hillary Potter (Lanham, MD: Lexington Books, 2007), 171–96; and Michael P. Powers, "A Matter of Choice: Historical Lessons for Disaster Recovery," in *There Is No Such Thing as a Natural Disaster: Race, Class, and Hurricane Katrina*, ed. Chester Hartman and Gregory D. Squires (New York: Routledge, 2006), 13–36.

Works Cited

Adams, William Hampton. "Dating Historical Sites: The Importance of Understanding Time Lag in the Acquisition, Curation, Use, and Disposal of Artifacts." *Historical Archaeology* 37, no. 2 (2003): 38–64.

Alexander, Michelle. *The New Jim Crow: Mass Incarceration in the Age of Colorblindness.* New York: New Press, 2010.

Allain, Mathe. "Slave Policies in French Louisiana." *Louisiana History* 21, no. 2 (1980): 127–38.

Althusser, Louis. *Lenin and Philosophy, and Other Essays.* New York: Monthly Review Press, 1971.

Anderson, Benedict. *Imagined Communities: Reflections on the Origin and Spread of Nationalism.* Rev. ed. London: Verso, 1991.

Appadurai, Arjun. *The Social Life of Things: Commodities in Cultural Perspective.* Cambridge: Cambridge University Press, 1986.

Arceneaux, Pamela. *Guidebooks to Sin: The Blue Books of Storyville, New Orleans.* New Orleans: Historic New Orleans Collection, 2017.

Arena, John. *Driven from New Orleans: How Nonprofits Betray Public Housing and Promote Privatization.* Minneapolis: University of Minnesota Press, 2012.

Arend, Orissa. *Showdown in Desire: The Black Panthers Take a Stand in New Orleans.* Little Rock: University of Arkansas Press, 2009.

Arnesen, Eric. *Waterfront Workers of New Orleans: Race, Class, and Politics, 1863–1923.* New York: Oxford University Press, 1994.

Asbury, Herbert. *The French Quarter: An Informal History of the New Orleans Underworld.* 1938. New York: Thunder's Mouth Press, 2003.

Bagert, Brod, Jr. "HOPE VI and St. Thomas: Smoke, Mirrors and Urban Mercantilism." Master's thesis, London School of Economics, 2002.

Barrios, Roberto E. "You Found Us Doing This, This Is Our Way: Criminalizing Second Lines, Super Sunday, and Habitus in Post-Katrina New Orleans." *Identities* 17 (2010): 586–612.

Barrows, Robert. "The Local Origins of a New Deal Housing Project: The Case of Lockfield Gardens in Indianapolis." *Indiana Magazine of History* 103, no. 2 (2007): 125–51.

Bartelt, David W. "Housing the 'Underclass.'" In Katz, *The "Underclass" Debate,* 118–58.

Barth, Fredrik. Introduction to *Ethnic Groups and Boundaries*, 9–38. Boston: Little, Brown, 1969.

Bauman, John F. *Public Housing, Race, and Renewal: Urban Planning in Philadelphia, 1920–1974*. Philadelphia: Temple University Press, 1987.

Baumann, Timothy. "Defining Ethnicity." *SAA Archaeological Record* 4, no. 4 (2004): 12–14.

Beath, Robert Burns. *History of the Grand Army of the Republic*. New York: Bryan, Taylor, 1888.

Beaudry, Mary C., Lauren J. Cook, and Stephen A. Mrozowski. "Artifacts and Active Voices: Material Culture as Social Discourse." In McGuire and Paynter, *The Archaeology of Inequality*, 150–91.

Bell, Caryn Cossé. *Revolution, Romanticism, and the Afro-Creole Protest Tradition in Louisiana, 1718–1868*. Baton Rouge: Louisiana State University Press, 1997.

———. "'Une Chimère': The Freedmen's Bureau in Creole New Orleans." In *The Freedmen's Bureau and Reconstruction: Reconsiderations*, edited by Paul Cimbala and Randall Miller, 140–60. New York: Fordham University Press, 1999.

Bennetts, David. "Black and White Workers: New Orleans, 1880–1900." PhD diss., University of Illinois at Urbana-Champaign, 1972.

Biehl, João, Byron Good, and Arthur Kleinman. "Introduction: Rethinking Subjectivity." In *Subjectivity: Ethnographic Investigations*, edited by João Biehl, Byron Good, and Arthur Kleinman, 1–23. Berkeley: University of California Press, 2007.

Bissell, William Cunningham. *Urban Design, Chaos, and Colonial Power in Zanzibar*. Bloomington: Indiana University Press, 2010.

Blassingame, John W. *Black New Orleans, 1860–1880*. Chicago: University of Chicago Press, 1973.

Borah, William, and Richard Baumbach. *The Second Battle of New Orleans: A History of the Vieux Carre Riverfront Expressway Controversy*. Tuscaloosa: University of Alabama Press, 1980.

Bordelon, Blair. "An Ethnic 'State of Mind': Historical Archaeology of Immigrant Identities in the New Orleans Irish Channel, 1850–1920." *Louisiana Archaeology* 40 (2015): 113–34.

Bourdieu, Pierre. *Outline of a Theory of Practice*. Cambridge: Cambridge University Press, 1995.

Bowly, Devereux, Jr. *The Poorhouse: Subsidized Housing in Chicago, 1895–1976*. Carbondale: Southern Illinois University Press, 1978.

Boyer, Paul. *Urban Masses and Moral Order in America, 1820–1920*. Cambridge, MA: Harvard University Press, 1978.

Bradley, Charles S. "Smoking Pipes for the Archaeologist." In *Studies in Material Culture Research*, edited by Karlis Karklins, 104–33. Tucson, AZ: Society for Historical Archaeology, 2000.

Brasseaux, Carl A. "The Administration of Slave Regulations in French Louisiana, 1724–1766." *Louisiana History* 21, no. 2 (1980): 139–58.

Brasseaux, Carl A., Keith P. Fontenot, and Claude F. Oubre. *Creoles of Color in the Bayou Country*. Jackson: University Press of Mississippi, 1994.

Breunlin, Rachel. *If Those Bricks Could Talk: A Collaborative Book and Film Devoted to the Lafitte Public Housing Development*. New Orleans: Cornerstones and the Neighborhood Story Project/Center for the Book at the University of New Orleans, 2015.

Breunlin, Rachel, and Helen A. Regis. "Putting the Ninth Ward on the Map: Race, Place, and Transformation in Desire, New Orleans." *American Anthropologist* 108, no. 4 (2006): 744–64.

Briede, Kathryn. "A History of the City of Lafayette." *Louisiana Historical Quarterly* 20, no. 4 (1937): 895–964.

Bring New Orleans Back Commission. "Urban Planning Committee: Action Plan for New Orleans: Executive Summary." January 30, 2006. Accessed October 2018. http://www.columbia.edu/itc/journalism/cases/katrina/city_of_new_orleans _bnobc.html.

Brubaker, Rogers, and Frederick Cooper. "Beyond 'Identity.'" *Theory and Society* 29, no. 1 (2000): 1–47.

Campanella, Richard. *Geographies of New Orleans: Urban Fabrics before the Storm.* Lafayette: Center for Louisiana Studies, 2006.

Campbell-Rock, C. C. "Hope VI Offers No Hope to St. Thomas Residents." *New Orleans Tribune*, October 2002.

Carter, Sam. *A Report on Survey of Metropolitan New Orleans Land Use, Real Property, and Low Income Housing Area.* Baton Rouge: Louisiana State Department of Public Welfare and the Housing Authority of New Orleans (HANO), 1941.

Castille, George J., Douglas D. Bryant, Joan M. Exnicios, William D. Reeves, and Susan de France. *Urban Archaeology in Old New Orleans: Historical and Archaeological Investigations within the Greater New Orleans Bridge No. 2 Right-of-Way.* Report prepared for the Louisiana Department of Transportation and Development. Baton Rouge, LA: Coastal Environments, 1986.

Castille, George J., David B. Kelley, Sally K. Reeves, and Charles E. Pearson. *Archaeological Excavations at Esplanade Avenue and North Rampart Street, New Orleans, Louisiana.* Report submitted to the National Park Service, Southwest Region, Santa Fe. Baton Rouge, LA: Coastal Environments, 1982.

Chase, John Churchill. *Frenchmen, Desire, Good Children, and Other Streets of New Orleans.* New York: Collier Books, 2001.

Chesney, Kellow. *The Victorian Underworld.* Harmonsworth: Penguin Books, 1970.

Christian, Marcus. "History of Negroes in Louisiana." n.d., Marcus B. Christian Collection, Archives, Earl K. Long Library, University of New Orleans.

Clark, Emily. *Masterless Mistresses: The New Orleans Ursulines and the Development of a New World Society, 1727–1834.* Chapel Hill: University of North Carolina Press, 2007.

Cohen, Lizabeth. *A Consumers' Republic: The Politics of Mass Consumption in Postwar America.* New York: Vintage Books, 2004.

——. *Making a New Deal: Industrial Workers in Chicago, 1919–1939.* Cambridge: Cambridge University Press, 1990.

Cohen, Lucy. *Chinese in the Post–Civil War South: A People without a History.* Baton Rouge: Louisiana State University Press, 1984.

Cohn, Bernard S. "The Census, Social Structure and Objectification in South Asia." In *An Anthropologist among the Historians and Other Essays,* 224–54. New York: Oxford University Press, 1987.

Colten, Craig E. *An Unnatural Metropolis: Wresting New Orleans from Nature.* Baton Rouge: Louisiana State University Press, 2005.

Comaroff, Jean, and John L. Comaroff. *Of Revelation and Revolution.* Vol. 1, *Christianity, Colonialism, and the Colonization of Consciousness in South Africa.* Chicago: University of Chicago Press, 1991.

Comaroff, John L., and Jean Comaroff. *Ethnography and the Historical Imagination.* Boulder, CO: Westview Press, 1992.

Cook, Bernard, and James Watson. *Louisiana Labor: From Slavery to "Right-to-Work."* Lanham, MD: University Press of America, 1985.

Corley, Florence Fleming. "Atlanta's Techwood and University Homes Projects: The Nation's Laboratory for Public Housing." *Atlanta History* 31, no. 4 (1987): 17–36.

Crutcher, Michael E., Jr. *Tremé: Race and Place in a New Orleans Neighborhood.* Athens: University of Georgia Press, 2010.

Davidson, James. "Deconstructing the Myth of the 'Hand Charm': Mundane Clothing Fasteners and Their Curious Transformation into Supernatural Objects." *Historical Archaeology* 48, no. 2 (2014): 18–60.

Davis, Mike. *Planet of Slums.* London: Verso Books, 2006.

Dawdy, Shannon Lee. *Building the Devil's Empire: French Colonial New Orleans.* Chicago: University of Chicago Press, 2008.

———. "Ethnicity in the Urban Landscape: The Archaeology of Creole New Orleans." In Young, *Archaeology of Southern Urban Landscapes*, 127–49.

———. *Madame John's Legacy (16OR51) Revisited: A Closer Look at the Archaeology of Colonial New Orleans.* Report submitted to Friends of the Cabildo and Louisiana Division of Archaeology. New Orleans: University of New Orleans, College of Urban and Public Affairs, 1996.

———. *Patina.* Chicago: University of Chicago Press, 2016.

———. "Understanding Cultural Change through the Vernacular: Creolization in Louisiana." *Historical Archaeology* 34, no. 3 (2000): 107–23.

Dawdy, Shannon Lee, D. Ryan Gray, and Jill-Karen Yakubik. *Archaeological Investigations at the Rising Sun Hotel Site (16OR225), New Orleans, Louisiana.* Vol. 1. Report prepared for the Historic New Orleans Collection (HNOC). Chicago: University of Chicago, Department of Anthropology, 2008.

Dawdy, Shannon Lee, and Juana Ibáñez. *Beneath the Surface of New Orleans' Warehouse District: Archaeological Investigations at the Maginnis Cotton Mill Site (16OR144).* Report submitted to Cotton Mill Limited Partnership and Historic Restoration. New Orleans: University of New Orleans, Greater New Orleans Archaeology Program, 1997.

Dawdy, Shannon Lee, and Richard Weyhing. "Beneath the Rising Sun: 'Frenchness' and the Archaeology of Desire." *International Journal of Historical Archaeology* 12, no. 4 (2008): 370–87.

De Certeau, Michel. *The Practice of Everyday Life.* Berkeley: University of California Press, 1984.

Deleuze, Gilles, and Felix Guattari. *A Thousand Plateaus.* Minneapolis: University of Minnesota Press, 1987.

Demerath, Nicholas J., and Harlan Gilmore. "The Ecology of Southern Cities." In *The Urban South*, edited by Rupert Vance and Nicholas J. Demerath, 135–64. Chapel Hill: University of North Carolina Press, 1954.

Dessens, Nathalie. *From Saint-Domingue to New Orleans: Migration and Influences.* Gainesville: University Press of Florida, 2007.

Domínguez, Virginia R. *White by Definition: Social Classification in Creole Louisiana.* New Brunswick, NJ: Rutgers University Press, 1994.

Dormon, James H. "The Persistent Specter: Slave Rebellion in Territorial Louisiana." *Louisiana History* 18, no. 4 (1977): 389–404.

Dougherty, Molly. "Southern Midwifery and Organized Health Care: Systems in Conflict." *Medical Anthropology* 6 (1982): 113–26.

Drake, St. Clair, and Horace R. Cayton. *Black Metropolis: A Study of Negro Life in a Northern City.* New York: Harcourt, Brace, 1945.

Du Bois, W. E. B. *The Souls of Black Folk.* 1903. Mineola, NY: Dover, 1994.

———. *The Philadelphia Negro: A Social Study.* New York: Oxford University Press, 2007.

Elliott, James, Kevin Fox Gotham, and Melinda Milligan. "Framing the Urban: Struggles over HOPE VI and New Urbanism in a Historic City." *City and Community* 3, no. 4 (2004): 373–99.

Epperson, Terrence. "Beyond Biological Reductionism, Ethnicity, and Vulgar Anti-Essentialism: Critical Perspectives on Race and the Practice of African-American Archaeology." *African Diaspora Archaeology Newsletter* 6, no. 2 (1999): article 4.

Evans, Freddie. *Congo Square: African Roots of New Orleans.* Lafayette: University of Louisiana at Lafayette, 2011.

Everett, Donald. "Free Persons of Color in Colonial Louisiana." *Louisiana History* 7, no. 1 (1966): 21–50.

Fairchild's Hand-Book of the Digestive Ferments. New York: Fairchild Brothers and Foster, 1894.

Fennell, Christopher C. *Crossroads and Cosmologies: Diasporas and Ethnogenesis in the New World.* Gainesville: University Press of Florida, 2007.

Ferguson, James. *The Anti-Politics Machine: "Development," Depoliticization, and Bureaucratic Power in Lesotho.* Minneapolis: University of Minnesota Press, 1994.

Ferleger, Louis. "Farm Mechanization in the Southern Sugar Sector after the Civil War." *Louisiana History* 23, no. 1 (1982): 21–34.

Fibbe, Toon. "Haunted Housing: An Interview with Toon Fibbe." Interview by Asher Kaplan. *Pelican Bomb*, June 27, 2016. http://pelicanbomb.com/art-review/2016/haunted-housing-an-interview-with-toon-fibbe.

Fifield, Rick, and Judy Bethea. *Investigation of St. Thomas Project Area prior to Construction of LA-1.* Manuscript prepared for Historic Restoration, Inc., New Orleans, 1999.

Fischer, Roger. "Racial Segregation in Antebellum New Orleans." *American Historical Review* 74 (1969): 926–37.

Fitts, Robert. "Becoming American: The Archaeology of an Italian Immigrant." *Historical Archaeology* 36, no. 2 (2002): 1–17.

Flores, Carol. "U.S. Public Housing in the 1930s: The First Projects in Atlanta, Georgia." *Planning Perspectives* 9, no. 4 (1994): 405–30.

Fogelson, Robert. *Bourgeois Nightmares: Suburbia, 1870–1930.* New Haven, CT: Yale University Press, 2005.

Follett, Richard. *The Sugar Masters: Planters and Slaves in Louisiana's Cane World, 1820–1860.* Baton Rouge: Louisiana State University Press, 2007.

Follett, Richard, and Rick Halpern. "From Slavery to Freedom in Louisiana's Sugar Country: Changing Labor Systems and Workers' Power." In *Sugar, Slavery, and Society: Perspectives on the Caribbean, Indian, the Mascarenes, and the United States,* edited by Bernard Moitt, 135–56. Gainesville: University Press of Florida, 2004.

Fortier, Alcée, ed. *Louisiana, Comprising Sketches of Counties, Towns, Events, Institutions, and Persons, Arranged in Cyclopedic Form.* 3 vols. Madison, WI: Century Historical Association, 1914.

Foster, Craig. "Tarnished Angels: Prostitution in Storyville, New Orleans, 1900–1910." *Louisiana History* 31, no. 4 (1990): 387–97.

Foster, Eugene, and Linda Nance, eds. *Archaeological Investigation Report: Allan Parkway Village, 41HR886, Houston, Harris County, Texas.* Report submitted to the Housing Authority of the City of Houston. Austin, TX: PBS&J, 2002.

Foster, Michael, John Lindly, and Ronald Ryden. "The Soiled Doves of South Granite Street: The History and Archaeology of a Prescott, Arizona Brothel." *Journal of Southwestern Archaeology and History* 70, no. 4 (2005): 349–74.

Foucault, Michel. *The Archaeology of Knowledge.* New York: Pantheon Books, 1972.

———. *Discipline and Punish: The Birth of the Prison.* New York: Vintage Books, 1977.

———. *The History of Sexuality.* New York: Pantheon Books, 1978.

———. "On Governmentality." *Ideology and Consciousness* 6 (1979): 5–21.

———. *The Order of Things: An Archaeology of the Human Sciences.* New York: Vintage Books, 1970.

Franklin, Maria, and Larry McKee, eds. "Transcending Boundaries, Transforming the Discipline: African Diaspora Archaeologies in the New Millennium." Special issue, *Historical Archaeology* 38, no. 1 (2004).

Fraser, Gertrude. *African-American Midwifery in the South.* Cambridge: Harvard University Press, 1998.

Frazier, E. Franklin. *Race and Culture Contacts in the Modern World.* Boston: Beacon Press, 1957.

Freedman, Leonard. *Public Housing: The Politics of Poverty.* New York: Holt, Rinehart, and Winston, 1969.

French-Marcelin, Megan. "Gentrification's Ground Zero." *Jacobin Magazine,* August 28, 2015, https://www.jacobinmag.com/2015/08/katrina-new-orleans-arne-duncan-charters/.

Gardner, Jeffrey W., Connie Huddleston, Dawn Reid, and Bobby G. Southerlin. *Material Culture and Consumer Choices at Tech Flats: Archaeological and Historical Investigations of the Techwood/Clark Howell Urban Revitalization Tract, Atlanta, Georgia.* Atlanta: Brockington and Associates, 1998.

Garreau, Joel. *Edge City: Life on the New Frontier.* New York: Anchor Books, 1992.

Germany, Kent. *New Orleans after the Promises: Poverty, Citizenship, and the Search for the Great Society.* Athens: University of Georgia Press, 2007.

Gill, James. *Lords of Misrule: Mardi Gras and the Politics of Race in New Orleans.* Jackson: University Press of Mississippi, 1997.

Godet, Aurélie. "'Meet de Boys on the Battlefront': Festive Parades and the Struggle to Reclaim Public Spaces in Post-Katrina New Orleans." *European Journal of American Studies* 10, no. 3 (2015), document 1.9.

Godzinski, Michael, Shawna Atkins, Dayna Bowker Lee, Donna Greer, Tegan Hanson, Aubra Lee, Marie Richards, Rhonda Smith, and Jill-Karen Yakubik. *Cultural Resource Investigations of Blocks I and F at the Iberville Housing Project, New Orleans, Orleans Parish, Louisiana.* Report prepared for HANO, New Orleans, 2013.

Godzinski, Michael, Zachary DeLaune, Jason Kennedy, Jeanne Marquez, Rhonda Smith, and Harriet Swift. *Phase I and II Cultural Resources Survey of the Lafitte Housing Project, New Orleans, Louisiana.* Report submitted to Louisiana Division of Archaeology, Baton Rouge, 2008.

Gomez, Michael A. *Exchanging Our Country Marks: The Transformation of African*

Identities in the Colonial and Antebellum South. Chapel Hill: University of North Carolina Press, 1998.

Gonzalez-Perez, Margaret C. "A House Divided: Public Housing Policy in New Orleans." *Louisiana History* 44, no. 4 (2003): 443–61.

Goodwin, R. Christopher, Paul C. Armstrong, Eric C. Poplin, David Moore, and Carol J. Poplin. *New Orleans Is Looking Forward to Its Past.* Report submitted to the Louisiana Division of Archaeology, Baton Rouge, 1987.

Goodwin, R. Christopher, Suzanne Sanders, Kathleen Child, and Katie Kosack. *Becoming New Orleanian: An Archaeological Perspective on Urbanization and Americanization in Lower Mid-City during the Late 19th and Early 20th Centuries.* Report submitted to the US Department of Veterans Affairs and Louisiana Division of Archaeology, Baton Rouge, 2016.

Gotham, Kevin Fox. *Authentic New Orleans: Tourism, Culture, and Race in the Big Easy.* New York: New York University Press, 2007.

———. *Race, Real Estate, and Uneven Development: The Kansas City Experience, 1900–2000.* Albany: State University of New York Press, 2002.

———. "Racialization and the State: The Housing Act of 1934 and the Creation of the Federal Housing Administration." *Sociological Perspectives* 43, no. 2 (2000): 291–317.

Gould, Virginia Meacham. "'A Chaos of Iniquity and Discord': Slave and Free Women of Color in the Spanish Ports of New Orleans, Mobile, and Pensacola." In *The Devil's Lane: Sex and Race in the Early South,* edited by Catherine Clinton and Michele Gillespie, 232–46. Oxford: Oxford University Press, 1997.

Gramsci, Antonio. *Selections from the Prison Notebooks of Antonio Gramsci.* New York: International, 1971.

Grand Army of the Republic. Joseph A. Mower Post No. 1 Records, 1875–1922. Manuscripts Collection 227. Louisiana Research Collection, Tulane University, New Orleans.

Gratz, Roberta Brandes. "Who Killed Public Housing in New Orleans?" *Nation,* June 2, 2015.

Gray, D. Ryan. "Identity and the Material Dimensions of Public and Private Practice: Archaeology of a Chinese Laundry in New Orleans." Master's thesis, University of Chicago, 2009.

———. "Incorrigible Vagabonds and Suspicious Spaces in Nineteenth-Century New Orleans." *Historical Archaeology* 45, no. 3 (2011): 55–73.

———. *Rediscovering the "Antiguo Cementerio": Archaeological Excavations and Recovery of Human Remains from the St. Peter Street Cemetery (16OR92), Orleans Parish, Louisiana.* Report submitted to the Louisiana Division of Archaeology, Baton Rouge, 2016.

Gregory, Steven. *Black Corona: Race and the Politics of Place in an Urban Community.* Princeton, NJ: Princeton University Press, 1998.

Gupta, Akhil, and James Ferguson. "Beyond 'Culture': Space, Identity, and the Politics of Difference." *Cultural Anthropology* 7, no. 1 (1992): 6–23.

Hair, William Ivy. *Carnival of Fury: Robert Charles and the New Orleans Race Riot of 1900.* Baton Rouge: Louisiana State University Press, 1976.

Hall, Donald E. *Subjectivity: The New Critical Idiom.* London: Routledge, 2004.

Hall, Gwendolyn Midlo. *Africans in Colonial Louisiana: The Development of Afro-*

Creole Culture in the Eighteenth Century. Baton Rouge: Louisiana State University Press, 1992.

Hall, Martin. *Archaeology and the Modern World: Colonial Transcripts in South Africa and the Chesapeake.* London: Routledge, 2000.

Hanger, Kimberly S. *Bounded Lives, Bounded Places: Free Black Society in Colonial New Orleans, 1769–1803.* Durham, NC: Duke University Press, 1997.

Hardee, T. S. *Topographical and Drainage Map of New Orleans and Surroundings.* New Orleans: Lewis Graham, 1878.

Harris, Leslie. *In the Shadow of Slavery: African Americans in New York City, 1626–1863.* Chicago: University of Chicago Press, 2003.

Harvey, David. "The Political Economy of Public Space." In *The Politics of Public Space,* edited by Setha Low and Neil Smith, 17–34. New York: Routledge, 2005.

———. *The Urban Experience.* Baltimore: Johns Hopkins University Press, 1989.

Hayden, Dolores. *Building Suburbia: Green Fields and Urban Growth, 1820–2000.* New York: Pantheon Books, 2003.

Heathcott, Joseph. "Black Archipelago: Politics and Civil Life in the Jim Crow City." *Journal of Social History* 38, no. 3 (2005): 705–36.

———. "'In the Nature of a Clinic': The Design of Early Public Housing in St. Louis." *Journal of the Society of Architectural Historians* 70, no. 1 (2011): 82–103.

Heitmann, John A. *The Modernization of the Louisiana Sugar Industry, 1830–1910.* Baton Rouge: Louisiana State University Press, 1987.

Herskovits, Melville. *The Myth of the Negro Past.* Boston: Beacon Press, 1941.

Hirsch, Arnold R. *Making the Second Ghetto: Race and Housing in Chicago, 1940–1960.* New York: Cambridge University Press, 1983.

Hirsch, Arnold R., and Joseph Logsdon, eds. *Creole New Orleans: Race and Americanization.* Baton Rouge: Louisiana State University Press, 1992.

Hochschild, Jennifer L., and Brenna M. Powell. "Racial Reorganization in the United States Census 1850–1930: Mulattoes, Half-Breeds, Mixed Parentage, Hindoos, and the Mexican Race." *Studies in American Political Development* 22, no. 1 (2008): 59–96.

Hogue, James K. *Uncivil War: Five New Orleans Street Battles and the Rise and Fall of Radical Reconstruction.* Baton Rouge: Louisiana State University Press, 2006.

Hollandsworth, James, Jr. *An Absolute Massacre: The New Orleans Race Riot of July 30, 1866.* Baton Rouge: Louisiana State University Press, 2001.

Hollman, Irene. "Techwood Homes." In *New Georgia Encyclopedia.* Georgia Humanities and University of Georgia Press. Article published June 20, 2008; last modified May 16, 2018. https://www.georgiaencyclopedia.org/articles/arts-culture/techwood-homes.

Holston, James. *Insurgent Citizenship: Disjunctions of Democracy and Modernity in Brazil.* Princeton, NJ: Princeton University Press, 2008.

Horne, Gerald. *The Deepest South: The United States, Brazil, and the African Slave Trade.* New York: New York University Press, 2007.

Horne, Jedidiah, and Brendan Nee. "An Overview of Post-Katrina Planning in New Orleans." Paper, Department of City and Regional Planning, University of California, Berkeley, October 18, 2006. http://www.nolaplans.com/research.

Housing Authority of New Orleans. *Report of the Housing Authority of New Orleans.* Annual vols. New Orleans: HANO, 1938–51.

Huber, Leonard, Peggy McDowell, and Mary Louise Christovich. *New Orleans Architecture*. Vol. 3, *The Cemeteries*. Gretna, LA: Pelican, 1997.

Hyatt, Harry. *Hoodoo, Conjuration, Witchcraft, Rootwork*. Vol. 2. Hannibal, MO: Western, 1970.

Ingersoll, Thomas N. "The Slave Trade and the Ethnic Diversity of Louisiana's Slave Community." *Louisiana History* 37, no. 2 (1996): 133–61.

Jackson, John L., Jr. *Harlemworld: Doing Race and Class in Contemporary Black America*. Chicago: University of Chicago Press, 2001.

Jackson, Joyce. "Declaration of Taking Twice: The Fazendeville Community of the Lower Ninth Ward." *American Anthropologist* 108, no. 4 (2006): 765–80.

Jackson, Kenneth T. *Crabgrass Frontier: The Suburbanization of the United States*. New York: Oxford University Press, 1985.

Jacobs, Claude F. "Benevolent Societies of New Orleans Blacks during the Late Nineteenth and Early Twentieth Centuries." *Louisiana History* 29, no. 1 (1988): 21–33.

Jankowiak, William R. *Black Social Aid and Pleasure Clubs: Marching Associations in New Orleans*. Cultural Resources Management Study, Jean Lafitte National Historical Park and the National Park Service, New Orleans, LA, 1989.

Johnson, Jerah. "Colonial New Orleans: A Fragment of the Eighteenth-Century French Ethos." In Hirsch and Logsdon, *Creole New Orleans*, 12–57.

Johnson, Matthew. *An Archaeology of Capitalism*. Oxford: Blackwell, 1996.

Johnston, Harry. *The Negro in the New World*. London: Methuen, 1910.

Jones, Siân. *The Archaeology of Ethnicity: Constructing Identities in the Past and Present*. New York: Routledge, 1997.

Jones, Steven L. "The African-American Tradition in Vernacular Architecture." In *The Archaeology of Slavery and Plantation Life*, edited by Theresa A. Singleton, 195–214. New York: Academic Press, 1985.

Joseph, J. W. "Archaeology and the African-American Experience in the Urban South." In Young, *Archaeology of Southern Urban Landscapes*, 109–26.

Jung, Moon-Ho. *Coolies and Cane: Race, Labor, and Sugar in the Age of Emancipation*. Baltimore: Johns Hopkins University Press, 2006.

Kaplan-Levenson, Laine. "'The Monster': Claiborne Avenue before and after the Interstate." May 5, 2016. In *TriPod: New Orleans at 300*, produced by Laine Kaplan-Levenson, podcast, MP3 audio, 10:16, https://www.wwno.org/post/monster-claiborne-avenue-and-after-interstate.

Katz, Michael. *In the Shadow of the Poorhouse*. New York: Basic Books, 1986.

———, ed. *The "Underclass" Debate: Views from History*. Princeton, NJ: Princeton University Press, 1993.

———. "The Urban 'Underclass' as a Metaphor for Social Transformation." In Katz, *The "Underclass" Debate*, 3–23.

Katz, Pete. *The New Urbanism: Toward an Architecture of Community*. New York: McGraw-Hill, 1994.

Keire, Mara. *For Business and Pleasure: Red-Light Districts and the Regulation of Vice in the United States, 1890–1933*. Baltimore: Johns Hopkins University Press, 2010.

Kelley, Robin D. G. *Hammer and Hoe: Alabama Communists in the Great Depression*. Durham: University of North Carolina Press, 1990.

———. *Race Rebels: Culture, Politics, and the Black Working Class*. New York: Free Press, 1994.

————. "'We Are Not What We Seem': Rethinking Black Working-Class Opposition in the Jim Crow South." In *The New African American Urban History*, edited by Kenneth Goings and Raymond Mohl, 187–239. Thousand Oaks, CA: Sage, 1996.

Kellogg, John. "Negro Urban Clusters in the Postbellum South." *Geographical Review* 67, no. 3 (1977): 310–21.

Kendall, John Smith. *The History of New Orleans*. Chicago: Lewis, 1922.

Kertzer, David I., and Dominique Arel, eds. *Census and Identity: The Politics of Race, Ethnicity, and Language in National Census*. Cambridge: Cambridge University Press, 2002.

Korn, Bertram Wallace. *The Early Jews of New Orleans*. Waltham, MA: American Jewish Historical Society, 1969.

Kowalsky, Arnold A., and Dorothy E. Kowalsky. *Encyclopedia of Marks on American, English, and European Earthenware, Ironstone, and Stoneware, 1780–1980*. Atglen, PA: Schiffer Books, 1999.

Krist, Gary. *Empire of Sin: A Story of Sex, Jazz, Murder, and the Battle for Modern New Orleans*. New York: Crown Press, 2014.

Kurtz, Donald V., and Mary Christopher Nunley. "Ideology and Work at Teotihuacan: A Hermeneutic Interpretation." *Man* n.s., 28, no. 4 (1993): 761–78.

Lachance, Paul. "The Foreign French." In Hirsch and Logsdon, *Creole New Orleans*, 101–30.

Lachoff, Irwin, and Catherine Kahn. *The Jewish Community of New Orleans*. Charleston, SC: Arcadia, 2005.

Lamb, Teresia R., and Richard C. Beavers. *Archaeology of the Stableyard Complex, Hermann-Grima House, New Orleans, Louisiana*. Report submitted to the Christian Women's Exchange and the Louisiana Division of Archaeology, 1983.

Landau, Emily. *Spectacular Wickedness: Sex, Race, and Memory in Storyville, New Orleans*. Baton Rouge: Louisiana State University Press, 2013.

Landphair, Juliette. "'The Forgotten People of New Orleans': Community, Vulnerability, and the Lower Ninth Ward." *Journal of American History* 94, no. 3 (2007): 837–45.

LaViolette, Forrest, and Joseph Taylor. *Negro Housing in New Orleans*. Special research report to the Commission on Race and Housing, New Orleans, LA, 1957.

Lee, Aubra, Gary Demarcay, Ryan Hale, Dayna Lee, Justine McKnight, Dorian Ray, Rhonda Smith, Elizabeth Williams, Jill-Karen Yakubik, and Chris Young. *Cultural Resource Investigations of City Squares 324 (16OR627), 349 (16OR628), 350 (16OR629), 357 (16OR630), 358 (16OR631), and 383 (16OR602) of the William J. Guste Housing Complex, New Orleans, Orleans Parish, Louisiana*. Report submitted to HANO and the Louisiana Division of Archaeology, Baton Rouge, 2018.

Lefebvre, Henri. *The Production of Space*. Oxford: Blackwell, 1991.

Leighninger, Robert D., Jr. *Building Louisiana: The Legacy of the Public Works Administration*. Jackson: University Press of Mississippi, 2007.

Lentz, Peggy. "Public Housing in New Orleans: Public Castles?" In *A Place to Live: Housing in New Orleans*, edited by James Bobo, 176–211. New Orleans: Urban Studies Institute, University of New Orleans, 1978.

Leone, Mark P. *The Archaeology of Liberty in an American Capital: Excavations in Annapolis*. Berkeley: University of California Press, 2005.

————. "Interpreting Ideology in Historical Archaeology: Using the Rules of Perspective in the William Paca Garden, Annapolis, Maryland." In *Ideology, Power and Prehistory,* edited by Daniel Miller and Christopher Tilley, 25–36. Cambridge: Cambridge University Press, 1984.

Lewis, Earl. *In Their Own Interests: Race, Class, and Power in Twentieth-Century Norfolk, Virginia.* Berkeley: University of California Press, 1991.

Lewis, Oscar. "The Culture of Poverty." *Scientific American* 215, no. 4 (1966): 19–25.

———. *Five Families: Mexican Case Studies in the Culture of Poverty.* New York: Basic Books, 1959.

Lewis, Peirce F. *New Orleans: The Making of an Urban Landscape.* 2nd ed. Santa Fe, NM: Center for American Places, 2003.

Logan, Onnie. *Motherwit: An Alabama Midwife's Story.* New York: E. P. Dutton, 1989.

Logsdon, Joseph, and Carolyn C. Bell. "The Americanization of Black New Orleans, 1850–1900." In Hirsch and Logsdon, *Creole New Orleans,* 201–61.

Lomax, Alan. *Mister Jelly Roll: The Fortunes of Jelly Roll Morton, New Orleans Creole and "Inventor of Jazz."* Berkeley: University of California Press, 2001.

Long, Alecia P. *The Great Southern Babylon: Sex, Race, and Respectability in New Orleans, 1865–1920.* Baton Rouge: Louisiana State University Press, 2004.

———. "Poverty Is the New Prostitution: Race, Poverty, and Public Housing in Post-Katrina New Orleans." *Journal of American History* 94, no. 3 (2007): 795–803.

Long, Carolyn Morrow. *A New Orleans Voudou Priestess: The Legend and Reality of Marie Laveau.* Gainesville: University Press of Florida, 2007.

———. *Spiritual Merchants: Religion, Magic, and Commerce.* Knoxville: University of Tennessee Press, 2001.

Lusignan, Paul. "Public Housing in the United States, 1933–1949." *Cultural Resource Management* 25, no. 1 (2002): 36–37.

Mahoney, Martha. "The Changing Nature of Public Housing in New Orleans, 1930–1974." Master's thesis, Tulane University, 1985.

———. "Law and Racial Geography: Public Housing and the Economy in New Orleans." *Stanford Law Review* 42, no. 5 (1990): 1251–90.

Marable, Manning, and Kristen Clarke. *Seeking Higher Ground: The Hurricane Katrina Crisis, Race, and Public Policy Reader.* New York: Palgrave Macmillan, 2008.

Marcuse, Peter. "The Beginnings of Public Housing in New York." *Journal of Urban History* 12, no. 4 (1986): 353–90.

Margavio, Anthony. "Residential Segregation in New Orleans: A Statistical Analysis of Census Data." PhD diss., Louisiana State University, 1968.

Marks, Gil. *Encyclopedia of Jewish Food.* New York: Houghton, Mifflin, Harcourt, 2013.

Marland, Hilary, and Anne Marie Rafferty, eds. *Midwives, Society, and Childbirth: Debates and Controversies in the Modern Period.* London: Routledge, 1997.

Massey, Douglas, and Nancy Denton. *American Apartheid: Segregation and the Making of the Underclass.* Cambridge, MA: Harvard University Press, 1987.

Matthews, Christopher N. *Management Report of Excavations at the St. Augustine Site (16OR148).* Report submitted to the Louisiana Division of Archaeology, Baton Rouge, 1999.

Maygarden, Benjamin. *Historical Background and Development Overview for the St. Thomas Housing Project Area.* Manuscript on file, Earth Search, Inc., New Orleans, 2001.

Maygarden, Benjamin, Jill-Karen Yakubik, Ellen Weiss, Chester Peyronnin, and Kenneth R. Jones. *National Register Evaluation of New Orleans Pumping Stations.*

Report prepared for New Orleans District, US Army Corps of Engineers, New Orleans, 1999.

Mayhew, Henry. *London Labour and the London Poor.* 1865. London: Penguin, 1985.

Mayne, Alan. *The Imagined Slum: Newspaper Representation in Three Cities, 1870–1914.* Leicester, UK: Leicester University Press, 1993.

Mayne, Alan, and Tim Murray, eds. *The Archaeology of Urban Landscapes: Explorations in Slumland.* Cambridge: Cambridge University Press, 2001.

McAtackney, Laura, and Krysta Ryzewski, eds. *Contemporary Archaeology and the City: Creativity, Ruination, and Political Action.* New York: Oxford University Press, 2017.

McCarthy, John. "Values and Identity in the 'Working Class' Worlds of Late Nineteenth-Century Minneapolis." In Mayne and Murray, *The Archaeology of Urban Landscapes,* 145–53.

McDavid, Carol, and David Babson, eds. "In the Realm of Politics: Prospects for Public Participation in African-American and Plantation Archaeology." Special issue, *Historical Archaeology* 31, no. 3 (1997).

McGuire, Randall, and Robert Paynter, eds. *The Archaeology of Inequality.* Oxford: Blackwell, 1991.

Meeks, Tomiko. "Freedmen's Town, Texas: A Lesson in the Failure of Historic Preservation." *Houston History* 8, no. 2 (2011): 42–44.

Merriman, John M. *The Margins of City Life: Explorations on the French Urban Frontier, 1815–1851.* New York: Oxford University Press, 1991.

Michney, Todd. "Black Middle Class Mobility and New Orleans East." Paper presented at the Annual Meeting of the Southern Historical Association, New Orleans, October 2008.

Miller, Daniel. *Material Culture and Mass Consumption.* Oxford: Basil Blackwell, 1987.

Miller, Monica. *Slaves to Fashion: Black Dandyism and the Styling of Black Diasporic Identity.* Durham, NC: Duke University Press, 2009.

———. "W.E.B. Du Bois and the Dandy as Diasporic Race Man." *Callaloo* 26, no. 3 (2003): 738–65.

Mills, Gary B. *The Forgotten People: Cane River's Creoles of Color.* Baton Rouge: Louisiana State University Press, 1977.

Mintz, Sidney, and Richard Price. *The Birth of African-American Culture: An Anthropological Perspective.* Boston: Beacon Press, 1992.

Mitchell, Timothy. *Colonising Egypt.* Los Angeles: University of California Press, 1991.

Moe, Richard, and Carter Wilkie. *Changing Places: Rebuilding Community in the Age of Sprawl.* New York: Henry Holt, 1997.

Moore, Donald. *Suffering for Territory: Race, Place, and Power in Zimbabwe.* Durham, NC: Duke University Press, 2005.

Moore, John Robert. "The New Deal in Louisiana." In *The New Deal: The State and Local Levels,* edited by John Braeman, Robert Hamlett Bremner, and David Brody, 137–65. Columbus: Ohio State University Press, 1975.

Morgan, Philip D. "The Cultural Implications of the Atlantic Slave Trade: African Regional Origins, American Destinations, and New World Developments." *Slavery and Abolition* 18, no. 1 (1997): 122–45.

Mrozowski, Stephen. *The Archaeology of Class in Urban America.* Cambridge: Cambridge University Press, 2006.

———. "Landscapes of Inequality." In McGuire and Paynter, *The Archaeology of Inequality*, 79–101.

Mullins, Paul R. "'A Bold and Gorgeous Front': The Contradictions of African America and Consumer Culture." In *Historical Archaeologies of Capitalism*, edited by Mark P. Leone and Parker B. Potter Jr., 169–93. New York: Kluwer Academic, 1999.

———. "The Optimism of Absence: An Archaeology of Displacement, Effacement, and Modernity." In McAtackney and Ryzewski, *Contemporary Archaeology and the City*, 244–61.

———. *Race and Affluence: An Archaeology of African America and Consumer Culture.* New York: Kluwer Academic, 1999.

———. "Racializing the Parlor: Race and Victorian Bric-a-Brac Consumption." In *Race and the Archaeology of Identity*, edited by Charles E. Orser Jr., 158–76. Salt Lake City: University of Utah Press, 2001.

Munn, Nancy D. "The 'Becoming-Past' of Places: Spacetime and Memory in 19th Century, Pre–Civil War New York." *Suomen Antropologi* 29, no. 1 (2004): 2–19.

Needham, Maurice d'Arlan. *Negro Orleanian: Status and Stake in a City's Economy and Housing.* New Orleans: Tulane, 1962.

New Orleans Annual and Commercial Register. New Orleans: Michel, 1846.

Nine Times Social and Pleasure Club. *Coming Out the Door in the Ninth Ward.* New Orleans: Neighborhood Story Project, 2006.

Ondaatje, Michael. *Coming through Slaughter.* Toronto: House of Anansi Press, 1976.

Orser, Charles E., Jr. *The Archaeology of Race and Racialization in Historic America.* Gainesville: University Press of Florida, 2007.

———. *The Material Basis of the Postbellum Tenant Plantation.* Athens: University of Georgia Press, 1988.

———. *Race and Practice in Archaeological Interpretation.* Philadelphia: University of Pennsylvania Press, 2004.

Osofsky, Gilbert. *Harlem: The Making of a Ghetto.* New York: Harper and Row, 1968.

Paccoud, Antoine. "Planning Law, Power, and Practice: Haussmann in Paris (1853–1870)." *Planning Perspectives* 31, no. 3 (2016): 341–61.

Palmié, Stephan. "Creolization and Its Discontents." *Annual Reviews in Anthropology* 35 (2006): 433–56.

Parker, Simon. *Urban Theory and the Urban Experience: Encountering the City.* London: Routledge, 2004.

Pauketat, Timothy R. "A New Tradition in Archaeology." In *The Archaeology of Traditions*, edited by Timothy R. Pauketat, 1–16. Gainesville: University Press of Florida, 2001.

Perry, Warren, and Robert Paynter. "Artifacts, Ethnicity, and the Archaeology of African Americans." In *"I, Too, Am American": Archaeological Studies of African-American Life*, edited by Theresa Singleton, 299–310. Charlottesville: University Press of Virginia, 1999.

Philpott, Thomas Lee. *The Slum and the Ghetto: Neighborhood Deterioration and Middle-Class Reform, Chicago, 1880–1930.* New York: Oxford University Press, 1978.

Piven, Frances Fox, and Richard Cloward. *Regulating the Poor: The Functions of Public Welfare.* New York: Vintage Books, 1971.

Pommer, Richard. "The Architecture of Urban Housing in the United States during the Early 1930s." *Journal of the Society of Architectural Historians* 37, no. 4 (1978): 235–64.

Popkin, Susan J., Bruce Katz, Mary K. Cunningham, Karen D. Brown, Jeremy Gustafson, and Margery Austin Turner. *A Decade of HOPE VI: Research Findings and Policy Challenges.* Washington, DC: Urban Institute and Brookings Institution, 2004.

Powell, Eric A. "Tales from Storyville." *Archaeology Magazine* 55, no. 6 (November/December 2002): 26–31.

Powell, Lawrence. *The Accidental City: Improvising New Orleans.* Cambridge, MA: Harvard University Press, 2013.

Powers, Michael P. "A Matter of Choice: Historical Lessons for Disaster Recovery." In *There Is No Such Thing as a Natural Disaster: Race, Class, and Hurricane Katrina*, edited by Chester Hartman and Gregory D. Squies, 13–36. New York: Routledge, 2006.

Praetzellis, Adrian, and Mary Praetzellis. "Faces and Facades: Victorian Ideology in Early Sacramento." In Yentsch and Beaudry, *The Art and Mystery of Historical Archaeology*, 75–100.

Praetzellis, Mary, ed. *SF-80 Bayshore Viaduct Seismic Retrofit Projects Report on Construction Monitoring, Geoarchaeology, and Technical and Interpretive Studies for Historical Archaeology.* Report prepared for the Office of Cultural Resource Studies, California Department of Transportation, 2004.

Praetzellis, Mary, and Adrian Praetzellis. *Putting the "There" There: Historical Archaeologies of West Oakland: I-880 Cypress Freeway Replacement Project.* Report prepared for California Department of Transportation. Rohnert Park, CA: Anthropological Studies Center, Sonoma State University, 2004.

Rabinow, Paul. *French Modern: Norms and Forms of the Social Environment.* Cambridge: MIT Press, 1989.

Rasmussen, Daniel. *American Uprising: The Untold Story of America's Largest Slave Revolt.* New York: Harper Perennial, 2012.

Reagan, Leslie. *When Abortion Was a Crime: Women, Medicine, and the Law in the United States, 1867–1973.* Los Angeles: University of California Press, 1997.

Regosin, Elizabeth. *Freedom's Promise: Ex-Slave Families and Citizenship in the Age of Emancipation.* Charlottesville: University Press of Virginia, 2002.

Riis, Jacob. *How the Other Half Lives: Studies among the Tenements of New York.* 1890. Mineola, NY: Dover, 1971.

Roberts, Kodi. *Voodoo and Power: The Politics of Religion in New Orleans, 1881–1940.* Baton Rouge: Louisiana State University Press, 2015.

Roberts, Robert. *The Classic Slum: Salford Life in the First Quarter of the Century.* London: Penguin Books, 1971.

Robinson, E., and R. H. Pidgeon. *Atlas of the City of New Orleans, Louisiana.* New York: E. Robinson, 1883.

Roediger, David. *Working toward Whiteness: How America's Immigrants Became White.* New York: Basic Books, 2005.

Rose, Al. *Storyville, New Orleans: Being an Authentic, Illustrated Account of the Notorious Red-Light District.* Tuscaloosa: University of Alabama Press, 1979.

Rosen, Ruth. *The Lost Sisterhood: Prostitution in America, 1900–1918.* Baltimore: Johns Hopkins University Press, 1983.

Rosenberg, Daniel. *New Orleans Dockworkers: Race, Labor, and Unionism, 1892–1923.* Albany: State University of New York Press, 1988.

Rothschild, Nan, and Diana diZerega Wall. *The Archaeology of American Cities.* Gainesville: University Press of Florida, 2014.

Ruechel, Frank. "New Deal Public Housing, Urban Poverty, and Jim Crow: Techwood and University Homes in Atlanta." *Georgia Historical Quarterly* 81, no. 4 (1997): 915–37.

Saalman, Howard. *Haussmann: Paris Transformed.* New York: G. Braziller, 1976.

Sanborn Map Company. *Insurance Maps of New Orleans, Louisiana.* New York: Sanborn Map, 1876–1937.

Saunders, James R., and Renae Shackelford. *Urban Renewal and the End of Black Culture in Charlottesville, Virginia.* Jefferson, NC: McFarland, 1998.

Saxon, Lyle, Edward Dreyer, and Robert Tallant. *Gumbo Ya-Ya: A Collection of Louisiana Folk Tales.* Boston: Houghton Mifflin, 1987.

Schafer, Judith Kelleher. *Becoming Free, Remaining Free: Manumission and Enslavement in New Orleans, 1846–1862.* Baton Rouge: Louisiana State University Press, 2003.

———. *Brothels, Depravity, and Abandoned Women: Illegal Sex in Antebellum New Orleans.* Baton Rouge: Louisiana State University Press, 2009.

Schlereth, Thomas. "Burnham's Plan and Moody's Manual: City Planning as Progressive Reform." *Journal of the American Planning Association* 47, no. 1 (1981): 70–82.

Schmidt, Robert, and Barbara Voss, eds. *Archaeologies of Sexuality.* London: Taylor and Francis, 2000.

Scott, James C. *Domination and the Arts of Resistance: Hidden Transcripts.* New Haven, CT: Yale University Press, 1990.

———. *Seeing like a State: How Certain Schemes to Improve the Human Condition Have Failed.* New Haven, CT: Yale University Press, 1998.

Scott, James C., John Tehranian, and Jeremy Mathias. "Government Surnames and Legal Identities." In *National Identification Systems: Essays in Opposition,* edited by Carl Watner and Wendy McElroy, 11–54. Jefferson, NC: McFarland, 2004.

Scott, Mel. *American City Planning since 1890.* Berkeley: University of California Press, 1995.

Scott, Rebecca J. *Degrees of Freedom: Louisiana and Cuba after Slavery.* Cambridge, MA: Belknap Press of Harvard University Press, 2005.

———. "Public Rights, Social Equality, and the Conceptual Roots of the *Plessy* Challenge." *Michigan Law Review* 106, no. 5 (2008): 777–804.

Segrave, Kerry. *Baldness: A Social History.* Jefferson, NC: McFarland, 1996.

Seifert, Donna J. "Mrs. Starr's Profession." In *Those of Little Note: Gender, Race and Class in Historical Archaeology,* edited by Elizabeth M. Scott, 149–73. Tucson: University of Arizona Press, 1994.

Semper Idem [pseud.]. *The "Blue Book": A Bibliographical Attempt to Describe the Guide Books to the Houses of Ill Fame in New Orleans.* Heartman's Historical Series no. 50 N.p.: Privately printed, 1936.

Shenkel, J. Richard. *Archaeological Investigations at the Hermann-Grima House.* Report submitted to the Christian Women's Exchange and the Louisiana Division of Archaeology, Baton Rouge, 1977.

———. *The Archaeology of Madame John's Legacy*. Report on file, University of New Orleans, Department of Anthropology, 1971.

———. *Oak Island Archaeology: Prehistoric Estuarine Adaptations in the Mississippi River Delta*. Report on file, Louisiana Division of Archaeology, Baton Rouge, 1981.

Shenkel, J. Richard, Robert Sauder, and E. R. Chatelain. *Archaeology of the Jazz Complex and Beauregard (Congo) Square, Louis Armstrong Park, New Orleans, Louisiana*. Report submitted to the City of New Orleans, 1980.

Shields, Rob. *Places on the Margin: Alternative Geographies of Modernity*. London: Routledge, 1991.

Silver, Christopher. "The Racial Origins of Zoning in American Cities." In *Urban Planning and the African American Community: In the Shadows*, edited by June Manning Thomas and Marsha Ritzdorf, 23–42. Thousand Oaks, CA: Sage, 1997.

Smith, Carl. *The Plan of Chicago: Daniel Burnham and the Remaking of the American City*. Chicago: University of Chicago Press, 2006.

Smith, Michael P., and Marlene Keller. "'Managed Growth' and the Politics of Uneven Development in New Orleans." In *Restructuring the City: The Political Economy of Urban Redevelopment*, edited by Susan Fainstein, Norman Fainstein, Richard Hill, Dennis Judd, and Michael Smith, 126–60. New York: Longman, 1983.

Smith, Neil. "Spaces of Vulnerability: The Space of Flows and the Politics of Scale." *Critique of Anthropology* 16, no. 1 (1996): 63–77.

Soja, Edward W. *Postmodern Geographies: The Reassertion of Space in Critical Social Theory*. London: Verso, 1989.

———. *Thirdspace: Journeys to Los Angeles and Other Real-and-Imagined Places*. Cambridge, MA: Blackwell, 1996.

Souther, Mark. *New Orleans on Parade: Tourism and the Transformation of the Crescent City*. Baton Rouge: Louisiana State University Press, 2006.

Spain, Daphne. "Race Relations and Residential Segregation in New Orleans: Two Centuries of Paradox." *Annals of the American Academy of Political and Social Science* 441 (1979): 82–96.

Spear, Jennifer M. *Race, Sex, and Social Disorder in Early New Orleans*. Baltimore: Johns Hopkins University Press, 2008.

Spencer-Wood, Suzanne, and Christopher Matthews. "Impoverishment, Criminalization, and the Culture of Poverty." *Historical Archaeology* 45, no. 3 (2011): 1–10.

Sprague, Roderick. "China or Prosser Button Identification and Dating." *Historical Archaeology* 36, no. 2 (2002): 111–27.

Stack, Carol. *All Our Kin: Strategies for Survival in a Black Community*. New York: Basic Books, 1974.

Stedman Jones, Gareth. *Outcast London: A Study in the Relationship between Classes in Victorian Society*. Oxford: Peregrine Penguin, 1984.

Sterkx, Herbert E. *The Free Negro in Antebellum Louisiana*. Rutherford, NJ: Fairleigh Dickinson University Press, 1972.

Stine, Linda, Melanie A. Cabak, and Mark D. Groover. "Blue Beads as African-American Cultural Symbols." *Historical Archaeology* 30, no. 3 (1996): 49–75.

Strachan, John. *Advertising and Satirical Culture in the Romantic Period*. Cambridge: Cambridge University Press, 2007.

Sugrue, Thomas. *The Origins of the Urban Crisis: Race and Inequality in Postwar Detroit*. Princeton: Princeton University Press, 2005.

Sullivan, Jack. "The Peruna Story: Strumming That Old Catarrh." *Bottles and Extras*, May–June 2007.

Susie, Debra Ann. *In the Way of Our Grandmothers: A Cultural View of Twentieth-Century Midwifery in Florida*. Athens: University of Georgia Press, 1988.

Suttles, Gerald D. *The Social Order of the Slums: Ethnicity and Territory in the Inner City*. Chicago: University of Chicago Press, 1968.

Sutton, Matthew. "Storyville: Discourses in Southern Musicians' Autobiographies." PhD diss., College of William and Mary, 2012.

Taylor, Henry Louis, Jr., and Walter Hill. Prologue to *Historical Roots of the Urban Crisis: African Americans in the Industrial City, 1900–1950*, edited by Henry Louis Taylor Jr. and Walter Hill, 1–26. New York: Garland, 2000.

Thompson, Shirley Elizabeth. *Exiles at Home: The Struggle to Become American in Creole New Orleans*. Cambridge, MA: Harvard University Press, 2009.

Tilley, Christopher. "Interpreting Material Culture." In *The Meaning of Things: Material Culture and Symbolic Expression*, edited by Ian Hodder, 185–94. London: Unwin Hyman, 1989.

Toledano, Roulhac, and Mary-Louise Christovich. *New Orleans Architecture*. Vol. 6, *Faubourg Tremé and the Bayou Road*. Gretna, LA: Pelican, 2003.

Tomaso, Matthew S., Richard F. Veit, Carissa A. DeRooy, and Stanley L. Walling. "Social Status and Landscape in a Nineteenth-Century Planned Industrial Alternative Community: Archaeology and Geography of Feltville, New Jersey." *Historical Archaeology* 40, no. 1 (2006): 20–36.

Tonkiss, Fran. *Space, the City and Social Theory: Social Relations and Urban Forms*. Cambridge: Polity, 2005.

Towles, John Ker. "Housing Conditions in the Vicinity of St. Mary's Market, New Orleans." Master's thesis, Tulane University, 1904.

Trotter, Joe William, Jr. *Black Milwaukee: The Making of an Industrial Proletariat, 1915–1945*. Urbana: University of Illinois Press, 1985.

———. *Coal, Class, and Color: Blacks in Southern West Virginia, 1915–32*. Urbana: University of Illinois Press, 1990.

Tulane School of Social Work. "A Housing Study of the Flint-Goodridge Hospital Area." Manuscript on file, Louisiana Collection, Tulane University, New Orleans, 1934.

Üngör, Uğur Ümit. "Creative Destruction." *Journal of Urban History* 39, no. 2 (2013): 297–314.

Upton, Dell. *Another City: Urban Life and Urban Spaces in the New American Republic*. New Haven, CT: Yale University Press, 2008.

———. "The City as Material Culture." In Yentsch and Beaudry, *The Art and Mystery of Historical Archaeology*, 51–73.

US Bureau of the Census. *Eighth Census of the United States, 1860*. National Archives, Washington, DC. Ancestry.com.

———. *Fifteenth Census of the United States, 1930*. National Archives, Washington, DC. Ancestry.com.

———. *Fourteenth Census of the United States, 1920*. National Archives, Washington, DC. Ancestry.com.

———. *Ninth Census of the United States, 1870*. National Archives, Washington, DC. Ancestry.com.

———. *Seventh Census of the United States, 1850*. National Archives, Washington, DC. Ancestry.com.

———. *Tenth Census of the United States, 1880*. National Archives, Washington, DC. Ancestry.com.

———. *Thirteenth Census of the United States, 1910*. National Archives, Washington, DC. Ancestry.com.

———. *Twelfth Census of the United States, 1900*. National Archives, Washington, DC. Ancestry.com.

US War Department. *Department of the Gulf: Map No. 5, Approaches to New Orleans*. Prepared by order of Major General N. P. Banks, February 14, 1863. Washington, DC: Government Printing Office, 1891.

Vale, Lawrence J. *From the Puritans to the Projects: Public Housing and Public Neighbors*. Cambridge, MA: Harvard University Press, 2000.

———. *Purging the Poorest: Public Housing and the Design Politics of Twice-Cleared Communities*. Chicago: University of Chicago Press, 2013.

Van Zante, Gary. *New Orleans 1867: Photographs by Theodore Lilienthal*. London: Merrell, 2008.

Vaz, Kim Marie. *The "Baby Dolls": Breaking the Race and Gender Barriers of the New Orleans Mardi Gras Tradition*. Baton Rouge: Louisiana State University Press, 2013.

Vella, Christine. *Intimate Enemies: The Two Worlds of the Baroness Pontalba*. Baton Rouge: Louisiana State University Press, 1997.

Wacquant, Loïc. *Urban Outcasts: A Comparative Sociology of Advanced Marginality*. Cambridge: Polity, 2008.

Walkowitz, Judith. *Prostitution and Victorian Society: Women, Class, and the State*. Cambridge: Cambridge University Press, 1980.

Wall, Diana diZerega. *The Archaeology of Gender: Separating the Spheres in Urban America*. New York: Plenum Press, 1999.

Wall, Diana diZerega, Nan A. Rothschild, and Cynthia Copeland. "Seneca Village and Little Africa: Two African American Communities in Antebellum New York City." *Historical Archaeology* 42, no. 1 (2008): 97–107.

Ward, David. *Poverty, Ethnicity, and the American City, 1840–1925: Changing Conceptions of the Slum and the Ghetto*. Cambridge: Cambridge University Press, 1989.

Ward, Martha. *Voodoo Queen: The Spirited Lives of Marie Laveau*. Oxford: University Press of Mississippi, 2004.

Waring, George E., Jr. *Report on the Social Statistics of Cities*. 1886–87. 2 vols. New York: Arno Press, 1970.

Warner, Mark S. "'The Best There Is of Us': Ceramics and Status in African American Annapolis." In *Annapolis Pasts: Historical Archaeology in Annapolis, Maryland*, edited by Paul A. Shackel, Paul R. Mullins, and Mark S. Warner, 190–224. Knoxville: University of Tennessee Press, 1998.

Watkins, T. H. *The Great Depression: America in the 1930s*. Boston: Little, Brown, 1993.

Webb, Julie Yvonne. "Louisiana Voodoo and Superstitions Related to Health." *Health Services and Mental Health Administration Health Reports* 86, no. 4 (1971): 291–301.

———. *Superstitious Influence—Voodoo in Particular—Affecting Health Practices in a Selected Population in Southern Louisiana*. New Orleans: published by author, 1971.

Wesson, Cameron. *Households and Hegemony: Early Creek Prestige Goods, Symbolic Capital, and Social Power*. Lincoln: University of Nebraska Press, 2008.

Wiese, Andrew. *Places of Their Own: African American Suburbanization in the Twentieth Century*. Chicago: University of Chicago Press, 2004.

Wilkie, Laurie A. *The Archaeology of Mothering: An African-American Midwife's Tale*. New York: Routledge, 2003.

———. "Expelling Frogs and Binding Babies: Conception, Gestation, and Birth in Nineteenth-Century African-American Midwifery." *World Archaeology* 45, no. 2 (2013): 272–84.

———. "Granny Midwives: Gender and Generational Mediators of the African American Community." In *Engendering African American Archaeology*, edited by Jillian Galle and Amy Young, 73–100. Knoxville: University of Tennessee Press, 2004.

Wilkie, Laurie A., and George Shorter Jr. *Lucrecia's Well: An Archaeological Glimpse of an African-American Midwife's Household*. Mobile: University of South Alabama, 2001.

Willmann, John B. *The Department of Housing and Urban Development*. New York: Frederick A. Praeger, 1968.

Wilson, Samuel, and Bernard Lemann. *New Orleans Architecture*. Vol. 1, *The Lower Garden District*. Gretna, LA: Friends of the Cabildo and Pelican, 1998.

Wilson, William Julius. *The Truly Disadvantaged: The Inner City, the Underclass, and Public Policy*. Chicago: University of Chicago Press, 1987.

Woldoff, Rachel A., and Brian J. Gerber. "Protect or Neglect? Social Structure, Decision Making, and the Risk of Living in African American Places in New Orleans." In *Racing the Storm: Racial Implications and Lessons Learned from Hurricane Katrina*, edited by Hillary Potter, 171–96. Lanham, MD: Lexington Books, 2007.

Woodward, C. Vann. *The Strange Career of Jim Crow*. New York: Oxford University Press, 1966.

Wright, Gwendolyn. *Building the Dream: A Social History of Housing in America*. Cambridge: MIT Press, 1981.

Yakubik, Jill-Karen. "Ceramic Use in Late-Eighteenth-Century and Early-Nineteenth-Century Southeastern Louisiana." PhD diss., Tulane University, 1990.

Yamin, Rebecca. "Alternative Narratives: Respectability at New York's Five Points." In Mayne and Murray, *The Archaeology of Urban Landscapes*, 154–71.

———. "Wealthy, Free, and Female: Prostitution in Nineteenth-Century New York." *Historical Archaeology* 39, no. 1 (2005): 4–18.

Yentsch, Anne, and Mary Beaudry, eds. *The Art and Mystery of Historical Archaeology: Essays in Honor of James Deetz*. Boca Raton, FL: CRC Press, 1992.

Young, Amy, ed. *Archaeology of Southern Urban Landscapes*. Tuscaloosa: University of Alabama Press, 2001.

Index

the African American experience,
24–25; constructivist/instrumentalist
approach to ethnicity, 42, 173n11,
180n12, 184n46; vs. documentary research, 22, 123; of immigrant communities, in New Orleans, 8; of midwifery, 105; in New Orleans, xiv–xv,
7–9, 26; power relations analysis and,
13; prehistoric sites, in the New Orleans area, 7; public engagement
and, 9, 11, 25; of public housing projects, in New Orleans, 9–12; of race
and consumption, in the United
States, 24, 80; Section 106 compliance and, in New Orleans, xv, 7, 8, 80;
of sex work, 136, 137–38, 139, 140, 144,
146, 148–50; of urban areas, 153, 154,
197n15; of urban poor, 15–16, 23, 75,
168. *See also* ceramics; faunal remains
in archaeological assemblages from
New Orleans; glass artifacts; material
culture; midwifery; *and individual sites*
Arlington, Josie, 124, 132
Asbury, Herbert, 127

Basin Street, xi, 121, 125, 131, 135, 193n24
Bayou St. John, 29, 96
Behrman, Martin, 66
Bellocq, E. J., 124, 146, 147
Belmont (neighborhood), ix, 17, 33, 67,
70, 77, *83, 84*, 90, 91, 93, 158–59,
187n34; archaeology of, 79; artifact assemblages, 82–84, 85, 86, 87–88, 89,
90, 91, 187n34; built environment,
92; characterized as slum, 79; demographics, 77–78, 85; excavations, 80–
81, 84, 86; housing patterns, 73–74,
76–77; Red Devil tenement, ix, 76,
78, 84–85, 187n34; residents as property owners, 78–79; residents as renters, 74, 76; as space of resistance, 70,
162–63; topography of, 69; Tulane
University study of, 75–78
Biehl, João, 13

Birth of African-American Culture, The
(Mintz and Price), 116
Black, 50–51, 57, 98; backswamp areas as
Black space, 69; Blackness, as site of
resistance, 12, 24; dandyism, 89, 162;
as ethnicity, xv; as racial category, ix,
134; separatism, 68–69; term, discussion of, xv–xvi; as United States Cen-
sus category, 85
Black Atlantic, 25
Black Creoles, 26, 28, 95, 101, 188n3. *See
also* Creoles of Color
Black Panther Party, 3, 165
Black Storyville. *See* Storyville
Boas, Franz, 115
Bolden, Buddy, 127, 191n3
bottles: from Belmont: 81, 82, 83, 84, *84,*
85, 86, 87, 92; from St. Thomas assemblage: 52, 55, 58, 59, 60, 65; from
Square 130: 136, 142, 146, 194n32;
from Square 252: 101, 105, 106–7,
108–11, 113. *See also* glass artifacts
Bourdieu, Pierre, 20, 21, 184n46
Bring New Orleans Back Commission,
1, 169n1
brothels, 124–25, 130–32, 134–41, 144, 145,
146–48, *147*, 150–52, 159, 161, 192n4
Bruenn family, ix, 54–56, 61, 66;
Bernard, 54–55, 65; material culture
of, 55–56, 64–65; unnamed woman
(Bernard's sister), 54, 56, 65; Zachary,
54, 65
Buchanan v. Warley, 31
Burnham, Daniel, 30, 131
B. W. Cooper Housing Project. *See* Calliope
(B. W. Cooper) Housing Project

Calliope (B. W. Cooper) Housing Project,
xi, 4, 35, *36*
Carondelet (Old Basin) Canal, 35, 96, 97,
99, 128, 129, 163
Carondelet Walk, 96
Catholicism, 38, 44, 52, 56; practices
of, 118, 119. *See also* cemeteries; St.